BEES AND BEEKEEPING

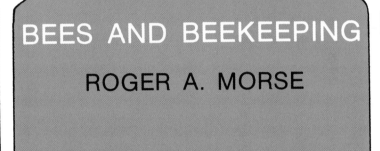

BEES AND BEEKEEPING

ROGER A. MORSE

COMSTOCK PUBLISHING ASSOCIATES, a division of

CORNELL UNIVERSITY PRESS

ITHACA AND LONDON

First published 1975 by Cornell University Press.
Published in the United Kingdom by Cornell University Press Ltd., 2-4 Brook Street, London W1Y 1AA.

International Standard Book Number 0-8014-0884-9
Library of Congress Catalog Number 74-27440
Printed in the United States of America by Cayuga Press, Inc.

Contents

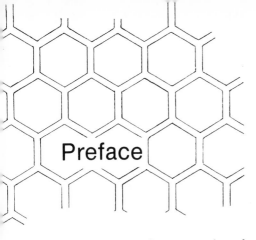

Preface

Within the past few years the wholesale price of honey has tripled. This change is in part a result of a greater demand for honey, not only in this country but abroad. The demand for general information about bees has also increased. This book is designed to answer questions about the science of apiculture and is an outgrowth of my course in the subject at Cornell University, which has had nearly 250 students enrolled during each of the last three years. It gives detailed biological information and the scientific background of beekeeping practices. My earlier book, *The Complete Guide to Beekeeping,* published by E. P. Dutton & Co., Inc., in 1972, now in its second edition, contains instructions for hobbyists and beginning beekeepers.

Interest in honey bees is not new. The ancient Egyptians were beekeepers, moving their bees up and down the Nile River to take advantage of the changing flora, source of the nectar and pollen which are the honey bees' food. Aristotle and other Greeks kept bees in hives with windows of thin horn, through which the bees could be observed. The Romans, too, kept large apiaries for honey production, especially in Spain; they also wrote about bees and beekeeping, though their knowledge of biology, like their knowledge of agriculture and medicine, was poor by our standards.

When men turned their minds to science, and their investigations into the nature of the universe became more profound, it was at first the presumed industriousness of the insects that aroused curiosity; later it was the harmony in which thousands of individuals lived together. That the honey bee colony was a predominantly female society resulted in many studies and in commentaries, both facetious and otherwise.

In this century exciting research on bee biology has been undertaken. Thousands of individual bees living together in a colony must have a system of communication. Order cannot exist without direction. As a result of studies on the dance language and odor communication system, we can say that only man has a communication system superior to that of the honey bee. Still, honey bees are not thinking animals. They respond to stimuli, dancing, for example, to convey information about food sources or potential home sites. Depending upon the circumstances, they may release an alarm odor to mark an enemy, or they may use a sweet, attractive scent to mark their home or their queen. These odors, called pheromones, evoke specific responses. Certain pheromones may be used in concert to reinforce or to negate one another. Although more pheromones have been identified for the honey bee than for any other insect, several are yet to be identified and their functions described. This text devotes considerable attention to the honey bee communication system.

In addition to its interest to biologists, the honey bee has an important part in our intensified agricultural system. Many persons make a living growing bees and producing honey and beeswax; others are pollination specialists, moving their bees into orchards or seed fields where bees are needed for cross-pollination. Production of certain seeds and fruits is dependent on honey bees under the conditions in which modern agriculturists force their crops to grow. Special pollination problems have arisen in recent years.

Americans are a practical people. They work and hoard; honey bees do the same. The societies of men and bees are similar in many respects; in part, this text is intended to point to certain of these similarities and differences so that men may better understand their own world. Above all, it is hoped that beekeepers will use their knowledge for the betterment of their bees.

ROGER A. MORSE

Ithaca, New York

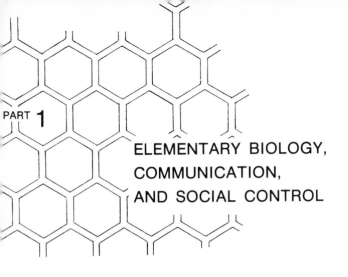

PART 1

ELEMENTARY BIOLOGY, COMMUNICATION, AND SOCIAL CONTROL

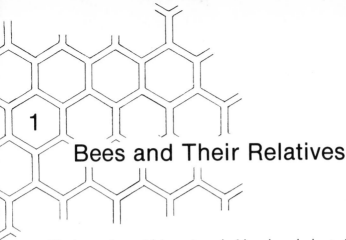

1

Bees and Their Relatives

The honey bee, which we keep in hives in apiaries today, is just as wild and untamed as it was when men first began to husband bees several thousand years ago.[1] We have not yet learned how to control bee breeding, although efforts are under way and systems for artificial insemination have been developed. Progress is slow.

There is also a great deal of uncertainty about what type of bee we want to develop. For example, some people suggest we should breed a bee without a sting, but many commercial beekeepers believe we should not. They fear that if we have bees without stings, beekeeping might become too popular and there would be too many bees! Some people think bees should be honey producers only; others take the view we should breed bees which are good pollinators; a few people feel that bees should be bred which do a superior job of pollinating one crop.

Given our present state of knowledge, and considering that the industry is migratory in some areas and that most beekeepers make

1. The spelling of honey bee as two words in this book follows the recommendations of the Committee on Common Names of Insects of the Entomological Society of America. This society, as well as its parent society, the American Association of Economic Entomologists, has had a committee on common names since 1908. The ruling of the present committee is that if a two-part insect name is used in a sense which is systematically correct that the name shall be spelled as two words. Some examples of common names of insects correctly spelled according to this rule are as follows: house fly, dragonfly, dobsonfly, butterfly, bumble bee, lady beetle. Most dictionaries spell honey bee as one word, as do some trade and foreign entomological journals; rarely the words will be hyphenated.

their living producing honey, I think that we need bees which will be both honey producers and pollinators, and which will thrive equally well both north and south.

Modern beekeeping developed because the honey bee is an adaptable animal which may be moved and kept almost anywhere, and because we have learned so much about bee biology. Beekeeping has been called an application of science and knowledge.

Over the years several beekeepers have attempted to select and breed a "gentle" bee, one which is not inclined to sting. By selecting gentle colonies from which to rear queens, one can have an effect on the resulting offspring of the queens. Every time a gentle bee has been produced, however, honey production has fallen, and it appears that the so-called gentle bees are either not good nectar gatherers or are less capable than more aggressive bees of protecting their nests against predators.

It is difficult for us to conceive of the seemingly infinite number of animal species on earth, for most people, based on their own experience, would be hard put to list many more than one hundred species. Yet there are at least a million species of insects alone, many so small that they can be seen only with a microscope. About 20,000 insect species are bees. A species is composed of a group of related individuals that resemble one another.[2] Animals of a single species can breed among themselves; however, they cannot mate with members of another species and in most instances do not show sexual interest in those of another species.

We define a bee as an animal (insect) that feeds during both its larval and adult life on pollen and nectar (insects do not feed in the egg or pupal stages).[3] Further, bees have plumose or branched hairs somewhere on their bodies. In addition to insulating the body of the insect, the plumose hair serves to entrap pollen grains and

2. A genus is a group of closely related species; a family, a group of genera; a superfamily, a group of families, etc. The divisions are arbitrary, but the men who make them (taxonomists) attempt to make logical or natural groupings. Accordingly, it may not be illogical for a genus to contain one or a hundred species.

3. Honey bee larvae are also fed royal jelly, a substance secreted by the pharyngeal and mandibular glands of young worker honey bees.

transport them from one plant to another. Thus, the lives of all bees are linked closely to the lives of plants.

The Hymenoptera

Because of their numerous varieties, insects are placed into 25 orders of the Linnaean classification system of binomial nomenclature for biology. The order Hymenoptera includes all social insects except one group, the termites (order Isoptera). However, not all Hymenoptera are social. The Hymenoptera are one of the larger groups of insects, and the order includes at least a quarter of a million species. For this reason they are subdivided into superfamilies. One of these is the Apoidea, the bees mentioned above. There are seven families in the superfamily Apoidea; from most primitive to most advanced they are: Colletidae, Andrenidae, Halictidae, Melittidae, Megachilidae, Anthrophoridae, and the Apidae. The Apidae, in turn, is broken into four groups or tribes, one of which is the Apini and contains the honey bees.

Two other important and related superfamilies are the Vespoidea (the vespoid wasps) and the Sphecoidea (the sphecoid wasps). Since wasps, like honey bees, are stinging insects and many of them are associated with plants, at least in their adult life, it is interesting and important to know something of the relationship of bees and wasps (see figure 1.1).

The wasps

The majority of wasp species, like those of bees, are solitary or subsocial, but it is among the social forms that some of the more interesting animals are found. These include the wasps that build paper nests, both above and below ground, some of which are enclosed in an envelope. The enveloped nests usually have several layers of paper that serve as insulation, especially in the fall when the reproductives are emerging.

The common yellow jacket and the white-faced hornet, *Vespula maculata,* are among the species that build architecturally fascinating nests (figures 1.2 and 1.3). Some of these are located high in trees, thirty to fifty feet above the ground. According to an old

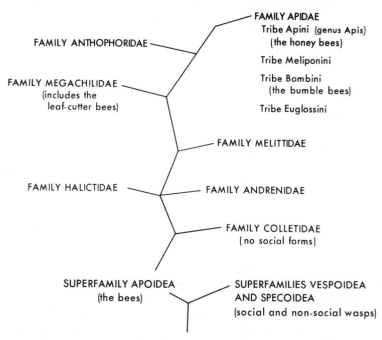

1.1. The major groups of bees and their relationships. (Modified after Charles D. Michener, 1974.)

wives' tale from New England, the severity of the coming winter may be predicted by the height at which the aerial wasps' nests are found in the fall: the lower the nests, the harsher the winter.

Both ground and aerial nests contain several thousand individuals in the fall. Persons who find the finished nests in their yards are amazed; their immediate reaction is that the nests must be new, that they have been constructed within a few weeks of being discovered. In fact, in most of the northern states and Canada, both the ground and aerial nests are started early in the year, usually in May. The wasps appear to do little to defend their nests until their populations reach several hundred or more. Often, homeowners mow the grass, week after week, over a ground nest but are

1.2. A wasp nest. This nest was made by *Vespula maculata*, the common white faced hornet. Note that the nest has a single entrance near the bottom.

1.3. A vespid (wasp) nest with the insulation (wasp-made paper) removed from one side. Note the air spaces between the layers of paper which offer the nest protection against changes in temperature. The combs in wasps' nests are horizontal, whereas those in honey bee nests are vertical. The arrow indicates the position of the nest's single entrance.

not attacked by the wasps until August or September, many months after the nest was first started.

None of the social wasps are fully social all year. In the fall, after mating, the males die and the females burrow into the gound, a hollow tree, or other cavity and survive the winter as individuals. Old nests are never reused but are abandoned, and new ones are started each spring.

Homeowners recognize the overwintering queens as a nuisance, for these insects may try to hibernate under the boards or shingles on the side of the house. If the house is not tight, they make their way inside. When the house is heated in the winter, the insects may be warmed, moving in the direction of the heat and responding to the warmth of the house as they would to the warmth of spring.

Wasps differ from bees in two important ways. Bees, as mentioned, have at least some plumose hairs on their bodies; wasps generally do not. One will occasionally find a wasp species with a few plumose hairs, usually on the thorax. Their lack of plumose hairs makes wasps less effective as pollinators than bees; they cannot transport as much pollen on their bodies as the average bee can. The plumose hairs found on honey bees are shown in figure 1.5.

The second major difference between bees and wasps is that bees feed exclusively on pollen and nectar in both the larval and the adult stages. Most wasps feed their larvae other insects. Some wasps that feed on other sources of protein are a nuisance in the summer at picnic tables, for they will feed on peanut butter, bread, hamburger, and other meats. Bees, requiring pollen for their young, have a closer association with flowers than do wasps. The wasps belonging to the genus *Nectarina* are an exception to this rule. The *Nectarina,* which are found only in Central and South America, collect and store honey. Presumably they feed their young pollen and nectar.

The solitary bees

Solitary bees, as their name indicates, are insects that have little or nothing to do with one another except during mating. The

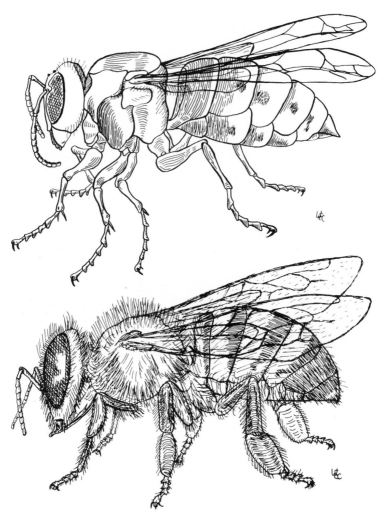

1.4. The chief differences between the bee and the wasp. The wasp (above) has fewer hairs on the body and a more pointed abdomen; it does not collect pollen and so lacks the pollen collection apparatus that the honey bee (below) has on her hind leg. (Illustrations by William E. Conner.)

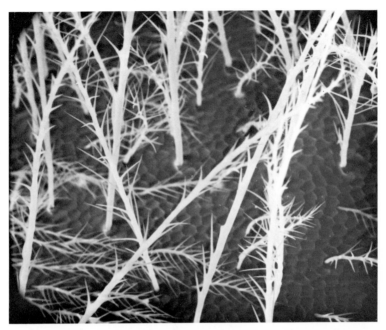

1.5. Plumose hairs on the thorax of a honey bee magnified by an electron scanning scope; a primary difference between wasps and bees is that wasps have simple hairs while those on solitary and social bees are branched. Presumably this aids in pollen transport.

typical solitary bee burrows into the ground, uses a hollow twig, or makes a nest under a rock or ledge where it is protected from the weather. The nest consists of cells that physically resemble those in a honey comb except that they are usually placed in a linear fashion. Probably the average solitary bee's nest contains six to ten cells. Some species build more than one nest, but they work on only one at a time. In each cell the female bee makes a ball of pollen moistened with nectar; when the cell is provisioned, she lays her egg, closes the cell, and never again has any contact with the cell, its contents, or her offspring. The great majority of solitary bees are ground nesters and many are rather selective about the type of soil in which they will nest.

Providing nests for solitary bees is an interesting hobby that enables one to trap the bees and study their biology. One drills holes of varying size in pieces of wood and puts these ready-made nests in protected areas. Some solitary bees nest only in hollow twigs which are horizontal; others nest only in twigs which are vertical, sometimes in those facing up, and sometimes in those facing down. Many wasps nest in similar situations, and nests made for solitary bees are often used by wasps.

With 20,000 species of bees in the world, obviously there are many species almost everywhere; in any part of the United States one should be able to find at least 500 species. Other than Arctic areas, there is no place where one cannot find at least several hundred species of solitary bees within a radius of 50 miles. Among the chief limits are nesting sites. Interestingly, one of the shortest check lists of bees on record is that from the vicinity of Miami, Florida, where the bees were collected and studied over a period of ten years. The wet, sandy soil around Miami is apparently not suitable for most ground-nesting bees.

Like any other group of animals, the solitary bees show some fascinating behavior characteristics. A few are nocturnal and have very large ocelli on the tops of their heads. The ocelli are three small eyes quite different from the compound eyes of insects. The nocturnal bees usually visit only specific flowers, and weather conditions must be rather precise for them to succeed. Other solitary bees are general feeders, taking pollen and nectar from a variety of flowers.

Solitary bees show great variation in size, color, and form. There is one large group of ground-nesting solitary bees known as the green bees because their bodies are a brilliant green. In this group are also a few bees that are bright blue. Other bees have bodies that are red or yellow, or combinations of red, yellow, and black; often these color variations may be used in identification.

A few species of solitary bees are parasitic, but parasitic in a rather unusual way. Parasitic solitary bees, after mating, seek out and enter the nests of other bees, usually the nests of a certain species. The egg laid by the host bee may be destroyed, though usually it is not, and the parasitic bee lays her egg alongside the existing egg on the ball of pollen and nectar. When the parasitic bee larva hatches, it attacks and kills, and sometimes consumes, the larva or egg of the host bee and then continues its development. Thus, even parasitic bees live almost exclusively on pollen and nectar, both in the larval and the adult stages. Parasitic bees, generally, tend to assume wasplike physical characteristics as adults. Their abdomens are more pointed than those of other bees, and their bodies less hairy. They are not so effective as pollinators.

Because there are so many species of bees and so few people to study them, the life histories of fewer than 10 per cent of our bees in the United States are known. On a world scale we know the life histories of an even smaller percentage of species. The solitary bees, like the honey bees, are important in the pollination of both agricultural crops and the wild fruit, seed, and nut crops useful for wildlife. Certain of these solitary bees are used commercially as pollinators in restricted areas and under specialized conditions. The role of bees other than honey bees in pollination is discussed further in Chapter 11.

The subsocial bees

How did social existence in insects come about? If a social animal has any advantages over one which is asocial in solving problems, then those advantages would create evolutionary pressure for the development of social forms. And social animals do apparently have advantages.

The problems that all plants and animals have in common are in the areas of food, protection, and reproduction. In the case of food, a honey bee colony must first find a source of food. The bee that finds the food needs to have a method of telling other bees where it is located. The bees must gather the food, carry it home, and then process it for storage; with regard to pollen, honey is added, and with regard to honey, both physical and chemical changes are made. The next step is to store the food and during storage to protect it. The bees must then distribute the food when it is needed, and after it has been distributed and eaten, the fecal matter that results from the food must be disposed of.

In the case of protection, a honey bee colony needs a way of alerting itself to danger, and once it is aware that danger exists, a way of combating the problem. Honey bees are required to protect themselves from men, bears, skunks, opossums, mice, wax moths, and bacterial, virus, and fungus diseases, to mention only a few of their predators and diseases. The bees in a colony must also protect themselves, their brood, and their food against extremes in temperature and humidity.

Finally, in the case of reproduction, some individual(s) in the honey bee colony must lay eggs, and there must be places to put the eggs and rear the young. Thus, it is necessary that the bees build cells for the purpose. Afterward, the young must be fed and, during their earlier stages, protected. Following this, the young take up the tasks done by the bees that reared them. As far as reproduction is concerned, the last requirement is a way to dispose of the bodies of dead bees.

But what has this to do with the social and subsocial bees? Before an animal can become social, it must go through social development. Animals cannot become social in a short period of time. One of the advantages of working with bees is that we can examine this evolutionary process, because there are so many species of them on earth.[4]

The biology of solitary bees has already been discussed, but we have still not answered the question of how they graduated from a solitary existence to a subsocial existence. The route may have

4. This statement is correct but might be misleading. The facts are the same whether we consider men or bees. The present apes, for example, may or may not resemble the ancestors of *Homo sapiens*. We did not descend from the apes found on earth today; however, present-day apes and men came from the same stock. So it is with bees. The honey bees and the other bees on earth today came from the same ancestors. We suspect that during the course of bee evolution the ancestors of the present-day honey bees passed through stages that resemble the life histories of many solitary and subsocial bees in existence today.

been somewhat as follows. Because certain ground-nesting bees found that certain soils were better for nest building, there came into existence nest aggregations, that is to say, groups of bees nesting in a small area. Following this, there was probably some advantage in having certain bees share a nest hole. The original nest probably looked like an upside down Y with a single entrance to the surface but a division below ground, so that one female would go down one branch of the Y to make her nest and the other female would go down the other branch. Next, perhaps three, four, or half a dozen females began to use the same nest.

Evolutionary evidence suggests that in the next step one of these bees acted as a guard, blocking the nest entrance during the night and perhaps in the day to protect it from predators—a division of labor.

So, labor was saved first by finding a suitable nesting site, next when the nesting hole was shared. The nest was better protected when there was a guard bee. This was followed by having one bee in the group specialize in egg laying. In all probability this step evolved rather slowly, after there had at first been two or three bees specializing in egg laying, but still no one dominant over the other. Finally, there was queen dominance.

Thus far, however, the bees in the story we are relating are a long way from being truly social. The bumble bee, for example, an insect with which most people are familiar, is really subsocial, not social. In northern climates only the young bumble bee queens live through the winter, hibernating in a hollow log, in the ground, or in a rotten tree. In the spring these females, which mated the previous fall, build a nest and rear half a dozen or so young. In the beginning the queen must be the nest builder, the food gatherer, the egg layer, and the protector. Obviously, this is a difficult stage in the life cycle of bumble bees, and many nests are destroyed because of a lack of protection. The first young that emerge from a bumble bee colony are small, much smaller than the queen. However, these young take over the routine work of the queen mother. They enlarge the nest, gather more food, and feed the young. As the season progresses, the queen bumble bee spends an increasing amount of time laying eggs. Successive broods are larger, better fed, and the bees themselves are bigger. By August, a bumble bee colony in the North may contain 50 or 100 adults, or even more. The social group consists of the queen and her workers of various sizes. By the latter part of the season the successful colony is large enough to devote its energies to the rearing of new queens and males. Mating takes place, the males die, the fertilized females hibernate during winter, and the cycle starts again the next spring.

The bumble bee colony does not have true social existence because the animals are not social all year. Bumble bees gather only a small quantity of honey, and even in the largest of the bumble bee nests one will rarely find more than a few grams. In the winter, the lone bumble bee queen is unprotected and vulnerable to attack by many predators. Clearly, the fully social honey bee has an advantage over the bumble bee in that it stores a large quantity of food and can survive the winter as a member of a colony.

In reviewing the long evolution of the subsocial bees, only a few of the animals involved have been mentioned. Evolution is a slow process, and along the route errors may be made and many species may perish.

Although honey bees are still evolving and will change in the future, it is doubtful if they or any other insect will ever develop to a very much higher level of sophistication than they have achieved at present. One of the limitations of insects is their size; all insects are small, at least relatively so. While some may have great wingspreads and elongated bodies, the maximum diameter of most insects' bodies is approximately a few centimeters. Honey bees have a poor oxygen distribution system, having neither lungs nor a circulatory system that can carry oxygen. It is for these physical reasons that we look to other forms of animal life for intelligence.

The social bees

It is difficult to say precisely what a social bee is. In addition to the honey bees, in many parts of the world there exist bees which are called social and which have colonies that survive the year round. These belong to the tropical bee family, Meliponidae.[5] In most of the species in this group, the bees are much smaller than our honey bee and they store less honey (though it has been recorded that some nests may contain several kilograms).

One of the more interesting aspects of these social bees is their defense system. They are commonly referred to as the stingless bees, but they do have a defense that is almost as effective as stinging. When attacked by a large mammal, some of the stingless bee species smear the victim with honey regurgitated from their honey stomachs. While this may at first appear amusing and odd, it is in fact effective. Other stingless bee species pull hair! A hundred or more of these bees may jump on a man's head, or on a bear's back, and begin to pull the hair out! That action is certainly sufficient to drive the intruder away. Other stingless bees run in and out of the ears, in and out of the nose, and in and out of the eyes, over the hands, and down the shirt collar. When hundreds of bees are doing this, there is no defense but to wipe them off and run.

An excellent text on the Meliponidae was published by Schwarz in 1948. More recently Kerr (1969) has studied many species of Meliponidae.

The genus Apis

Apis mellifera is not the only honey bee. There are three other species of *Apis,* all Asian. Of the four species, unquestionably our own, the European species, is the best honey producer and the most practical animal to keep in a commercial agricultural system where we are concerned with pollination.

Apis florea is the smallest bee in the genus *Apis*. This bee builds a single comb in an exposed area, not in a hollow tree or cave as does our own bee. *Apis florea* stores honey, but because the nest is exposed, the brood and the stored food are subject to predation. Thus, this bee must use 60 to 80 per cent of its popula-

5. Honey bees belong to the family Apidae.

1.6. A comb built by *Apis dorsata* in the Philippines. The brood pattern is very compact in this nest, indicating a young queen. *Apis dorsata* builds only a single comb.

1.7. The same *Apis dorsata* nest, end view. Note that the honey storage cells in the upper portion of the comb are eight to ten centimeters deep; thus, even though there is only a single comb, the storage cells will hold a large quantity of honey.

tion for protection, and because so much of its energy is devoted to protection, the animal cannot spend much time gathering food, and its nest is small and poorly provisioned. When we examine the biology of *Apis florea*, it is evident that one of the chief advantages held by *Apis mellifera* is the fact that it nests in a protected area, where it is shielded not only from inclement weather and changes in temperature but where it may better guard against predators.

Apis dorsata is the largest in size of the four species of honey bees (figures 1.6 and 1.7). A colony sometimes contains as many as 80,000 individuals and its population may exceed that of any other *Apis. Apis dorsata*, like *Apis florea*, builds a single exposed comb under a large branch, or on a rock. People who have traveled throughout Asia are familiar with the fact that this bee may also nest under the eaves of buildings. While *Apis dorsata* colonies have sizeable populations, one seldom finds a nest that contains more than a few kilograms of honey. Like *Apis florea*, the workers devote a large part of their efforts to nest protection. The protection system is remarkable to watch. Under circumstances in which one to five bees from an *Apis mellifera* colony might attack, it is not uncommon for 5,000 *Apis dorsata* to attack. When alerted to danger, thousands of bees fall from the nest, taking wing as they fall, and they return to the nest only if they do not find some predator to sting. When they sting a predator, they mark it with an oderiferous compound, which warns other *Apis dorsata* of an enemy in the vicinity that they too should attack.[6]

Ingenious men have found that they can build small screened wire cages into which they can climb and can carry from the inside.

6. During the Viet Nam conflict, it is recorded that the North Vietnamese booby-trapped colonies of *Apis dorsata* so that the bees would be disturbed and attack when someone walked on a nearby path. Unlike our own species, the giant Asian bee will fly into shaded areas and has been known to chase people through the woods and jungle for long distances. Martin Lindauer (1971) records that during his expedition to India and Ceylon he was pursued for a kilometer and a half (about a mile) through a eucalyptus woods by bees from an *Apis dorsata* colony which he had disturbed.

A cloth skirt around the bottom prevents the bees from entering underneath the cage and stinging the occupant. In this way it has been possible to observe the biology of the *Apis dorsata.* In certain parts of the world where *Apis dorsata* is common, the inhabitants harvest the honey and beeswax. They have learned that, if they build a smoking fire under a nest of *Apis dorsata,* the bees will abandon the nest and will soon build another. During the centuries men have used fire and smoke to raid the nests of *Apis dorsata,* the animals that could take wing quickly survived and those that attempted to resist, perished; thus, in the evolution of this bee there has been sufficient time for this characteristic to evolve.

A third Asian species of honey bee is *Apis indica.* This is a bee similar to our own honey bee but smaller in size. *Apis indica* is used for commercial honey production in India and other parts of Asia. Because of its small size, however, colonies of *Apis indica* seldom store much more than five to eight kilograms of honey. In countries where labor is cheap and honey and sweets in short supply, it is profitable to keep *Apis indica.*

Few attempts to carry the Asian honey bees into other parts of the world have been successful. As we have learned recently, the Asian bees have diseases which, when introduced into colonies of *Apis mellifera,* quickly destroy the European honey bees. Certain Asian bees have been carried to Europe for experimental purposes in recent years, and Asian bee diseases now present in Europe, as a result of these importations, may have a disastrous effect upon the beekeeping industry in some areas there.

The evolutionary success of the honey bee has been demonstrated by its tremendous adaptability. Honey bees can live almost anywhere that men can. They are successful in the tropics and equally so in northern climates, though not in the extreme north. They have been taken to all the continents, and while European honey bees do not thrive in tropical and subtropical Asia, this is apparently because they cannot withstand certain diseases common to Asian honey bees.

Races of honey bees

There are many races of honey bees.[7] The geographic isolation that has led to the development of racial differences in people in Europe, Africa and the rest of the world, has also led to profound differences in honey bees (see also Chapter 8, under Africa). A few people have treated the races as subspecies, calling, for example, those bees from central Africa, *Apis mellifera adansonii,* those from the southern tip of Africa, *Apis mellifera capensis* and those from Germany, *Apis mellifera mellifera.* I believe that it is much more logical to speak of African bees, cape bees (from the southern tip of Africa), German bees, and so forth. However, all honey bee races will interbreed, and show many physical and behavioral characteristics in common.

Certain extremes in physical and behavioral characteristics among races of bees are well known to beekeepers. African bees and Cyprian bees (from the island of Cypress) are more inclined to sting than most races. They will also pursue those who molest their colonies for greater distances. Caucasion bees (originally from the Caucausus Mountains in Russia) use excessive quantities of propolis; this habit makes the removal of frames and the inspection of their colonies more difficult.[8] Bees of the German race run on the combs; they are the darkest of the honey bees and are often called *blacks.*

In the early stages of the development of commercial beekeeping in the United States (1850–1880), the German bee was most common. However, in an intense commercial management scheme, the Germans are susceptible to European foulbrood, a bacterial

7. It is almost impossible to buy purebred bees. There have been so many shipments of bees from one country and continent to another in the past 100 years as to almost preclude the possibility of any race's being pure. Many queen breeders, through selection for color and behavioral characteristics, sell queens which are predominately of one race or another. A buyer should be aware that not only may the queen be slightly different from her ancestors but that she may not have mated with drones of her own race.

8. *Propolis* is the name given the gums and resins collected by honey bees and used by them as a varnish and to seal cracks and crevices (see Chapter 3).

disease of honey bee larvae. An extensive search for a better race of bees was started about 1870, and by 1900 the Italian race, especially from the vicinity of Bologna in North Italy, became the favorite. Italians are relatively gentle bees, use little propolis, and are more or less resistant to European foulbrood; they are a distinctive light brown or yellow in color. They have some faults, the chief one being that they will rear brood, even when it is not needed (from the beekeeper's point of view), so long as food is available to them. Other races are said to slow brood rearing when the honey flow stops though this varies. The Italian bee is the race most commonly used and the one I recommend. However, many beekeepers continue to search for a better race of bees. Because so many races (in fact, probably all) have been brought to the United States at one time or another, we have in this country a tremendous gene pool from which to work. (Since 1923 it has been illegal to import bees into the United States; see Chapter 12.)

I have stated my opinion many times and in many places that in beekeeping, management is more important than the race of bees or type of hive. Still, testimonials on both better hives and better bees abound.

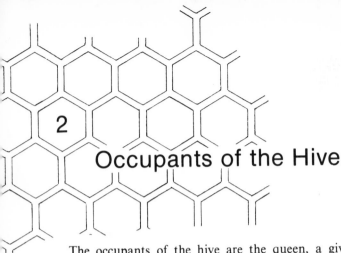

2

Occupants of the Hive

The occupants of the hive are the queen, a given number of workers, and when food is abundant and the colony is growing, a certain number of males or drones (see figure 2.1). The number of workers and males present depends upon a great variety of factors, and only a so-called expert would risk saying how many of each will be present without defining the circumstances. One must make a thorough examination of a honey bee colony to determine what exists within. A judgment based on the number of bees flying or carrying pollen at the colony entrance may be helpful, but such estimates are fallible. It is important to understand how the number of occupants within a hive changes throughout the year and how this may affect colony management.

The normal colony

Perhaps the easiest way to define a normal colony is to talk first about the extremes in population that can occur in the honey bee colony. By so doing we indicate that a normal colony is one whose population falls between these limits. In the northern states the largest possible population in the honey bee colony would usually occur during June; such a colony would contain a single queen, probably about 60,000 worker bees, and not many more than 3,000 drones. It should be emphasized that a colony with about 60,000 bees is definitely larger than normal. Under extreme circumstances the number of workers might be slightly greater.

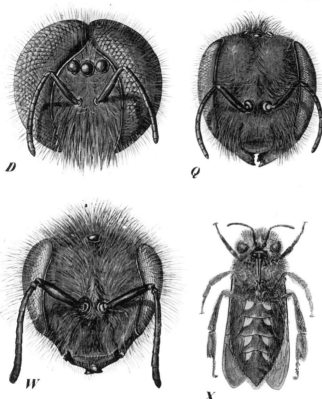

2.1. The faces of the drone (D), the queen (Q), and the worker (W) showing the positions and relative sizes of the ocelli, compound eyes, and the antennae. X illustrates the underside of a worker's abdomen and shows, in the lighter color, the position of the four pairs of wax glands. (Illustrations by A. G. Hammer in Anna Botsford Comstock's *How to Keep Bees,* 1905).

The minimum size for a colony would be one queen and about 150 to 200 worker bees since, when there are fewer worker bees, there is no social order and no food exchange. A smaller number of bees will not cluster, and while 200 or 300 bees sometimes cluster without a queen, the cluster formation will not be normal. The worker bees of a colony are capable of undertaking a great number

2.2. An egg. In laying eggs the queen positions and glues them to the bottom center of the cell where they remain in an upright position until they hatch. (Photo by Karl Weiss.)

of tasks over a long period of time, but individual bees cannot survive very long.

What is normal insofar as population size is concerned also depends upon the time of year. This is discussed further in Chapter 4, where the cycle of the year is covered.

The castes and their development

The females in the honey bee colony are divided into two castes, the queens and the workers. The male or drone does not constitute a caste though it is incorrectly referred to as such in many texts. Among some species of ants and other social insects one may find a greater number of castes. However, the worker honey bee has built in her body a number of modifications that allow her to undertake a variety of tasks, and so there would appear to be no evolutionary advantage in the development of another caste among the females in a honey bee colony.

2.3. An egg on the left and the five instars (growth stages) of worker larvae. (Photo by Karl Weiss.)

An egg can develop into either a queen bee or a worker (see figure 2.2)—a fact that is demonstrated every time a queen breeder removes a worker larva from a worker cell and grafts it into a queen cell, and as a result, rears a queen. (figs. 2.3, 2.4, 2.5).

The body of the worker bee is modified in ways that aid in its work in the hive. Workers have wax glands whereas queens do not, the active head glands of workers differ greatly from those of queens, and queens have no pollen-carrying apparatus on their hind legs whereas workers do. In brief then, the worker is designed for her tasks, and the queen is aptly suited for her role in the hive. (figs. 2.6, 2.7).

In addition to the differences in the development time and the morphological differences (see Chapter 10), the life spans of the queen and worker differ greatly. Generally it is stated that worker honey bees live either for six months in the winter or six weeks in the summer. The statement is reasonably accurate, though both estimates may be a little long for the average worker. Workers live a short time in the summer because they work harder at that time of the year and actually wear out their bodies. The bodies of

2.4. Brood, eggs, and larvae in various stages of development. Note that brood of more or less the same age are in close association with one another. (Photo by Karl Weiss.)

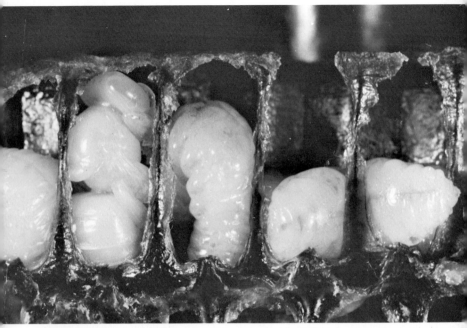

2.5. Brood in advanced stages of development. The sides of cells have been cut away to reveal their contents. Note that the three cells on the left, which contain more advanced larvae and a pupa, are capped. (Photo by Karl Weiss.)

old worker bees will have fewer hairs, and their wings may be frayed. Despite her very active life in the hive, the queen is not subjected to the rigors of inclement weather; instead, she remains in the center of the brood nest protected by the workers, fed by them and in a climate which obviously favors her longer life span. Queens have been known to live five years but two to three years is probably more common.

The drone

The drone is a much maligned animal. While Webster's dictionary correctly defines a drone as a male honey bee, an alternate definition is "a person who lives on the labors of others." Certainly

2.6. A worker honey bee. Note the empty pollen basket on rear leg. (Photo by Karl Weiss.)

2.7. A queen honey bee. The body of the queen is more elongate than that of the worker, and it can be seen that the leg structure is somewhat different. (Photo by Karl Weiss.)

2.8. A drone honey bee with a full complement of hair. Older bees lose their hair and often have frayed wings. (Photo by Karl Weiss.)

a drone is a specialized animal and among animals on earth, perhaps one of the most specialized. His genitalia, proportional to his body size, are larger than those of almost all other animals. Only a few species of fleas have genitalia which might be larger proportional to their body size.

A drone honey bee is a specialist: as far as we have been able to determine, his sole function is to mate. When drones are in the hive, they cluster at the side of the brood nest, and their position suggests that they have been driven from the active brood rearing area by the worker bees. Drones, like queens, fly only on warm, sunny afternoons. Presumably, the fact that they both fly only during this limited time facilitates mating.

Queen honey bees mate several times, but drones mate only once. In fact, the explosive shock which everts the male genitalia out of the abdomen, in which it is contained, kills the male almost immediately upon mating. It is believed that after mating, the queen usually removes the genitalia without assistance.

The rearing of drone brood starts later in the spring than does the rearing of worker brood. Drones are usually not produced until there is an abundance of pollen available, and there appear to be far more drones produced in colonies that are about to swarm than in those which are not. In the fall, worker honey bees cease to feed the males, and they are slowly driven from the hive. The discharge of drones from the hive was not studied until recently.

A popular book, written at the turn of the century by Maurice Maeterlinck, entitled *The Life of the Bee,* describes in vivid terms a massacre of the males in the fall. There is no real massacre of the males or drones in the fall, but at that season one may find several starved drones at a colony entrance and on the grass in front of a hive, and some people have thought that these drones were the victims of such a massacre. Maeterlinck's portrayal of this aspect of the life of the honey bee is so well written that many people came to believe it. Discharge of drones in the fall usually takes place over a period of several weeks and even months, but if there is a shortage of food, it is speeded up. This has been studied by Morse, Strang, and Nowakowski (1967).

The males of a colony congregate in an area away from the hive to which the queen goes. They are presumably attracted to it for the purpose of mating. Cyprian Zmarlicki wrote on this peculiar aspect of the life of the drone in 1963.

We are also aware that space, and evidently a large space, is necessary for mating to take place. Several people have attempted to mate queen honey bees in captivity using cages and indoor flight rooms of various designs and shapes, and with varying lighting and other conditions. Maurice Smith (1961) of Guelph University records that he had a mating take place in an indoor flight room, but he was unable to have the event repeated. Jan Nowakowski (Nowakowski and Morse, 1971) and John Harbo (1971) pursued the subject, and although they saw males follow queens in flight in cages of various design, mating did not take place.

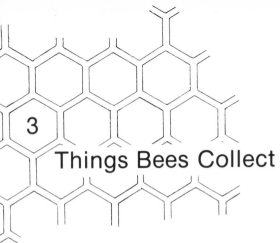

3
Things Bees Collect

The lives of bees and flowers are interwined. All bees, not just the honey bee but the solitary and subsocial bees too, are dependent upon flowers for their food. Not all flowering plants are dependent upon bees or other insects for cross-pollination; many have evolved methods using other animals or wind or water to transfer their pollen from the male to the female parts.

Honey bees collect four substances in the field: nectar, pollen, propolis, and water. Nectar provides bees with the carbohydrate portion of their diet, while pollen provides them with the protein and fat that they need. Both pollen and nectar are rewards given by the plant in exchange for pollination, and of course the system makes certain plants and bees wholly dependent upon one another. Propolis, which is the gum and resin secreted by trees, especially poplars and pines, and brought back to the hive by the bees in their pollen baskets, is used to close cracks and crevices, and as a varnish over rough wood. Sometimes bees use propolis to narrow the hive entrance.

Water is collected by bees for two purposes: first, to dilute the honey that they feed to their young; and second, to cool the hive. In warm weather, they sometimes place droplets of water around the hive at strategic points and then, by fanning their wings move large volumes of air through the hive, so that the water is evaporated and the hive cooled. While honey bees hoard pollen and nectar, they do not hoard or store propolis and water. The latter are collected only when needed.

3.1. A worker bee collecting saw-dust in the early spring when no plants have yet flowered. Note the small load in her pollen basket and the small particles on her body. She does not collect the large wood chips, which were made by a chain saw, but only little particles, which she mistakes for pollen. This fresh, hardwood sawdust had a pleasant odor.

Exceptions

Hard and fast statements are seldom tenable in biology. Having just stated that bees collect only certain substances, we must note that there are exceptions which, however, have to do with what bees "think" they are collecting. Of course, bees do not think, but they do have thresholds. Honey bees have a threshold of perception and also a threshold of acceptance. They are capable of determining the difference between a 10 per cent and a 20 per cent sugar solution, but what they will collect depends upon what is available to them.

It is interesting to watch bees collect sawdust as a substitute for pollen, in the early spring in the northern states (see fig. 3.1). During late March and early April there may be one or two days when the temperature will rise above 21° C (70° F) and sometimes above 27° C (80° F), but on these first spring days there are no flowering plants from which bees may collect either pollen or nectar. While the buds on the pussywillows may be swollen and almost ready to open, flowering is delayed a day or more until the temperature is sufficiently warm. On such days one may see honey bees burrowing into a sawdust pile [1] in much the same way that they will wallow across the head of a dandelion flower. When collecting pollen, the bee covers or dusts her body with pollen and then, using her legs, cleans the body and rakes the pollen from it into the pollen basket. Sawdust-collecting bees follow the same pattern, first dusting themselves with very small grains of sawdust, then packing the smaller bits into the pollen basket. The sawdust will be more attractive to the bees if it is freshly cut and has a fragrant odor from the early spring sap.

Similarly, bees have been observed collecting grain dust from bird feeders or even from around granaries in the early spring. Honey bees have been seen active in coal dust piles, too. We do not know if these materials are rejected by other bees once they are carried back to the hive, but we do know that bees do return to the hive with them. Obviously these substances have no food value, and this fact is an excellent indication of the bees' low threshold of acceptance.

Honey bees have been observed collecting bits of road tar in place of propolis, and it is not uncommon to find a piece of tar mixed in with propolis in a hive. They will similarly collect droplets of fresh paint in place of propolis. Taber and Barker (1974) found bees collecting caulking compound in Arizona.

In Europe honeydew honey is a favorite. Aphids, small insects which feed on coniferous trees, secrete a substance that is sweet but that is also high in gums and dextrins; this is called honeydew. Because this aphid secretion contains sugar, it attracts honey bees, and they collect it. The resulting honey is dark in color and strong in flavor; but, many people like, and sometimes prefer, strongly flavored foods. Thousands of colonies of honey bees are carried

1. Several people mention having seen bees collect sawdust in the spring, but there are few records of the type of wood from which the sawdust has been cut. They may collect sawdust from hardwoods only.

into the forests of Europe for the express purpose of storing honey-dew honey. It commands a good price on the local market although most Americans, who are accustomed to milder, lighter flavored honeys, would reject it. Honey bees, too, prefer floral nectar to aphid honeydew; however, it is all a question of their threshold of acceptance, and when nothing else is available, they will collect honeydew. Honeydew honey is produced in only small quantity in North America and then not intentionally. In this part of the world it is sold to the bakery trade and is not used as a table honey.

Collection, storage, and utilization of nectar

Nectar is the sweet secretion which the flower of a plant produces for the express purpose of attracting the insects or birds that will pollinate the flower and distribute its pollen to other flowers of the same species. A few people have suggested that nectar might serve another function; however, documentation of any other purpose is lacking. Biologists generally agree that plants and animals do not waste energy; when something is produced, or when some change takes place in nature, there is usually a positive reason for it, and in explaining biological processes, it may be assumed that the simplest and most obvious explanation is the correct one until shown otherwise.

Nectar, as mentioned, is a source of carbohydrate for honey bees. After nectar has been collected, modified, changed into honey, and stored in the honey comb, it has a long life. Honey that is a few years old is a perfectly satisfactory food for both bees and men. Fresher honey may have a slightly better flavor as some of the flavoring ingredients are volatile. Honey that is several years old darkens and slowly loses its flavor.

Field bees which collect nectar give the food to hive bees. We presume that both field and hive bees add enzymes to the nectar in the process, but apparently it is the hive bees which are active in reducing the water content of nectar. In an observation hive one can watch hive bees forcing droplets of nectar in and out of their

3.2. Honey bees ventilating a colony force air out of the hive on the right hand side of the entrance. There are several standing, fanning bees under the waving strip of tissue paper. On the left hand side of the entrance, which is used for air intake, there are no fanners. This photograph was taken in the afternoon as some drones are visible.

honey sacs and onto their tongues, an action which probably serves to mix the enzymes with the honey and to reduce its moisture content. Following such activity, hive bees place droplets of nectar in storage cells; then, by fanning their wings, the bees move large volumes of air through the hive, and the moisture content of the new honey is in this way further reduced. Worker bees ventilating are shown in figure 3.2.

Cells of stored honey are covered with cappings made of beeswax. The cappings probably facilitate the movement of worker bees over the comb and prevent the contamination of the honey by any loose particles or debris.

As bees need honey for food, they eat that which is closest to the brood nest. Only a small percentage of the storage cells are opened at one time. As the bees consume the honey, they continue to move the brood nest or cluster in an upward direction. Interestingly, the cells that are opened are always in close proximity; cells are not opened at random over the face of the comb when food is needed.

Honey versus nectar

Nectar is secreted from a mass of plant cells (a gland) called a nectary, usually at the base of the male and female parts of the flower. In their search for nectar, the hairy honey bees pass over the male parts and/or sometimes the female parts, and their bodies become covered with pollen. As the bees move from one flower to another, they transport pollen from one to the other. The nectar that the bees collect is predominately sucrose, and honey bees apparently prefer it to other sugar solutions. Honey bees begin the digestive process immediately and add the enzyme, invertase, to the nectar. Invertase acts to convert the twelve-carbon sucrose into two six-carbon sugars, levulose and dextrose.[2]

In addition to adding an enzyme to nectar, honey bees also reduce its water content. Nectar may contain as little as 5 to 10 per cent, or as much as 50 to 60 per cent, sugar. Nectar with more than 50 per cent solids is uncommon. As will be discussed later, honey bees can detect differences in the total solid content of a nectar and will choose the sweeter when two or more are offered to them.

Honey bees make at least two changes in nectar, one a chemical change, the conversion of the twelve-carbon sugar to two six-carbon sugars, and the other a physical change involving the re-

2. There is some confusion over the terms *levulose* and *dextrose,* and *fructose* and *glucose.* Levulose is the same as fructose; dextrose is the same as glucose. If one were talking to a chemist or biologist he would be more inclined to use the terms *fructose* and *glucose* when speaking about the two, six-carbon sugars that are made when honey bees add the enzyme invertase to the twelve-carbon sugar sucrose; sucrose is the predominate sugar in nectar, whereas levulose and dextrose are the common sugars in honey. The terms *levulose* and *dextrose* occur more commonly in beekeeping texts, and several years ago were in more popular use.

duction of moisture to less than about 19 per cent. A third change, the addition of the enzyme glucose oxidase, is discussed in Chapter 12 under Natural systems protecting honey bees and their food.

The substance bees collect from flowers is nectar, and the substance finally stored in a hive is honey. The change from nectar to honey is a process that may take several hours to complete. The important thing to remember is that in the beginning and at the end we have two quite different materials. Unripe honey is the usual appellation for that which is neither nectar nor true honey.

Collection, storage, and utilization of pollen

It is evident why bees collect nectar: they respond to both the taste of the sugar and the odor of the flower. Until recently, however, it has not been understood why bees collect pollen. We now know, as a result of observations by Stephen Taber III [3] and Rolf Boch, that those pollens which bees collect contain chemical substances attractive to them. Taber has demonstrated that one may extract these chemicals from pollen, put the extracts on sawdust, and in this way make the sawdust attractive to bees. It was Rolf Boch and his associates who identified the first such chemical substance. Boch also found that certain pollen colors are more attractive than others to honey bees and that they have a preference for the yellow pollen; there is a great variation in pollen colors. Last, there is a question of particle size. While the size of pollen grains does not serve to attract bees, they will not collect substitutes of a grain size which is larger than that of normal pollen.

When honey bees collect nectar, they suck it from the flower with their mouthparts and store it in their honey sacs. To collect pollen, however, the worker bee burrows in and around the anthers of the flower and dusts herself with pollen. Following this she hovers, and using her legs, combs the pollen from her hairy body

3. The only record of Taber's discovery is an abstract in the program of the December 1963 meeting of the Entomological Society of America held in St. Louis. At that meeting I vividly remember a film which Taber presented showing bees collecting sawdust coated with an extract of pollen washed with the solvent hexane.

and packs it into the pollen baskets on the hind legs. Most bees are either nectar collectors or pollen collectors, but occasionally one finds a bee which will collect both on the same trip. As Aristotle noted over 2,000 years ago, on a single trip bees usually visit flowers of the same species. Thus, when they return to the hive, the color of the pollen balls on their hind legs is usually uniform throughout. This is not true of certain solitary bees, which may collect pollen from several different species of plants on the same trip.

Worker honey bees themselves place the pollen pellets that they have collected into the storage cells, but the pollen is finally packed into the cells by house bees,[4] which use their heads as rams. Whereas honey cells may be filled to the brim, pollen cells are filled only three-fourths full. If the pollen is for immediate use, nothing further is done, but if it is to be stored for a long time, it is usually covered with honey. Even so, pollen loses some of its nutritive value in storage. (See Chapter 12 for more information on the protection of stored food.)

Not all pollens are equal in food value for honey bees. Only recently it has been found that dandelion pollen is deficient in certain materials and by itself does not make good food for bees. While individual bees collect pollen from only one species of flower, together, the bees in the hive collect from many sources, and thus, sources that are superior compensate for those that are deficient.

Collection and utilization of water

Honey bees do not store water in the hive; they collect large quantities of it, as it is needed, to dilute the food of the larvae and also to cool the hive during warm weather. What stimulates bees to collect water is not known, but it is suggested that the bees merely respond to a shortage of water in larval food or to high temperatures.

Although bees show a remarkable flower fidelity (that is, an

---

4. *House bees,* sometimes called *hive bees,* are the young bees which do all the work in the hive; *field bees* are the older bees which are scouts and/or collect nectar, pollen, water, and propolis.

interest in only one species) when collecting pollen or nectar, they may interrupt their collection of either to collect water when it is needed. They have been observed collecting alternate loads of nectar and water, depending upon the needs of the colony.

The worker bees carry water in their honey sacs. On returning to the hive they give it to the house bees, which in turn distribute it among themselves to be used for larval feeding or deposit it in cells or on wooden parts in the interior of the hive where it subsequently evaporates during warm weather. Bees appear to prefer contaminated or slightly salty water to pure water, and they have even been observed collecting water with a small amount of urine in it from around barns. It is highly probable that the odor aids them in finding the water, though this is not clear. The urine in the water does not pose a health hazard to the honey bee since very few microorganisms that might live in a water-urine solution would have an adverse effect on an insect, but the thought is repugnant to man. This is one of the reasons that many beekeepers have a dripping water spout or a source of fresh water in the apiary.

In villages and cities honey bees, in search of water, are sometimes a serious nuisance around bird baths and swimming pools. In fact some municipalities have enacted anti-bee ordinances. Usually bees will collect water from the nearest source, and if water is provided in the apiary they will not fly longer distances for it. If running water is not available in the apiary, water may be made available from an open tank or can which has a proper float to prevent the bees from drowning as they collect the water. A rural area often has good natural sources of water, but a water collection station for bees can save the beekeeper in an urban area many a headache.

Collection and utilization of propolis

The collection and manipulation of propolis is not an easy task for the bee because the material is very sticky and gummy. Certain races of bees use far more of it than others. Bees of the Caucasion race will use propolis to restrict the colony entrance, thereby making it easier for bees in the colony to protect their hive.

It is not known what stimulates honey bees to collect propolis, but if a beekeeper uses a frame that is not properly planed or sanded, or if the interior of a hive body has a rough surface, the bees will soon varnish the rough area with this substance. Sometimes they use propolis of several colors, and an interesting pattern emerges. The material has an antiseptic effect in the bee hive just as it has on a tree wound: it is both bactericidal and bacteriostatic. We presume that by covering cracks and crevices in the bee hive, the honey bees eliminate places that might harbor microorganisms as well as larger pests and predators such as beetles, flies, and wax moths.

Bees carry propolis in their pollen baskets. A load of it takes the shape of a load of pollen. The bees that collect propolis do not remove it from their pollen baskets themselves. Rather, they go to that part of the hive where the propolis is needed and wait for other bees to take it from them, bit by bit. G. A. Rosch, as recorded by von Frisch (1967b) once watched a honey bee that had to wait seven hours before the propolis was removed from her legs; during this time she made no effort to take it off her legs herself. Presumably, propolis is removed in a more rapid fashion under normal circumstances. As is the case with water, bees do not store propolis in the hive though they may redistribute a small quantity of it from time to time.

When old comb is rendered (melted) for the wax it contains, excessive quantities of propolis may adversely affect both the color and the quality of the resulting beeswax. In fact, propolis is probably responsible for part of the odor of wax. A light-colored beeswax, with a mild odor, commands a higher price on the market than does a darker wax.

Fresh propolis is plastic at about 21°C (70°F) and melts at approximately 66°C (150°F); these qualities vary considerably depending upon the source. Propolis collected by honey bees, like those plant gums and resins left in place on tree wounds, solidifies in time, giving a hard, glossy appearance to the surface on which it is placed.

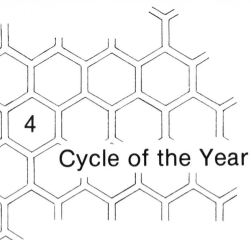

4

Cycle of the Year

In the cycle of the year, the changes that we are concerned with are those that take place in a colony rather than those in individuals. Since only the queen lives for more than a year, part of the cycle involves the continual replacement of worker bees within the hive.

Several people have suggested that it is sometimes appropriate to consider a honey bee colony not as a collection of individuals but as a single individual, with worker bees being constantly replaced in a system just as cells are replaced in another animal's body. The thought has merit, for great changes do take place in the honey bee colony during the year. A normal colony of honey bees may have a population as low as 10,000 to 15,000 individuals at one time of year and a peak population of about 60,000 at another time.

The cycle of the year varies with the latitude. In Florida, for example, in most years the peak population is reached in March, but in the northern states it would be found in late June or July. However, the populations of colonies in the southern parts of the United States usually do not attain the size of those in the northern United States and Canada. As one moves from south to north it appears that honey flows intensify, and certainly bees are able to work more hours because of longer periods of daylight in the North. Though there are no precise data on the question, commercial beekeepers state that swarming is more intense in the northern states than in the South. The great stimulation given brood rearing in the northern states by the tremendous quantities of pollen available in April from pussy willow and other plants unquestionably influences the cycle of the year.

The normal cycle

At one time egg production and brood rearing in midwinter in the northern states were thought to be abnormal and brought about by poor food or other adverse conditions. This theory has been discarded; we now believe that brood rearing in the winter is normal.

Perhaps it is unreasonable to talk about a normal cycle of the year, for on paper we can obtain a smooth curve only by taking data over a period of several years and from several colonies. All the factors that affect the growth and development of any plant or animal enter into the honey bee's cycle, including weather, the availability of food, and physical condition. In the average hive bees can withstand great extremes in temperature, especially low winter temperatures, but shortages of pollen or nectar, or both, will have a profound effect on brood rearing. Honey bees have been observed to remove and discard larvae when there is insufficient pollen to feed them. The worker bees do not remove eggs and pupae from their cells during a time of dearth since there is no feeding in these stages. It is a curious situation to find only eggs and capped pupae in a honey bee colony, but this condition has been observed by many beekeepers at various times of the year.

The selection of the site to keep a colony of bees is of major concern to the commercial beekeeper because it will affect the health and productivity of the bees. Some diseases are associated with faulty environment, and local climatic conditions may have an adverse effect on colony development. Bees need fresh water in which other bees have not deposited fecal matter from which they might pick up disease-causing microorganisms. Similarly, bees need exposure to the sun on a southern slope so that their hives are warmed early in the morning and they may take flight as early as possible, either to cleanse themselves or to collect food.

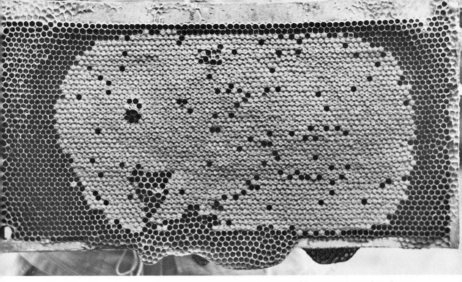

4.1. A brood comb with a reasonably compact brood pattern. The queen has missed very few cells in the process of laying eggs in this frame.

Flight from a colony starts when temperature reaches 18° C (65° F). Full flight does not occur until the temperature is about 21° C (70° F). The selection of an apiary site is under the beekeepers control. It behooves him to select sites which encourage maximum flight.

All of these factors affect the normal cycle of the year. As in the case of norms for most animals, we may talk about the normal cycle of the average colony, but normality is actually a hypothetical concept.

Data on brood production

Egg laying and the production of brood by colonies during the spring, summer, and fall months have been studied by several people. It is well established, for example, that in Florida brood production starts around the first of the year and reaches a peak about the time of the orange honey flow in March or early April. If another honey flow follows in April or May, the colony population does not begin to wane until June or after. A frame of capped brood is shown in figure 4.1.

In the northern states, the first pollen, which becomes available about the middle of April, stimulates brood production, and colony populations peak about the beginning of July or shortly after. If there is a good honey flow in August, colony populations may reach another peak during that month and then begin to decline.

Until the mid 1950's most authorities on bees and beekeeping agreed that brood rearing started in earnest when the earliest fresh pollen and nectar were brought into the hive in the spring. Most people felt that any colonies which reared brood in the inactive season were not normal and those which had brood during the winter suffered from poor stores, a lack of bees, or insufficient insulation, or in some way had been disturbed; presumably any one of these four conditions was sufficient to initiate brood rearing.

Data to the contrary were presented by Edward P. Jeffree in 1956. He stated that there is a "very strong tradition that bees should be left strictly alone during the winter," and this, he felt, is responsible for the lack of data. He next stated that "with discretion and common sense," one might inspect colonies in midwinter. He cited those people who had suggested that in the northern states, or in a place such as Scotland, brood rearing might begin about the first of the year. Jeffree found that in Aberdeen, Scotland, approximately 57° north latitude, there was the least amount of brood in October and November. Over a period of seven years he made 367 colony examinations during the months of September through March. His data are summarized in table 4.1 below.

Table 4.1.   Brood production observed over a seven-year period in Scotland (modified after Jeffree, 1956).

Month	Brood mean square inches	Number of examinations	Per cent colonies with brood
September	76	45	78
October	2	106	14
November	2	114	25
December	10	31	58
January	14	18	50
February	48	10	100
March	50	43	91

Jeffree offers no explanation of why brood rearing begins in December, as it apparently does, judging by his data.

Several items in the Jeffree data need further exploration. It is interesting that there were always some colonies with brood, presumably throughout the year. Everything we know about the queen and her role in the colony suggests that her age and the pheromones she secretes may have a controlling influence on brood production. Also evident, as several people have suggested, is the extreme importance of pollen, the bee's source of protein, in winter brood rearing. The last figure in the lower right hand corner of table 4.1 is most telling in this regard. Jeffree found that whereas all his colonies had brood in February, only 91 per cent had brood in March. He did not explain the 9 per cent decrease, but I suspect it occurred in colonies that had depleted their pollen stores. There is also the question of the value of certain pollens as bee food. Some pollens provide many more of the nutrients needed by bees than do others, and it is possible that some may stimulate brood rearing more than others. If there is any substance to this last remark, knowing which materials might be stimulating would be of great value to the beekeeping industry.

Does day length control the normal cycle?

In my opinion brood rearing and colony reproduction (swarming) are controlled by day length. This hypothesis is in part based on the data of Jeffree, which shows that brood rearing begins in December. While this may be before the day length is actually increasing, there is no change in day length at the time, and if we postulate that increasing day length stimulates brood rearing, we may equally postulate that decreasing day length slows it. These thoughts are also based on the fact that in the northern hemisphere most swarming occurs before about the first of July, the exact date depending upon the latitude. From an evolutionary point of view, prohibiting swarming after the first of July makes biological sense, and so does the old farmer's ditty: "A swarm of bees in May / is worth a load of hay, / a swarm of bees in June / is worth a silver spoon, / and a swarm of bees in July / isn't worth a fly." A swarm of bees which initiates its nest in May in the northern states would certainly have sufficient time to build comb and gather a surplus of honey for winter; a swarm of bees which starts its nest in June is also likely to do so. But as the season progresses, and certainly after the first of July, a swarm does not have sufficient time to build comb, and collect and store the 60 to 80 pounds of honey required to survive the winter in the northern states. Of course, the modern-day beekeeper with his knowledge of bee behavior and food requirements would supplement the food of a late swarm, and so perhaps it is worth a little more than a "fly"; however, this was not true years ago before colonies could be opened and given needed care.

People who believe that day length is not the controlling factor in the cycle of the year are careful not to deny the idea categorically, but they point out, for example, that although most swarming takes place in the early part of the season, it does sometimes occur in the summer and even fall. This varies with latitude; Burgett and Morse (1974) have presented data for Ithaca, New York. They also suggest that queen production, which is mentioned below, and which is one of the early signs of the swarming process, may occur at any time of the year. Another suggestion is that there is a closer correlation with honey production than with day length. My own observations seem to cast doubt on this suggestion. I have seen swarms in the area of Ithaca in early June, after the dandelion and yellow rocket nectar flows and before the flowering of clovers (June 20–25), when there is often a dearth of nectar.

Clearly, this seemingly simple question needs much examination.

Pollen in the diet

Our limited knowledge of honey bee nutrition permits us to make only very general statements about their dietary requirements. We can state that without pollen bees cannot rear brood. In some parts of the country, and in some seasons, or under severe climatic conditions, there may be a serious pollen shortage. Interestingly, the reverse may also occur. Under good growing conditions certain plants may produce a great surplus of pollen. The bees may store so much pollen that they leave no room for brood rearing. Colonies with too much pollen are said to be pollen-bound.

Beekeepers in the northern states are all too familiar with the fact that bees may remove larvae of various ages from their cells and discard them in front of the hive if they have no pollen in the hive. Interestingly, the queen continues to lay eggs. If a food shortage lasts long enough, egg laying may diminish, but no diminution is visible in the early stages of pollen starvation.

Presumably both worker and queen larvae are fed royal jelly, a secretion from the pharyngeal and mandibular glands of worker honey bees, for the first two days or so of their lives, and thereafter the larvae of workers receive less royal jelly, if any at all, while those destined to become queens are fed lavish amounts. Research has shown that, in a second or third generation of confined bees fed only a sugar solution, pharyngeal glands do not develop. In a normal worker bee the pharyngeal glands are fully developed at eight to ten days of age.

Several experimenters have developed pollen substitutes in order to spur brood rearing before pollen is naturally available and also to carry bees through pollen shortages. Both pollen substitutes and pollen supplements have been devised; the former contain no bee-collected pollen, while the latter usually contain some bee-collected pollen and other materials. Among the foods that have been fed to bees are egg white, dried yeast, distillers' corn solubles, and soy flour. These materials seem to work very well; adding a small amount of bee-collected pollen appears to encourage the bees to accept the supplements or substitutes more readily. Some people add honey to the mixture to make it more palatable. The studies undertaken to date suggest that the attractiveness and palatability of the supplements and substitutes are very important. Some researchers have suggested that, if a suitable pollen attractant could be identified, synthesized, and added to these materials, it would enhance their practical use.

In any event, the availability of pollen has a profound effect upon the normal cycle of the year. Being able to assess when to and when not to feed bees a high protein additive is part of the art of beekeeping. Such judgments are usually made on the basis of the weather, the pollen-producing plants available to bees, and an estimate of the amount of pollen stored in the hive.

Swarming as part of the cycle

Swarming is a natural phenomenon that occurs when a colony of honey bees divides into two parts. Not every colony swarms every year, but it is probably safe to say that the average colony swarms once every two or three years. As long as queens lay eggs and colony populations increase, there must be swarming or colony division for species perpetuation. We do not have any data to show what percentage of swarms fail after having left the parent colony.

In the northern hemisphere most swarming occurs during the spring months. In southern Florida a colony may sometimes swarm as early as late February; however, more often the swarming season in Florida is in March and early April, and to a lesser extent in May and June. In New York State it is estimated that 80 per cent of swarming takes place in May and June. It would appear, as one moves north, that not only does the swarming season come later in the year, but the tendency to swarm is intensified.

Steps in swarming

The actual process of swarming, during which the old queen and 30 to 70 per cent of the workers and the drones in the hive leave, takes place in 10 to 20 minutes, but signs that swarming is about to happen are visible to the careful observer several days, perhaps even weeks, beforehand.

When the colony population increases in the spring, the building of queen cups by worker honey bees is the first indication that the colony may swarm. A queen cup is the base of a queen cell, and it will later be made into a queen cell if the colony continues with its efforts to swarm. Queen cups, like queen cells, are placed in a position perpendicular to the worker and drone cells in the hive. Usually, the queen cups are constructed at the lower edge of the brood nest. Space, however, is as important as position; because a queen cell is much larger than other cells in the hive, it can be built only where there is enough space to accommodate it. Commercial beekeepers, when they wish to inspect a colony, split the two hive bodies at the point where the brood nest exists and check between the upper and lower frames for queen cells and queen cups, since bees favor this place for building them. Bees sometimes construct queen cups and queen cells between two frames that are side by side, but more often they build them below the bottom bar of one frame and above the top bar of the frame below. Queen cups may be visible in a colony several weeks before the queen lays eggs in them. The number of cups constructed varies; the greater the number, the greater the chances the colony will swarm. We presume the number of queen cups constructed relates to the pheromone balance in the hive; this theory is developed in Chapter 7.

In the next step of swarming, the queen lays eggs in the queen cups, but this still does not mean that the colony will swarm and, in fact, even after first instar [1] larvae have hatched from eggs in the cells, the process of swarming may still be reversed. We suspect that worker honey bees remove some of the first eggs placed in queen cups by queens, though there are no quantitative data on this question.

If one finds larvae two or more days old in queen cells, especially in May and June in the North and earlier in the South, swarming may occur, however, this is not always the case, and the question is discussed in greater detail below. The primary swarm will usually emerge anytime after the queen cells have been capped.

When the larvae in the queen cells are two days old, the queen begins to lose weight. Queens lose about one-third of their weight in the three to five days before they take flight and emerge from the colony with a swarm. This weight loss is apparently necessary for

1. Honey bee larvae pass through four instars, or growth periods, moulting at the end of each. They moult again at the end of the prepupal stage, and a sixth moult occurs just before they emerge as adults. The subject was researched by Bertholf (1925).

the queens to be able to fly. Meanwhile the worker honey bees begin to engorge. A swarm carries with it sufficient food for several days. This fact also means that there is a slowing of food gathering by the colony, another reason why beekeepers wish to prevent swarming.

The irreversibility of swarming

Once larvae two days or older are found in queen cells during the swarming months, commercial beekeepers tend to believe that the process of swarming is irreversible (May and June in the North and earlier in the South). However, Gary and Morse (1962) found that queen rearing can be aborted repeatedly and that production of mature queen cells is not necessarily followed by swarming or supersedure. Queen replacement was observed in ten colonies during a six and one-half month period. Traps were attached to the colony entrances to collect queens that died within the colony. Three of the ten experimental colonies showed no change during the period. A fourth reared one virgin queen but did not replace its old queen. Changes took place in the remaining six colonies, but the process can indeed be complicated as table 4.2 indicates. Of special interest in this table is colony 7, which reared and discarded six virgin queens over a period of three weeks before the old queen was found dead in the trap. Following this, sixteen more virgins were reared before the colony was requeened; however, the colony did requeen itself without any outside assistance.

Secondary swarms

Some colonies cast secondary or even tertiary and quaternary swarms. Each is usually successively smaller. The tendency to cast more than one swarm is highly variable and appears to be affected by the bees' race. I believe it occurs less often with the Italian race. Whereas the first swarm is accompanied by the old queen, the secondary swarm must await the emergence of a virgin queen. Its departure can occur as long as eight days after that of a primary swarm which left when the queen cells were first capped.

Sometimes more than one virgin queen will emerge at the same time, and two or more young queens may accompany a secondary

Table 4.2. Queen bodies found in dead-bee traps (after Gary and Morse, 1962).

Colony no.	Virgin queens	Laying queens	Date		Maximum brood count (¼-frames)	Seasonal honey yield (lb.) [1 lb. = 0.454 kg.]
1	0	0	—		32	152
2	0	0	—		29	187
3	0	0	—		25	215
4	1	0	Aug.	4	25	115
5	1	–	June	11	51	135
	1	1	"	12		
	1	–	"	30		
6	1	–	June	3	32	61
	–	1	"	10		
	colony swarmed		"	17		
	1	–	"	19		
	1	–	"	20		
	1	–	"	21		
	1	–	"	22		
	–	1	Sept.	16		
7	1	–	April	29	31	117
	2	–	May	2		
	1	–	"	6		
	1	–	"	17		
	1	1	"	19		
	2	–	"	21		
	1	–	"	28		
	4	–	"	29		
	1	–	"	31		
	3	–	June	1		
	1	–	"	2		
	1	–	"	3		
	1	–	"	5		
	1	–	"	6		
	1	–	"	8		
8	–	1	Sept.	15	16	45
	3	–	Oct.	26		
	4	–	"	27		
	1	–	Nov.	1		
9	queen removed		July	29	32	234
	queen introduced		Aug.	2		
	1	–	"	9		
	8	–	"	10		
	6	–	"	11		
	1	–	"	18		
	–	1	"	28		
10	queen lost		April	14–19	28	92
	1	–	May	20		
	queen introduced		June	3		
	1	–	"	3		
	1	–	"	6		
	–	1	"	26		
	combined with nucleus		"	27		

swarm. A secondary swarm captured at Dyce laboratory at Cornell a few years ago contained four virgin queens. A beekeeper wrote me recently that he once captured a swarm, which he thought to be a secondary swarm, that contained 14 virgins; the details in his letter showed that he was a careful observer, and presumably his figure was accurate. Probably these large numbers of virgin queens in secondary swarms occur rarely, but we have no data to show whether or not this statement is correct.

Within a colony, virgin queens will seek out and fight with each other, one attempting to sting the other to death. Usually, the first virgin to emerge will destroy other queen cells or at least open them so that they will be destroyed by worker bees. It is thought that virgin queens recognize each other and queen cells, through a pheromone not yet identified. During inclement weather bees have been observed containing or holding virgin queens in their cells, presumably to prevent them from fighting. Workers do so by feeding the virgins as they begin to emerge and chew their way out of their cells. Feeding apparently slows or prevents the virgins from chewing further. It appears that, in a swarm, virgin queens are less prone to attack one another or at least less quick to do so. Presumably, after the swarm has moved to its final destination the virgin queens seek out one another, and only one survives. In later swarms, the virgin queen does not mate until after the swarm has moved to its final destination. (At least, this is the present belief. Drones may take mating flights from a swarm, and return to the swarm's temporary nesting site, just as they would from a colony; however, it is difficult to believe a virgin queen would do so though this may be the case.) If, however, a secondary swarm does not appear, the virgin queen which first emerges in the colony kills her adversaries, destroys queen cells, subsequently mates and then becomes the "queen" of the colony.

Behavior of a new swarm

The new swarm, whether it be primary, secondary, or other, leaves the hive rapidly and becomes an airborne mass of bees 15 to 30 meters (approximately 50 to 100 feet) in diameter. Certain workers in the swarm then proceed to settle on a nearby bush or tree and soon after five or ten of them have done so, a few start to expose their scent glands, thereby attracting the remaining bees in the swarm. The queen does not lead the swarm in flight but behaves as though she were a worker bee, responding to the worker scent herself and settling in the swarm with the rest of the bees. The swarm cluster takes the shape of a sphere which may become oblong depending upon the number of branches on which it has to cluster. During the first few minutes when the swarm cluster forms, the presence of the queen is not required. However, if the queen does not soon join the growing cluster, it will break up and may attempt to settle elsewhere in the vicinity. If the queen does not leave the hive or is lost, the bees return to the parent colony. On occasion, a newly emerged swarm may start to form two or more clusters; however, only the cluster with the queen remains intact. This activity is controlled by pheromones and is discussed in greater detail in Chapter 7.

Under normal circumstances, bees in a swarm do not forage. They carry with them food sufficient for several days, and presumably because they are engorged, their wax glands are stimulated to produce beeswax. Settled swarms are attractive to other bees and may be joined by drones and foragers from other colonies, including the occasional pollen collector which is sometimes seen on the surface of the cluster. This is probably true because the scent gland pheromone, used so extensively by swarms, is attractive to all bees and is the same for all bees.

Soon after the swarm cluster settles, scouts depart from it and visit the potential homesites that have been searched out before the swarm left the hive. Infrequently, though it is not known how infrequently, swarms may move directly from the old hive to a new home. The circumstances under which this may occur are not clear. Usually 50 to 100 scout bees from the swarm do the home searching for the rest. After the scouts return from suitable homesites to the swarm cluster, they dance, using the wag-tail dance described below, and indicate to other bees the location and quality of the homesite. When all of the scouts are dancing the same dance and thus have agreed upon the new home, the swarm again becomes airborne, usually within two or three minutes, and moves as a mass to the new homesite. The rapidity with which the swarm can become airborne is amazing, and it is a fascinating process to watch. Again, the queen does not lead this flight, but follows or proceeds in the midst of the workers; however, the workers are aware of the presence of the queen and will seldom go more than about 200 meters (apx. 200 yards) without her. Should she be lost in transit, the bees will return to where she was last known to be and search for her.

In the new homesite, the bees begin to construct comb, rear brood, and gather food. If the swarming process is to be successful, the new swarm must gather enough food to survive the following winter; if the location it has picked is satisfactory, and if there is abundant food, the colony will continue to prosper. It is my opinion that the old queen is usually replaced within two to four months by a young virgin queen which takes over the duties of egg laying and the production of queen pheromones. The new colony will itself cast a swarm in two to three years in all probability.

Swarm prevention

The two major problems of beekeepers in the northern states are swarming and winter losses. Although it is difficult to say which of these causes the greater dollar loss it is probable that beekeepers in these states could produce 25 to 50 per cent more honey if they could prevent all winter losses and control all swarming. In the southern states, swarming is less of a problem.

In the case of swarming, beekeepers think in terms of prevention or control, two distinct entities: swarm prevention refers to those actions taken to prevent the production of queen cells and virgin queens, and swarm control refers to those steps which must be taken after larvae have been found in queen cells when the swarming process is considered to be irreversible.

tion of too many drones and a sudden emergence of brood are discouraged both by having good combs in the hive and young queens present.

The favorite swarm prevention technique is called "reversing." There is a natural tendency for bees within a colony to move their brood nest continually upward. In fact, it is not uncommon to find a colony in two or three supers with the top super full of brood and the bottom one or two supers empty. Under these circumstances the colony brood nest may be congested, and as the bees will not relieve the congestion themselves by moving in a downward direction, the beekeeper must do it for them. Reversing entails taking the bottom super and placing it on top of the super above. In this way bees are given additional room to move their brood nest upward. They may be encouraged to move in an upward direction by taking one frame of brood from the brood nest and moving it into an empty super above. This is called "spreading the brood," and it also serves to relieve congestion. There is danger in doing this too early in May (in the northern states) for if the weather suddenly becomes cold the bees may not be able to cluster around the brood sufficiently well to protect it.

Commercial beekeepers sometimes reverse their colonies three or four times during May and June in New York and other northern states. To determine whether or not reversing should be done, they check between the supers and watch for the construction of queen cups.

Swarm control

Once two-day, or older, larvae are found in queen cells in May and June in the North, and earlier in the South, swarming is likely to take place. At this time the swarm prevention methods outlined above are inadequate, and the beekeeper must take more drastic steps. There are only three things he can do, though each has some variations: he can remove the queen, he can remove the brood, or he can separate the queen and the brood.

Removal of the queen: One method advocated by old-time comb honey producers is to cage the queen for about ten days, leaving

We still do not know precisely what makes bees swarm, tho u
we understand why swarming must occur, and that it is part of 1
natural cycle of the year. The most popular theory is that swarm
is caused primarily by congestion of adult bees in the brood n
It is thought that congestion upsets the normal distribution of s
chemicals (pheromones) that the queen produces. We know t
food exchange, which is probably also a method of exchang
pheromones, is necessary for the continued existence of a col
(The chemistry of pheromones is discussed in Chapter 7.) H
ever, long before we began to think about and understand
chemistry of the swarming process, beekeepers had designed t
niques to prevent swarming. It is suggested that a lack of ven
tion, insufficient shade, too many drones, too much honey, in
ficient room, and a sudden emergence of young bees may be
tributory factors in swarming. Perhaps the best of the thousan
publications on swarm control is by George S. Demuth, prep
in 1921.

To prevent swarming, commercial beekeepers take step
relieve congestion and improve the physical situation within
colony. Although the steps are simple to describe, conside
experience is required to assess colony conditions accurately
to know when to act. In addition to making certain standard n
pulations, it is known that a queen two years old is approxim
twice as likely to head a colony which will swarm as is a one-
old queen. This question was well researched by James Sim
(1960). The chief method of discouraging swarming is to
plenty of room for colony expansion, both for expansion
brood nest and for honey storage. Most colonies come int
spring in two supers, or boxes. The third super of combs is u
added in April, sometimes early May, in the northern stat
fourth, fifth, and sixth super may be added during May and
Sometime in May the entrance cleat (reducer) is removed fro
colony entrance so as to improve ventilation. The entrance
is left in place until this date to help the bees protect the bro
cool nights; an entrance cleat may also deter robbing. The p

her in her own colony during this time. Meanwhile, the queen cells are cut from the colony, an operation that usually must be repeated six or seven days later. After the ten days have elapsed, the queen is released and resumes egg laying. In effect, caging the queen serves to limit the brood, and thus to relieve congestion of adult bees in the brood nest area of the colony. Caging the queen may possibly hasten her supersedure later in the summer or fall.

One may also remove the queen and allow the bees to rear a new queen. If, at the time the queen is removed, all the queen cells are removed from the colony, the bees are forced to rear a new queen from a one or two-day-old larva. It will therefore be ten or eleven days before the new queen will emerge, and by this time congestion will have been relieved because of the break in the brood rearing. Under these circumstances it is presumed that the colony will not swarm, and that the first virgin to emerge will become the active queen in the colony. This method probably has more disadvantages than advantages, especially if it is done at a time when increased brood rearing is needed for the impending honey flow. The method is dangerous because queen rearing is not always successful under these circumstances, and the colony may become queenless. Also, it is presumed that during this period of queenlessness, while the bees are rearing a new queen, food gathering may be slow. Our knowledge of bee behavior suggests that the physical presence of the queen encourages food gathering.

Some beekeepers attempt requeening at the same time the queen is removed; this is sometimes possible though it is difficult at this time of the year (May–July). It is nearly impossible to introduce a young queen by way of a queen cage and have her accepted. Under these circumstances, it is far better to place a nucleus colony with a young queen on top of the old hive, after the old queen has been removed, putting a piece of newspaper between the two units. By the time the newspaper is chewed away by the bees, the hive odor in the two units is similar, and there is usually little fighting. In effect, however, the new queen is occupying her own brood nest, or at least not the one that was presumably congested and on the verge of swarming. Thus, in part, requeening under these circumstances really involves a separation of the queen and the brood. Most beekeepers and researchers agree that we need a better method of queen introduction than the one now existing.

Removal of the brood: Removing the brood from the colony relieves the congestion by dispersing the adult bees, or at least causes them to be less congested in the brood rearing area. It is probably preferable to removing the queen. The beekeeper has several options at this point. He may give the brood to another colony, together with some adhering bees. (One must always be wary of giving brood to a colony if the colony does not have a sufficiently large population to keep the brood warm.) Some beekeepers take a few frames of brood and adhering bees, together with the queen cells, and place them in a nucleus box where the new colony is allowed to rear its own queen. This is a good method, and the result will be a nucleus colony which may be used to requeen another colony at a later date, perhaps even the parent hive. The process can be accelerated by removing some of the brood and the adhering bees, and giving the nucleus colony a young queen, since young queens are usually accepted by small colonies more readily than by large colonies.

Separation of the queen and brood: Separation of the queen and the brood is known to most beekeepers as Demareeing, after George W. Demaree, a beekeeper who first wrote about the system in 1884. Again, there are many variations on the system, but basically it involves placing the queen below a queen excluder in a single super on the bottom of the hive. One to two supers are placed above this, and the brood is placed on top of the hive in the third, fourth, or fifth super, depending upon the strength of the colony. The method has the advantage of keeping the hive population intact and of allowing the colony to grow to maximum strength. Since it is agreed that populous colonies produce more honey, the method has merit.

The chief disadvantage of the Demaree method is that it requires considerable time and skillful management. One must first find the queen in order to place her in the lower super, and in a colony about to swarm this may be difficult, for the colony population may be in the vicinity of 40,000 to 60,000 bees. The bees will often produce queen cells from brood placed on top of the hive making this method still more difficult. Six to eight days following separation of the queen and brood it is necessary to remove these queen cells; otherwise, a second queen will emerge and swarming will occur. Usually, by the time the brood emerges above, the honey flow is in progress, and the bees begin to place honey in the cells left by the emerging brood.

In the two-queen system, a variation of the Demaree method, a second queen is introduced into the colony. Two excluders are used instead of one, the second excluder placed immediately below the brood so that the two queens are separated by at least one empty super. Usually, two-queen colonies have two entrances. Under these circumstances the colony will not swarm, and both the queens will survive. The colony may then be combined at the start of the honey flow with, usually, the older of the queens being killed by the bees. Again, the amount of management involved in the two-queen system discourages its use by most beekeepers.

Queen supersedure

Although not part of the normal cycle of the year, replacement of the queen, called supersedure, may take place during the year and have an effect on the cycle. Replacement sometimes takes place during May and June, but it occurs more frequently during July, August, or September in the northern states and in spring and autumn in the southern states. However, what starts out to be queen supersedure may result in swarming and vice versa so far as we are aware.

The phenomenon of queen supersedure needs more study; commercial beekeepers have long sought methods of encouraging natural supersedure, especially in July or August, knowing that such queen replacement could be beneficial to their management systems and could relieve them of much work.

Production of males

Drones have been discussed in Chapter 2, but a few additional remarks about their relation to the cycle of the year are in order. The honey bee colony is clearly a female society, and the absence of males during the greater part of the year is no deterrent to colony prosperity or development. So far as we can determine, the presence or absence of males has no effect on food gathering.

It is believed that the queen has exclusive control over male production, but this assumption may be incorrect. Worker honey bees can tell the difference between male and female larvae, and will remove the larvae if they are placed in the wrong cells. It is entirely possible that production of males in the spring is delayed, not only by the queen, but also by the workers who remove male larvae if there is insufficient food for them. In any event, large-scale production of males is delayed until pollen is available to the colony in quantity. In the fall, the discharge of males appears to be dictated by both a decreasing day length and the scarcity of available nectar sources.

Just as it appears that swarming occurs more often in colonies with older queens, so it appears that these colonies have more drones. There are no precise data, for drones drift from one hive to another far more often than workers do, at least so it seems, and thus the number of males found in a single colony may not be precisely indicative of the number of males that have been reared in that colony.

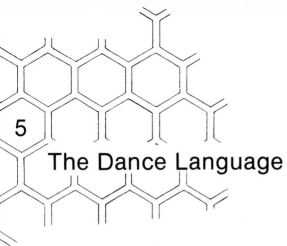

5

The Dance Language

A colony of honey bees has the same basic problems that men face in their own society: food, protection, and reproduction. To cope with these problems honey bees have developed an elaborate communication system involving physical movements (including dances), food exchange, and the distribution of chemicals that dictate social control.

By examining the other species of solitary, subsocial, and social bees which exist, we know reasonably well how the present, well-organized social system of honey bees has evolved. (This is discussed in greater detail in Chapter 1.)

The dance language

The dance language of the honey bee is an intricate method of communication that can be used to relay various bits of information. There are two basic dances. The round dance indicates that food is to be found near the hive, and the wag-tail dance that food is to be found more than 100 meters from the hive (as is discussed below, the precise distance indicated by this dance varies).

Bees apparently use the same chemicals and same systems to communicate different pieces of information under slightly varying circumstances; in doing so they display a remarkable conservation of energy. This is true of the round and wag-tail dances. The same dance is used to communicate information about nectar, pollen, propolis, and water; additionally, honey bees use the wag-tail dance to communicate information about a new homesite when the colony swarms. Since honey bees appear to prefer homesites some distance from the parent hive, no one has ever seen them using the round dance to convey this type of information.

When the dance is used to communicate information about food, propolis, or water, the recruit learns what the dance is about from traces of the material (or its odor) on the dancer's body, or from a taste of the material given her by the dancer. When the wag-tail dance is used to communicate information about homesites, it is performed on the surface of the swarm cluster at a time the bees are engorged and do not normally collect any of the four things that they gather from the field.

By placing honey bees in glass-walled observation hives it is possible to observe them dancing. We can read the dance as easily as bees do by watching the direction indicated in the wag-tail dance and the rapidity of the dance. However, we still do not know how the bees gain all the information they do from the dance. Dietrich Mautz (1971) of Germany has demonstrated that the longer a recruit bee follows a dancing bee the more certain she is to find the food source. Not all bees that follow dancing bees necessarily leave the hive, let alone find the food source. Some recruits, after one unsuccessful foraging venture, return to the hive and again follow a scout; their second trip to the field may be successful.

During the past three decades we have come to understand much about dance communication in honey bees, but many questions still remain, and the limits of the dance communication system are not yet fully known.

Karl von Frisch

Von Frisch was born in Vienna in 1886. His father was a physician, as were several other members of his family, and he continued their interest in science and biology. Several of von Frisch's first papers were concerned with fish and fish sensory systems. It was not until 1913 that he wrote his first paper on honey bees.

During the 1920's and 1930's, he made observations on the sensory systems of honey bees and was especially concerned with their perception of color and their sense of taste and smell.

One of his more fascinating books is his autobiography, *A Biologist Remembers,* published in 1957. He records that on the fifteenth day of June, 1945, at about midday, he made the observation that honey bees are able to indicate the actual direction of a food source from their hive by the use of a wag-tail dance. This earned him the Nobel prize in 1973. At the time of this important discovery he was 59 years old.

He also tells about an error he once made. He had first described the wag-tail dance of the honey bee as a dance made only by pollen collectors. He continues, explaining why the error had been made, and reading between the lines, one understands his pleasure in being able to correct the error himself.

Von Frisch is interested in many aspects of biology, not just honey bees, and he hopes that his research will have practical applications that will benefit beekeepers and agriculture in general. He surrounds himself with books and keeps an excellent museum in his home. Perhaps more impressive than these facts, however, is his enthusiasm when he demonstrates his observation hive, the same hive which he has used for several years in studying the dance language of the honey bees. While the study of biology today often requires great sums of money and sophisticated laboratory apparatus, it is evident that there is still much to be discovered by observation and experimentation with simple equipment. The amount of money which von Frisch has invested in bees and beekeeping equipment over the years is relatively small; his discoveries have stemmed from the investment of time and knowledge.

The detractors

The discoveries by von Frisch have elicited expressions of surprise and skepticism from many people, and, at first glance, there is every reason to question whether or not honey bees have a true and accurate system of communication. Insects are low on the evolutionary ladder. Animals that are more advanced in other ways should logically be the ones to develop a refined communication system. So far as we are aware, however, only man has a system of communication more intricate and highly evolved than that of the honey bee.

If Karl von Frisch can be accused of any one thing, it is that in his writing he makes honey bee communication systems sound overly simple. In none of his works does he devote much time to techniques, which to him are obvious. But for others, especially for those with no experience with honey bees, there is a great deal to learn about the hive, its physical construction, and the organization of bees within it.

Starting in 1967, a series of papers have formally expressed doubt that bees do have a dance language. Their authors complain that some of the von Frisch experiments lacked the necessary controls, and that the dance as described seemed to be too accurate. Von Frisch has replied to these objections, but the best proof that honey bees do have a dance language is contained in papers he published decades earlier. In the early 1920's von Frisch studied the scent gland of worker bees and reported that scouts exposed it at feeding stations, thus aiding recruits to find the food.[1] Some of his students, including Martin Lindauer, have also investigated communication among bees further, and they have refuted these criticisms. Others, notably Goncalves (1969) have contributed, too.

The criticism of von Frisch and his research, although it has dismayed many people, has not detracted from the value and importance of his work. Our knowledge of the dance language has come, for the most part, from the work of von Frisch, his students, and their students. There are few people elsewhere in the world, and especially in the United States, who have made important contributions to our knowledge of the honey bee language. Any papers that stimulate activity in this area are valuable, even though they may take a negative approach.

What follows are summaries of the highlights of the observations

1. The subject is thoroughly discussed in von Frisch's 1965 text (see below), which also contains references to the earlier work.

made by von Frisch and his students over several years. The results of his more than 50 years of research on honey bees were compiled and published in a comprehensive volume in 1965. This text of von Frisch has been translated into English by Leigh E. Chadwick under the title, *The Dance Language and Orientation of Bees,* 1967.

The round dance

The round dance is a rapid, almost violent dance. It is intended to convey information to the effect that food may be found within about 100 meters (app. 100 yards) of the hive. The area of the comb on which the bee dances is small, its total diameter being less than twice the length of the worker bee undertaking the dance. During the course of the dance the bee reverses her position; she does so again at the end of the dance. However, though the dance is performed in a small area, the dancing bee may move and shift her position on the comb.

During the dance, recruits, seldom more than one to six in number, follow the dancing bee, touching her with their antennae, but not following her in such a way as precisely to imitate the dance. More than anything else, the round dance tells of an abundant food supply near the hive; the dance contains no information about the direction or the precise distance of the food, except that it is within about 100 meters. Therefore, if one sets up an experiment, as von Frisch did, and trains bees to visit a feeding station close to the hive, it will be observed that recruits will turn up about equally at any feeding station, any direction from the hive, and within the short distance indicated by the dance. One factor that may affect the number of bees which arrive at any one station is the scent gland which, if exposed at a food source, will make that food source more attractive. The scent gland of the honey bee is described in greater detail below. Suffice it to say at this point that the scent gland on the abdomen of the worker honey bee is used only outside of the hive and as a precise means of attracting bees to a food source, to their queen, and to a clustering site or a home site.

An intermediate dance

Races of honey bees show profound differences, as we have seen. In the process of swarming, for example, one race of bees may typically rear five queens whereas another may rear 30. Certain races use far more propolis than do others. Twenty years before and after the turn of the century, most beekeepers were concerned with the production of comb honey, and this led them to select bees that collected little propolis and therefore capped their honey with unstained, almost pure white wax. The selection of bees for this characteristic allowed the beekeeper to make a cleaner, whiter, and better appearing section of comb honey.

The race of bees with which von Frisch did his early work on language showed a rapid transition from the round dance to the wag-tail dance. However, in other races, for example those found in Switzerland, there is a slow transition which is called the sickle dance. Variations of it are performed when the food source is between about 25 and 100 meters from the hive.

The bees in the United States are a conglomerate, a mixture of many races brought to this country from various parts of Europe, Africa, and the Near East. Because of this mixing, color cannot be depended upon as an infallible indication of the race of bees being used in experiments; however, in identifying the experimental bees, there is almost no designation other than color which can be used. In performing experiments on honey bees one must be alert to the fact that behavioral differences occur in bees.

The intermediate dance is discussed later in this chapter under the heading Dialects.

The wag-tail dance

When the food source is more than about 100 meters from the hive, successful foragers use the wag-tail dance to convey information about the food source to the other bees in the hive (figure 5.1). Like the round dance, the wag-tail dance takes place in an area not much more than twice the length of the bee's body. However, the dancing bee does not necessarily remain on the same

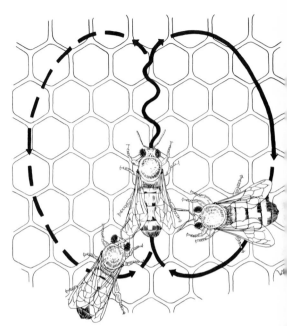

5.1. The wag-tail dance. When dancing to indicate food (or a home site) more than about 100 meters from the hive, worker bees follow the dance pattern shown here. By dancing straight up on the comb, as in this illustration, the bee indicates food is in the direction of the sun. (Illustration by William E. Conner.)

spot of the honey comb while she dances; she may perform several cycles of the dance in one location and then move several centimeters away to continue her dancing.

The wag-tail dance contains several pieces of information that we can read. The direction taken by the tail wagging part of the dance indicates the direction of the food source from the hive. If, for example, the food source is in the direction of the sun, the bees dance straight up the comb; if it is away from the sun, the bees dance straight down. Correspondingly, they dance to the left or right, showing by the angle of the dance the number of degrees away from the sun the food source is located. The distance of the food source from the hive is indicated by the rapidity of the dance: the greater the number of the cycles in the given time, the closer the food source is to the hive. Thus, a very slow dance, indicates a food source a mile or more away from the hive, whereas a rapid one means that a food source is close to the hive. Periodically, the dancing bee stops and gives up food to recruits who are following the dance. In this way, the floral odor, in the case of nectar, is conveyed to the recruit. When the food source is close to the hive, the floral odor may adhere to the outside of the dancer's body as well. Last, the liveliness of the dance indicates whether or not the food is available in great quantity. Additionally, at the food source, the scout or a recruited bee may expose her scent gland, thus further orienting recruits which have followed a dance.

In 1971 Dietrich Mautz used small colonies of bees, with each individual bee marked and numbered, to determine how many recruits were successful in finding a food source. In his experiments, Mautz learned that 32 per cent of the bees which followed dancers found the feeding station. However, over half of the bees which followed dancers did not leave the hive; of those that left, 60 per cent did find the feeding station. Mautz observed that, on the average, recruits follow seven to thirteen dances; the more dances followed, the greater the chances that the food source will be found. However, one bee found a food source at 400 meters after following only five wag-tail dances.

The dance language is not infallible. Von Frisch and his students have devoted a great deal of time to studying the limits of the dance and have found there are indeed, certain pieces of information that bees cannot convey to one another.

The around-the-hill, or detour, experiments

What direction and distance do recruits indicate when the food source is on the opposite side of a hill, or when a large building lies between the hive and the food source? Von Frisch answered this question very simply. He first found, near his summer home in the Austrian Alps, a sharp, high ridge. He placed his observation bee hive on one side of the ridge and trained the bees by moving the food source, step by step, around the ridge so that eventually it lay on the opposite side. When the feeding station was at its final destination, the scouts indicated the proper distance, that is, the distance they flew around the hill from the hive to the food source. However, they indicated to the recruits that they should fly straight through the hill to reach the food source. The recruits responded by flying over the hill and successfully found the food source. When an extra food source was placed on top of the hill, some of the recruits stopped at this site and did not fly the full distance. Whereas the recruits flew over the hill, the scout bees, trained to fly around the hill, continued to follow their original route.

The same experiment was repeated in Munich, Germany. In this case the observation hive was placed on one side of a building 35 meters high and 74 meters long (a 12-story building). Again, the feeding station was first placed in front of the hive. After it had been found by a given number of bees, it was moved slowly around the building. Again, the scouts indicated the correct distance, that is, the distance around the building. However, their dance indicated that recruits should fly straight through the building. The recruits responded by flying over the building. When they were offered food on top of the building also, some of them stopped there and did not fly down the other side.

It is interesting that in both of these experiments, although recruits flew over the hill and over the building, the scout bees, which had been originally trained to the food source, continued to fly about the same distance and path around the building. When the recruits became scouts, having made several flights over the building, they performed the same dance as the original scouts which continued to fly around the building.

Up and down

Dancing honey bees are unable to convey to recruits that a food source can be found "up" or "down." If the source of the food is on the side of a mountain above the hive, or in a valley below it, the natural flight of the recruits leads them up or down; however, if the food is placed on a man-made object above or below the hive on top of a water tower, for example, or under a bridge, the bees have no way to convey the necessary information, and the food source will not be found under normal circumstances.

In his 1965 (Frisch, 1967b) text, von Frisch reviews several experiments he conducted on the bees' ability to convey information about up and down. He used a high bridge over a gorge in Bavaria, Germany; bees were placed on the bridge and scouts trained to the valley floor 76 meters below. To do so it was necessary to train the bees down the side of the gorge. When they returned to the hive, these bees conveyed information about the food source, indicating the correct distance, but recruits flew on a plane level with that of the bridge. The project was reversed, with the bees in the valley and the food source on the bridge; in this case the recruited bees searched for food on the valley floor, not above it. The scouts continued to move back and forth between the hive and the food source and to dance enthusiastically about its existence while the recruits sought in vain for the food.

The various species of the more primitive social bees, Meliponidae, make odor trails from the food source to the nest and so are able to convey information about up and down and, for example, to lead recruits successfully to the top of a water tower, but they are not able to direct recruits to a food source across a lake, whereas *Apis mellifera* can do so. Experiments on this question were conducted by Lindauer (1957). Perhaps one of his more interesting experiments to show the limitations of the odor trail communication system was to train bees from the family Meliponidae from one side of a lake to the other side. To do so he moved the feeding station around the lake slowly, and the scout bees made an odor trail as they proceeded along the lake shore. However, there came a point where it was expedient for the scouts to return to the nest by flying over the water. When they did so, they could no longer make their odor trail, and recruits could not find the food. When Lindauer had finally moved the feeding station to the side of the lake opposite the nest, he placed a rope across the lake and tied branches, at close intervals, on the rope. The scouts then resumed their normal habit of making an odor trail on the dry branches and recruits could once again find the food source across the water. Thus, a more primitive communication system, on the part of certain species of the Meliponidae, enables them to find food sources in an up or down situation where the more advanced *Apis mellifera* are unsuccessful. Of course, there is little need to convey this type of information in the day-to-day existence of honey bees.

Walking versus flying

Von Frisch has concluded that the tempo of the dance is an indication of the energy required to fly the distance between the food source and the hive. He states that this is "a yard stick that truly is strange to man." Interestingly, when bees are forced to walk to a food source, they perform the tail-wagging dance when the feeding station is only three to four meters from the hive. Research on this subject was conducted by A. R. Bisetsky (see Frisch, 1967b), also a von Frisch student.

Bisetsky also conducted experiments forcing bees to walk in semicircles between the food source and the hive. In part, this work paralleled the earlier detour experiments by von Frisch and his students. It was shown that in the case of the bee forced to walk in a semicircle, the dance indicated the direction straight from the food source to the hive.

Other experiments by Bisetsky showed that it was important for the bees to see the sun or blue sky when moving to and from a food source. An L-shaped corridor was constructed between the hive and the food source, and the bees were forced to walk in this corridor. When the bees could see the sunlight while walking the entire length of the corridor, the direction of the wag-tail dance indicated the hypotenuse of the triangle even though the bees were forced to walk the legs of the triangle. However, when one or the other leg of the L-shaped corridor was darkened with a cloth, the direction danced by the scout bees was that in which the sky was visible to them.

In conversation with Bisetsky I have learned that it is not an easy matter to train bees to walk in a corridor under glass. Training recruits to take food in this unnatural way is a laborious process. However, the many experiments performed under these conditions give us insight into the orientation and the dance language of the honey bee.

Dialects

There are several races of *Apis mellifera*. Beekeepers have long known of their existence and have selected certain of these because of their particular traits as regards honey production, foraging methods, gentleness, winter survival, propensity to swarm, and so forth.

In the 1950's one of von Frisch's students, Rolf Boch, undertook a systematic study of six races of honey bees for the purpose of determining what differences might exist in their dance language. Boch found that only one of the six races does not make use of the intermediate sickle dance. Of particular interest is the distance from the hive at which he observed the bees start to use the wag-tail dance. The Egyptian bee, one of the races studied, uses the round dance when food is within about three meters of the hive and uses the wag-tail dance when the food is more than about ten meters from the hive; however, the Carniolan bee, another of the races observed, does not start the wag-tail dance to indicate a a food source until it is almost 90 meters from the hive. The other four races studied were intermediate between these two extremes.

Boch also made observations of the distance indicated by the bees dancing in the hive when the feeding station was several hundred meters from the hive. Again, profound differences were observed. One race of bees dancing to indicate a food source 500 meters from the hive might be interpreted by another race to mean that the food source is only 200 or 300 meters from the hive. Thus, just as we find dialects in our language, so do we find them in the dance language of the honey bee.

The evolution of the dance language

Despite the wealth of material available for study (the approximately 20,000 species of bees ranging from strictly solitary to subsocial and social forms), it is not clear how the species themselves evolved or how they developed communication systems. However, we may make some reasonable assumptions that will serve as guidelines in thinking about the evolution of the communication system of the honey bees. Many bees and wasps have evolved a system whereby certain females dominate others and the males; in the more advanced forms, a single female dominates the rest and becomes the chief egg layer and source of certain chemical substances that have to do with maintenance of social order. The division of labor is advantageous to colony life. However, concomitant with the emphasis on social existence and large colonies is the problem of food collection.

Our present knowledge suggests that the dances of honey bees evolved from more primitive dances of their ancestors, in which one bee incited other bees to search for food. We believe the first dancing bees were unable to give any information about direction and distance of the food source from the hive. Our knowledge of evolutionary processes suggests that, as the honey bee evolved, it became beneficial for the species to give more specific information, and that those animals which did so prospered, whereas the others did not.

It has been learned that the Meliponidae, or social bees of the tropics, perform a dance, but this dance only excites the bees to leave the hive and does not indicate the direction of the food source from the hive. Certain species of the family make an odor trail, stopping periodically as they return from a food source to the hive to impart a bit of scent on leaves and twigs along the trail. Clearly, the fact that the bees must stop to mark their trail slows down the actual process of food collection. Thus, we believe that the dance language of *Apis mellifera* is superior to the communication system of any other bee or social insect.

The dance languages of the Asian bees, *Apis florea, Apis dorsata* and *Apis indica* have been little studied. Martin Lindauer (1957) observed that *Apis florea,* commonly thought of as the most primitive of the four species of *Apis,* dances on top of its nest in the same way that *Apis mellifera* would dance if the comb were turned into a horizontal position Thus, the running part of the wag-tail dance points directly to the food source.

Lindauer found that, if he placed a book on top of the *Apis florea* nest, the bees would dance on top of the book. If he placed a notebook over the nest in such a fashion as to make a peaked roof, he would then frustrate the dance of *Apis florea*; the bees are not able to perform their dance on any surface other than a horizontal one. Although the dances of the Asian *Apis* appear similar to those of *Apis mellifera,* it is likely that there are greater differences in the dances of the three Asian species than in the dances of *Apis mellifera.* The question deserves further investigation, and observation of the behavior of these bees will no doubt contribute greatly to our understanding of evolution in bees.

Learning in honey bees

Actions by animals may be as a result of reasoning, learning, instinct, or reflex. Among the higher animals reasoning and learning are more important than instinct and reflex, while the reverse is true with the simpler animals. Learning takes place when an animal's behavior changes as a result of experience. Some animals learn much more rapidly than others.

For many years it was widely held that insects could not learn. However, among honey bees and other highly evolved social bees, it is a simple matter to undertake experiments that demonstrate learning.

When honey bees first fly outside of the hive they learn the location of their hive by its color, size, shape, and relationship to surrounding objects such as trees, stones, and other hives. The bees fly up and down, back and forth in front of the hive. This learning process takes many minutes; bee-keeping texts often refer to these first learning flights as "play flights." This learning becomes very evident to the beekeeper when, in rearranging the supers of combs on his hives, he sometimes thereby changes the color of the hives. His bees will become confused and may enter the wrong hive.[2] Also, if a colony of bees is moved several feet, foraging bees returning from the field go to the old location, finding it by markers other than the hive itself. They will hover in the vicinity, moving back and forth over the terrain until they finally recognize their own hive by its shape and color.

Reinhardt (1952) demonstrated that honey bees can avoid the explosive tripping mechanism of the alfalfa flower. Alfalfa is different from other clover-like flowers: the sexual parts are enveloped under pressure in a sheath between two petals. When a bee alights on these petals, the sexual column is released, snapping upward, and it usually strikes the bee on the underside of the head. At this point, the bee may be caught between the large standard petal and the sexual column. Reinhardt reports that most bees free themselves rather quickly, but he observed one bee which took 45 seconds to free herself from this situation.

Because nectar-collecting honey bees learn to avoid the exploding sexual column of the alfalfa flower, only about 1 per cent of the flowers visited by honey bees are tripped and pollinated. The chief reason that certain of the solitary ground nesting and twig nesting bees are important in alfalfa pollination is that they do not learn to avoid the exploding sexual column and therefore trip and pollinate almost every flower they visit.

More recently, Pessotti (1972) showed that *Melipona rufiventris,* one of the more advanced social, stingless bees found in South America, would respond to a light stimulus and press one of two levers to receive food. A long training period was required, and the bee's ability to discriminate between the two levers was never perfect; however, it was statistically significant.

2. Beekeepers paint their hives a variety of colors; a few imprint a design on them to aid the bees in orientation.

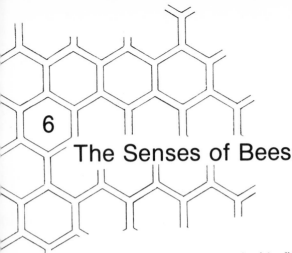

6
The Senses of Bees

In this chapter we are concerned with, first, the sensory system of the honey bee, its physical description and location; and second, those colors, odors, and tastes (in terms we can understand) that honey bees are able to detect.

It has been demonstrated that honey bees have preferences and sensory thresholds just as do men and other animals. These vary with the circumstances and depend especially upon what is available to the bees in the way of food and other necessities.

Honey bees have an elaborate sensory system. However, as indicated in Chapter 3, bees often collect items, such as sawdust, grain dust, and contaminated water, that have no food value to them. This is not because the sensory system fails under the circumstances. Rather, the items collected are substances that the bees did not encounter during the course of their evolution but that have been made available to them by man, and even then in only the last thousand, or two thousand, years.

The primary sensory receptors

The primary sensory receptors in honey bees are those of smell, sight, taste, and touch. Honey bees have no organs sensitive to sound, and so far as we have been able to determine, they are not responsive to sound; however, they do detect and respond to substrate-borne sound (several hundred cycles per second), though what role these vibrations play in their communication system is not clear to us.

The development of the electron scanning scope has made it possible to take pictures of receptors at magnifications of several thousand times, and has greatly increased our knowledge of certain of these sense organs. More detail may be found in books by Karl von Frisch and Robert E. Snodgrass.

Insofar as odor is concerned, the primary odor receptors are on the antennae. Worker and queen antennae have 12 segments, and those of the drone have 13. Von Frisch (1967b) showed that he could remove the eight terminal segments on one antenna of a worker and the seven terminal segments from the second antenna, and the bee could still detect odors. This indicates that the shock of the operation is not such that it destroys the odor sense of the honey bee. However, when von Frisch removed the terminal eight segments from both antennae, bees could no longer detect odors. There are several types of odor receptors on the antenna. The number of receptors was counted by Cheshire (1886). He observed that queens had approximately 1,600 sensory receptors of various types on each antenna, workers 2,400, and drones 37,800. One may question why the drone has so many sensory receptors on his antennae; indeed, our observations suggest that, in the day-to-day functioning of the colony, the worker comes into contact with a great variety of circumstances and would appear to have need for a more elaborate sensory system. The answer probably lies in the fact that drones are able to detect the queen's sex attractant at very low levels. This is discussed in greater detail below. Suffice it to say, with honey bees and most other animals, reproduction is probably more important for the survival of the species than is the day-to-day collection of food by individuals.

Honey bees have five eyes. Two are compound eyes with several thousand ommatidia. Whereas the human eye has a single lens, in the honey bee each ommatidium has its own lens. Thus, the picture the bee sees, must be markedly different from that seen by man. It has been suggested that the multifaceted eye of the honey bee is used for orientation and that bees are aided in this regard by their ability to perceive polarized light.

In addition to the two compound eyes, honey bees have three ocelli on the top of their heads, each of the three having only a single lens. Their function is not clear. However, in certain species of solitary bees that fly at night, the ocelli are much enlarged and this suggests that these may be used, and are important, under conditions where the light level is reduced.

The sensory cells responsible for taste in honey bees are less well known. We are aware that workers, and perhaps queens and drones, have sense organs for taste on their mouthparts and can recognize sweetness only by direct contact. As indicated below, the honey bee's sense of taste is not so refined as that of man; however, honey bees do respond to a variety of taste sensations.

The vibrations that honey bees are able to detect, because of their frequency (cycles per second), are in a range audible to man and are called *substrate-borne sound,* a term which at first appears confusing. The bees presumably detect these vibrations by as yet undescribed sensory receptors on their feet. Substrate-borne sounds are associated with the wag-tail dance and occur when swarms depart from a hive or a temporary resting place; they are produced by virgin queens before they emerge and when they are confined in their cells, and by mated queens in cages (and perhaps under other circumstances, too). Bees also make sounds when flying, but so far as we can determine, these have no meaning either to the bees making the sounds or to those in the vicinity.[1]

1. An angry bee flying around one's head makes a buzzing sound quite different from a curious bee doing the same thing. A neophyte might think an experienced beekeeper's behavior a curious thing when he suddenly raises his hand and strikes down one bee. There may be thousands of bees in the air in an apiary, flying to and from their hives, still, the beekeeper hears the distinctive sound made by an angry bee, and experience has taught him that he must move away, eliminate the bee, or be stung, and which he does must be decided upon quickly. It is interesting to us that not infrequently a single bee, in an apiary of thousands or even millions, may choose to attack; of course, there are times when many may do so too, but in this footnote we have reference to the attack by a single individual. When many bees attack, the beekeeper uses smoke, dresses properly, and usually takes steps to calm the offending colony(s).

Certain man-made sounds or vibrations will cause bees to "freeze" and remain still on a comb for long periods of time. Still, the function of these sounds is not understood, and the subject needs much more study. The effect of one substrate-borne sound, drumming (beating on the hive with the hands or a hammer), is discussed in Chapter 13.

Color vision

Honey bees have a color sense and use color in orienting to food sources in the field and to their hive. Demonstrating that such a sense is present, but that it is much less well defined than that of man, is a relatively simple matter. Several experiments are outlined by Karl von Frisch in his book, *Bees, Their Vision, Chemical Senses and Language.*

One need not own a hive of bees to undertake experiments with the color sense, provided there is a hive nearby. A small quantity of honey placed on a table or feeding station will attract bees to the vicinity where one wishes to undertake the experiments. Interestingly, and depending upon the number of bees in the vicinity, the food source may be visited by wasps and other unwanted insects before it is eventually found by the honey bees.

To demonstrate that honey bees have a color sense, a dish containing diluted honey or a scented sugar syrup is placed on the feeding station on a piece of blue cardboard. After several bees are observed feeding, and after most of them have made at least six or eight round trips between the hive and the feeding station, that station is replaced by two feeding stations, one marked with cardboard of the same shade of blue and the second with a piece of red cardboard. The bees should now alight on the blue cardboard since they associate this color with this food source.

As von Frisch (1967b) points out, this does not necessarily show that bees have a true color sense, for they might be distinguishing shades of gray. To disprove this possibility, one may use several pieces of cardboard of different shades of gray to surround a single piece of blue cardboard to which the bees are trained. It will be noted that after a suitable training period the bees will again light on the blue, indicating that they are not interested in any shade of gray. An objection to this experiment has been that some odor might be associated with one or more of the pieces of paper. To negate this possibility one may cover the feeding station with a large piece of plate glass.

Another variation of this same experiment is first to train bees to a feeding station where syrup without scent is offered and, when ten or more bees are feeding, to cover the feeding station with a box that has a hole in the side (a round, one-gallon ice cream container with a hole about two or three centimeters in diameter bored through the side with a cork borer works well). One may either paint the box a color or glue or staple a piece of colored paper to the outside so that again the bees associate a color with the food. It is now necessary to allow the bees to take several round trips between the covered feeding station and the hive. To test whether the bees have a color sense, one removes the feeding station and the colored box, and substitutes two or more new, empty boxes, each of which bears a different color. In the next minute or two, one counts the number of bees going through the holes and in the boxes. In our experiments we have always found that most bees enter the correct box, again showing that they have a color sense.

According to von Frisch, honey bees see only four colors distinctly: yellow, blue-green, blue, and ultraviolet.

Reinforcement to certain Colors

For a number of years I have performed the above experiment with students in an elementary class on the biology of the honey bee. The method outlined by von Frisch was followed, and the bees were trained to a feeding station on a blue cardboard or inside of a blue box. One year, for no good reason, the procedure was changed and the bees were trained to a feeding station on a red piece of cardboard. Bees see red as black. After a reasonable training period, a piece of red cardboard and a piece of blue cardboard were substituted for the single piece of red cardboard and empty feeding jars placed on each. The bees landed on the blue cardboard, not the red to which they were presumably trained. In searching the literature, nothing could be found that explained the behavior of the bees under these circumstances.

The answer lies in the fact that bees prefer certain colors over others (blue is their favorite), and they prefer colored objects to those which are grey or black. To train bees to visit and remain with a feeding station on red cardboard, one must reinforce the experiment. This is done by making two feeding stations available to the bees at the same time, only one of which has food in it. One is on red cardboard, the other on blue, and they are side by side. Thus, even though the bees have at first a preference for the blue cardboard and may move to it, they soon come to learn there is no food to be associated with the blue cardboard. Thus reinforced, the bees will visit the red cardboard to which they are trained. In performing experiments of this nature, one must also be careful that there is no training to a location.

The odor sense

The odor sense of the honey bee is well developed and remarkably similar in sensitivity to that of man; in general, the substances that are odorless to man are odorless to bees as well.[2] Despite the fact that their sensory systems are different, men and bees detect about the same odors.

To demonstrate that honey bees have a sense of odor, one may use boxes with holes in the sides, the same as those used in testing the color sense.

It is first necessary to attract bees to the area where the experiments are to be undertaken. In these experiments an odoriferous oil or substance is added to the sugar syrup at the outset. After a suitable number of bees have been trained to the feeding station,

2. One of the very interesting and notable exceptions to this statement is queen substance, 9-oxodec-*trans*-2-enoic acid, discussed in Chapter 7. This substance, which is odorless to man, is detected as an odor by bees under a variety of circumstances.

usually ten or twenty bees, the station is covered with a box with a side hole about two or three centimeters in diameter. Again, the bees being trained to a scented feeding station should be allowed to make six or eight trips between the feeding station and the hive so that they clearly associate the correct scent with the food. (The time involved in a round trip may be recorded, including the time taken for bees to engorge and to rid themselves of the food in the hive.) If marked bees are used for this experiment, it must be remembered that the paints used on the bee's body will have volatile components that may have an odor when they are first applied. Thus, before the experiments begin, the paint marks on the bees must be allowed to dry thoroughly. (In timing the trips made by marked bees, it will be noted that the round trip time, including the time spent engorging and disposing of the food, is remarkably similar. Usually a bee required only 60 to 90 seconds to engorge, but in the field and when collecting food from natural sources, a bee may take 30 or more minutes to fill her honey stomach with nectar. The practical importance of this difference is that those flowers which have sufficient sugar to attract bees but yet which are parsimonious in the quantity which they make available to the bees, will have a better chance of being visited by a bee and therefore of being cross-pollinated merely because the bees are forced to visit so many flowers.) After the bees have been trained to the scented food station inside the box, one may substitute two or more similar boxes, only one of which has the correct scent inside. The number of bees that enter the correct box during the next one, two, or three minutes may then be counted. If there is no food in the scented box, the bees will come out and may then search for food in the other boxes even though they do not carry the proper scent (figure 6.1).

An obvious sequel to these experiments was performed by von Frisch to determine which is more important in orientation in the field, color or odor? As above, the feeding station must first be established and bees trained to it; then the feeding station is covered with a box with the hole in the side; other boxes are placed

6.1. Gallon-size ice cream containers cover food sources in this laboratory demonstration of bee behavior. There is much more activity around the hole in the ice cream container on the left, indicating that the bees associate the color of this container with their food.

nearby. As bees approach the feeding station, they are first attracted to the box with the correct color. However, if no scent emanates from the box, the bees will fly up and down the line of variously colored boxes and enter the box that emits the correct scent.

In the 1918 *Gleanings in Bee Culture,* under the title, *Two Remarkable Odor Experiences,* the following was pointed out by C. E. Fowler of New Jersey and Mel. T. Pritchard, then the queen breeder for the A. I. Root Company.

In the first experience it is recorded that in the process of requeening a colony, a presumably old queen was removed and crushed against the trunk of a tree. A short while later a mass of bees had clustered on the spot where the queen had been crushed and killed. The observer washed the spot with soap and water, but when it was dry, the bees again clustered there. Phenol was then used to wash and paint the tree; however, as soon as it was dry, bees again lit on the spot where the queen had been killed; her odor remained despite the washing and phenol.

The second observation concerned Pritchard's son, who had an insect collection. Included in this collection was a queen bee which had been dead for more than a year. The boy brought his insect collection into the apiary to show it to some visitors. The box was left open. At the time Pritchard had been making up nuclei, and there were a number of stray, queenless bees in the air. Despite the fact that there had been mothballs in the box during the whole year, the dead queen (through her odor) was still attractive to the worker bees, and several minutes after she was exposed, many of them clustered about her.

These are only two of the many accounts which demonstrate that queen honey bees produce chemical substances that are attractive to worker bees and that, in turn, dictate social order. In the late 1940's and early 1950's the terms *social hormone* and *ectohormone* first appeared in the literature. However, it was not until 1959 that the term *pheromone* was coined. In 1918, at the time the observations by Fowler and Pritchard were written, men still used the word "instinct" and did not understand the role that odor plays in the day-to-day life of the colony.

The taste sense

The taste sense of honey bees may be studied in much the same manner that one studies the color and odor senses. Again, it is not necessary to own a hive of bees to make such tests but only to be in the vicinity of a bee hive and to attract bees from the hive to a feeding station. Testing the taste sense of the honey bee, like testing any of the other senses, is difficult because the bees prefer natural sources of food, and so long as nectar is abundant in the field, they will go to flowers. In fact, in the area of Ithaca, New York, I have often had difficulty training bees to artificial sources. Europe is not one of the major honey-producing areas in the world; although at some times of the year nectar is available in quantity, in general, experiments on the senses of honey bees can be conducted much more easily in Europe than in the United States because there are fewer natural sources of nectar on which the bees may feed.

To research the taste sense of the honey bee, one must offer the bees food at least as attractive as, and usually more attractive than, that which is available in the field. During a major honey flow, bees will pay scant attention to any artificial food source.

To demonstrate that honey bees have a sense of taste and a threshold of acceptance, one first trains bees to a feeding station and then offers them, side by side, sugar syrups of different concentrations. One then records the amount of time required for the bees to empty two feeders containing food with different sugar concentrations. The results are not always perfect and depend on what is available to the bees locally in the form of nectar from natural sources. Usually, however, the richer food station will be emptied first, and the bees will move rapidly to the second. During the course of the experiment one may also count the number of bees at each feeding station, and it will be noted that there are usually at least some bees feeding at the lower sugar concentration, these being bees which have not yet learned which is the richer of the food sources.

Using a similarly designed experiment, it is possible to demonstrate that bees are not only able to distinguish sweet but also salt, sour, and bitter. However, they do not taste all the bitter materials that man tastes. Again, a simple experiment is to add a small amount of quinine, an extremely bitter material, to a sugar syrup and to note that, although the quinine does not discourage the bees from feeding, a small drop of it on the tongue of a man will cause him to reject the food.

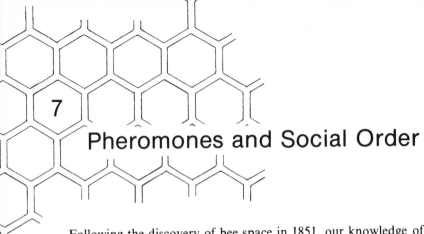

7

Pheromones and Social Order

Following the discovery of bee space in 1851, our knowledge of honey bees increased rapidly, and beekeeping became a vocation and an avocation for thousands of people. By about 1880 the life cycles of both individual honey bees and the honey bee colony were reasonably well known, and while men had not changed bees, they had learned how to manipulate them for their own profit. It was understood that the queen is the most important individual, and papers and books romanticizing her presence and activities within the colony were written. During the next several decades hundreds of papers appeared on the biology of the honey bee, and for the commercial beekeepers the most important of these concerned swarming. Great emphasis was placed on having young queens in the hive. Many papers were written about how social order might be maintained within the colony, but no explanation of precisely how it is maintained was forthcoming.

In retrospect, an examination of the literature makes it evident that the answers to this question were really known. However, the knowledge had not been fitted together properly. Also, certain terminology was lacking in our own communication system which prevented men from better understanding the biology of the honey bee.

As early as 1859 it was noted that drones pursue queens in the field for mating, but no one thought that there might be a chemical substance that attracts the males to the females. In 1927 Lloyd

Watson wrote his thesis on a practical method of artificial insemination of queen honey bees. Almost as an addendum Watson pictured and described a comet of males following a flying queen. The words *sex attractant* were not known to him (and others of the time) and he did not think in terms of chemical communication.

In 1959 Peter Karlson and Adolf Butenandt proposed the term *pheromone*. Their definition, which stands today, is as follows: "Pheromones should designate substances that are secreted by an animal to the outside and cause a specific reaction in a receiving individual of the same species, e.g., a release of certain behavior or a determination of physiologic development." Pheromones are messengers among individuals. They are not hormones as hormones are released within an animal and cause a response in that animal only. Alarm odors, sex attractants, substances that stimulate grooming and cleaning, food exchange, recognition, and caste determination are all pheromones.

Since 1959 hundreds of researchers around the world have turned their attention to the study of pheromones in insects, a study of tremendous scientific interest and esoteric value that, it appears, may also aid in the practical control of certain noxious insects. In the study of pheromones, the honey bee has been a popular laboratory animal; it can be kept in a hive, moved into an experimental area, and in addition it is almost world-wide in distribution. Today we know more about the pheromones in honey bees than in any other insect, and research on honey bee pheromones has served as a model for pheromone research in other insects.

Food exchange

Before pursuing the question of pheromones further, food exchange, another aspect of honey bee biology, should be explored; it, too, is an integral part of hive life. Many pheromones are odoriferous, but some may not work in this manner. Many are thought to be exchanged along with food and to have an effect internally on the receiving individual. Additionally, food exchange serves to alert those within the hive as to the availability of food and the need for it.

The idea that among social insects food exchange may occur between adults and larvae has been postulated and the subject researched, but there is yet no proof that this does take place. The food exchange with which we are concerned is that which takes place between adults.

The most widely quoted experiment concerned with food exchange between adult honey bees was undertaken by H. L. Nixon and C. R. Ribbands (1952). They used a colony containing 24,600 adult worker bees. They trained six marked bees to a feeding dish outside of the hive and from this station fed the bees 20 milliliters, about two tablespoonfuls, of radioactive sugar syrup. The six bees made 379 round trips and took three and one-fourth hours to collect this quantity of sugar syrup. Samples of bees within the colony were taken five hours and twenty-nine hours after all the food had been taken back to the hive. It was observed that the radioactive sugar syrup was widely distributed throughout the hive. Tests were also made of the legs and wings of workers within the hive to make certain that the researchers were not just measuring external contamination which might have accidentally taken place. The results obtained by Nixon and Ribbands are shown in table 7.1.

Table 7.1. Percentage of hive population of 24,600 honey bees radioactive after six have been fed treated sugar syrup (after Nixon and Ribbands, 1952).

Location of bees	After 5 hours	After 29 hours
Foragers	62	76
Brood chamber	18	43
Lower super	16	53
Upper super	21	60

The Nixon and Ribbands experiment was undertaken in August when bees were consuming more food than they were collecting; thus, food exchange would be encouraged at this time of year. Forty-eight hours after the test was completed, the older unsealed larvae were examined, and it was determined that 85 per cent of these were radioactive and thus had received a small portion of the radioactive sugar syrup. Although there is apparently no reciprocal feeding between larvae and adults, larvae may receive pheromones from the adults together with their food.

At this stage we can only suggest many reasons why food exchange benefits the colony. Certainly it seems to be a method through which pheromones may be exchanged; perhaps bees of a particular age are in greater need of certain pheromones than others. It has been demonstrated that, in time of dearth, when a colony starves, all the bees starve together; food exchange allows all the bees in the colony to live as long as possible, and on the other end of the spectrum, it also permits the bees to prosper together.

The role of pheromones in reproduction

Reproduction in any animal is never a simple matter; in the honey bee it is complicated by the fact that there are two female castes, each specialized but both capable of laying eggs. In honey bee reproduction pheromones play an important role; several of these chemical substances are known, and others are yet to be discovered.

Queen recognition

As has been indicated, honey bees recognize a queen not as a living object but because of the chemicals she produces. The materials may be extracted with alcohol or ether, that is, the queen may be placed in either of these materials and the chemicals washed from her body. The extract may then be placed on a stick, or other inanimate object, and the bees will surround and attend the stick as though it were a living queen.

In 1961, C. G. Butler, R. K. Callow, and N. C. Johnston isolated and identified 9-oxodec-*trans*-2-enoic acid, which they called queen substance and which they felt was responsible for queen recognition. The substance has been synthesized and tested by many people under a variety of conditions. It is attractive to honey bees,

7.1. Bees in a small swarm marked with numbered, colored discs for experimental purposes. These bees have settled on a cage which contains their queen.

and though it may be the primary material by which bees recognize their queen, it is not the only substance responsible for queen recognition. Pain (1961) wrote that at least two pheromones are active in queen recognition.

H. H. W. Velthuis (1972) has pointed out that not all honey bees within a colony are attracted to their queen. Many of them avoid her though why they do so is not clear. In the field, a swarm of honey bees may be attracted by its queen or queen substance. Bees finding their queen after she is apparently lost, or finding an object anointed with queen substance, will expose their Nassanoff glands and thereby emit a scent that is highly attractive to other bees in the vicinity. By using synthetic queen substance and synthetic scent one may force a swarm of honey bees to settle where it is wanted. The scent gland pheromone, discovered by R. Boch and D. A. Shearer in 1962 and 1964, contains geraniol, geranic and nerolic acids, and citral. It has been found recently that the worker's alarm pheromones, isopentyl acetate and 2-heptanone, may cause worker bees to stop emitting Nassanoff scent.

A colony of honey bees normally contains a single queen. If a second queen is placed in it, bees are able to recognize their own queen, and the foreign queen will be killed. Likewise, in the case of a swarm, the bees are able to distinguish their own queen from a foreign queen; however, the foreign queen is not killed, at least not immediately.

The fact that a swarm may not kill a foreign queen makes biological sense. It is important for bees in a swarm to identify their own queen so that the swarm will remain a coherent group. However, if their queen is lost, and if the swarm cannot return to the parent hive, it is reasonable to assume that any queen is better than no queen at all. Clearly, queen recognition and the pheromones other than 9-oxodec-*trans*-2-enoic acid involved in it need further study.

Research on how bees recognize their queen has been carried on for many years. The question fascinated Francis Huber, who wrote about it in his *New Observations Upon Bees* in 1814.[1]

Huber noted that only an hour after the loss of the queen, "disquiet commences to be manifested among the workers." He noted further that after 24 hours of queenlessness, the construction of emergency queen cells in the colony was evident.

Huber undertook an experiment as follows:

I divided the hive into two equal parts by means of a grated partition; this was done with so much celerity and care that no disturbance was noticed at the time of this operation, and that not a single bee was wounded. The bars of this grating were too close for passage of the bees

1. There are several translations of Huber's book, but the one made in 1926 by C. P. Dadant, editor of the *American Bee Journal,* is considered the best; the remarks here are found on page 210 of this translation.

from one to the other side; but admitted the free circulation of air in all parts of the hive. I did not know which half contained the queen, but the tumult and the buzzing in No. 1 soon apprized me that she was in No. 2, where tranquility prevailed. I then closed the entrances of both, so that the bees seeking their queen should not find her, but I made sure that outside air should continue to circulate in the hives.

At the end of two hours the bees calmed and order was restored.

On the 14th, we visited hive No. 1, and found 3 royal cells begun. On the 15th we opened the entrances of both hives; the bees went to the field and we noticed that they did not mix, upon their return, and that those of each half kept to their respective hives. On the 24th we found two dead queens at the entrance of hive No. 1, and in examining the combs we found the young queen that had killed them. On the 30th, she emerged from the hive and was fecundated and thenceforth the success of the swarm was assured.

The apertures which I had preserved in the partition allowed the bees of hive No. 1 to communicate with their old queen by means of smell, hearing or any unknown sense; they were separated from her only by a space not exceeding a third or a fourth of an inch, which they could not pass, yet they had become agitated, had constructed royal cells and reared young queens, therefore they had conducted themselves just as if their queen had been truly taken away and lost to them forever. This observation proves that it is not by means of sight, hearing or smell that the bees notice the presence of their queen; another sense is necessary; but since the grating used in this occasion had only removed the contact with her, is it not probable that they must touch her with their antennae in order to make sure of her presence among them, and that it is through the use of this organ that the feeling of their combs, of their companions, of their brood and of their queen is communicated to them?

Huber then conducted further experiments and observed that when the bees on the two sides of a divided hive could have antennal contact that the side without the queen did not act in a queenless fashion. He caged a queen in a double-screened cage so that the queen was separated from the workers by such a distance that there could not be antennal contact. Under these circumstances he again noted that the bees built queen cells. This substantiated his theory that antennal contact was most important, and thus he missed the point that food exchange might also be involved.

The observations of Huber are basic to our present understanding of queen recognition. Although Huber's writings have been cited by many persons interested in bees and bee research, this particular observation, which may have been his most important, remained unnoticed until the pheromone theory was advanced.

Queen replacement

New queens are reared under one of three circumstances: when the queen is accidentally lost, when the queen is old or failing and is superseded, and when the colony swarms.

Although a queen may be lost or accidently killed in various ways, most frequently she is accidentally injured or killed by the beekeeper while he is making routine manipulations. As Huber noted and others have subsequently recorded, a few hours after the bees discover their queen has disappeared, they begin to enlarge a few cells containing day-old or two-day-old worker larvae and to feed these larvae lavishly with royal jelly, thus transforming them into queens. The number of queens raised under these circumstances is variable and depends upon many factors but especially the race of the bees. It has been noticed that the synthetic queen substance will prevent queen rearing by small groups of queenless bees; however, no one to date has been able to give synthetic [2] queen substance to a large colony of bees and thereby to prevent queen rearing. It has been thought that this was true because men have not yet learned exactly how queen substance is distributed within the colony; however, this explanation is no longer believed to be correct, and present evidence suggests that one or more pheromones in addition to queen substance are responsible for queen recognition.

2. In attempts to substitute queen substance for a natural queen, it has been fed in sugar syrup or in water and placed on wicks, dead queens, and/or worker bees. In experiments with small groups of bees it was on wicks. Morse and Boch (1971) mixed the substance with paraffin oil which was placed on porous polyethylene blocks, 5 x 5 x 20 mm.

It is suggested that the circumstances promoting swarming and supersedure are quite similar. It is thought that the queens which are superseded are old or injured and are not producing a natural or normal complement of queen substance and the other pheromones responsible for queen recognition. In the case of swarming, it has been suggested that congestion of the bees within the colony is such that the normal distribution of queen substance breaks down. Though possibly neither of these theories is correct, they are the two most plausible that we have to work with at the present time.

In any event, in the process of supersedure and/or swarming, the bees first construct queen cups, usually at the edge and more frequently at the lower edge of the sphere-shaped brood nest. This is followed by the queen's laying a single egg in each of these cups and their subsequent development into queen cells.

An old queen which is superseded is not always killed. Beekeepers find that mother-daughter combinations in colonies are not uncommon. The older of the two, the mother queen, is usually much smaller, and her physical condition suggests she does not lay eggs as frequently as does her daughter; however, this question has been little researched. The old queen may remain in the colony for several months, and this is the only circumstance under which there may be two queen bees living side by side in the same brood nest. It has been suggested that under these circumstances the mother queen is producing queen substance and other pheromones at a much lower level, if at all, and that she is not recognized as a queen by the workers. She is probably successful in soliciting food, as are males, but she contributes little to the colony. Further investigation of this question would be very helpful and could lead to a better understanding of how pheromones function within the honey bee colony.

Worker ovary development

The ovaries of queens and workers differ considerably. In a fully developed queen, Robert E. Snodgrass (1956) states that each ovary contains 160 to 180 ovarioles or tubules. Eggs originate in the upper end of each of these ovarioles; as they move down the ovarioles, they continue their development and finally pass into a common oviduct and are then deposited (laid) one per cell, by the queen. Worker honey bee ovaries contain four to eight ovarioles each, and in *Apis mellifera* it is generally agreed that these usually become functional only when the queen is absent. Worker honey bees do not mate, and they do not have a developed spermatheca; thus, eggs laid by workers are not fertilized, and usually only males develop from them. Like many other aspects of honey bee biology, the development of laying workers has been the subject of much speculation.

In 1942, Gertrude Hess wrote about the ovary development of worker bees in colonies that she had dequeened. She found that, after queen removal, eggs begin to develop in the ovaries of about 10 per cent of the bees in the hive within about a week, and several days thereafter worker eggs may be found in cells in the hive. Eggs laid by workers are smaller and more slender than are queen eggs. They are seldom deposited in the bottom center of the cell as are eggs laid by the queen but are sometimes found on the bottom and more frequently on the sides of the cell. Often a cell in which workers are laying will contain a dozen or more eggs. Although Hess's work in 1942 is widely quoted, and has laid the basis for our present understanding of how pheromones control worker ovary development and egg laying, the thought that this aspect of honey bee biology might be chemically controlled was not suggested until 1956 when C. G. Butler incorporated it into his queen substance theory. Butler later showed that worker ovary development can be inhibited by synthetic queen substance. In 1970 Cameron S. Jay observed that the presence of brood, even without a queen, has some effect on worker ovary development. He concluded that, in addition to queen substance, there is also a brood pheromone that inhibits the development of the workers' ovaries. Although this is not unlikely, and the inhibition would be of benefit to the colony while brood is present and while the bees can still rear a queen, the identification of this pheromone has eluded researchers.

Several people have stated that some normal, queenright colonies contain a small percentage of laying workers. This is probably true; however, the circumstances under which such laying workers may appear are not clear.

Mating and the sex attractant

In 1961, while he was perusing some of the earlier literature, Norman E. Gary noted that Lloyd R. Watson, in his 1927 Cornell University thesis, had pictured a comet-shaped group of males pursuing a queen in flight. Watson understood that mating was taking place. Gary recognized the importance of Watson's observations and as a result became the discoverer of the fact that queen substance, 9-oxodec-*trans*-2-enoic acid, is the primary, and perhaps the only, honey bee sex attractant.

Gary first conducted his studies using a fishpole, a nylon line, and a helium-filled balloon under which he suspended queens and queen parts. He demonstrated that honey bee queens have a sex attractant and that it is extractable. He found that all parts of the queen's body are attractive to drones but that the head is especially so. This led to the discovery that the mandibular glands are the source of the sex attractant. Since these glands are also the source of the queen substance discovered only a short while earlier by C. G. Butler, R. K. Callow, and N. C. Johnston, Gary contacted Callow and was given some of the synthetic queen substance for testing. Gary's paper, published the 26th of December, 1961, is a classic in honey bee and insect biology and is much referred to. While the whole subject seems to be clear enough to us today, Gary's paper is testimony to the fact that, to make important advances, a researcher must be knowledgeable both in literature and in techniques and have the ability to make use of the two together.[3]

In all his studies, Gary has observed only two tethered queens that have mated successfully and lived to lay eggs. Reluctance to mate seems to be with the queen alone since Gary has demon-

3. As an interesting aside, Gary's first attempts were on the quadrangle of the College of Agriculture. Questions from friendly but bothersome bystanders forced him to move to the vicinity of the apiary at the head of Beebe Lake, on the edge of the Cornell campus. Fortunately, drones were active in the area selected (see Drone congregation areas, below).

strated that males will mount and attempt to mate with dead queens and dummy queens made of wood or metal but annointed with the sex attractant.

An interesting aspect of mating in honey bees is that mating usually takes place fairly high above the ground, from 8 to 30 meters. Worker honey bees normally fly within about three meters of the ground; when workers fly over a forest, they fly just at tree top level. Thus, queens and drones have one flight lane and workers another; the two female castes seldom come in contact with each other in the field. Gary noted, as have others, that worker honey bees will attack and attempt to sting queens in the field. Workers are not antagonistic toward flying drones so far as we are aware; still, drones fly higher than workers and in the same flight lanes as queens. The fact that workers are able to recognize their own queen in a swarm is discussed below. I suggest that the antagonism of worker bees toward queens not their own is pheromonal in origin, but the pheromones in question are unknown.

Drone congregation areas

Mating in honey bees takes place only in the afternoon; at this time of day the males and those virgin queens about to mate take wing and fly some distance from the apiary. While mating may take place in the apiary and has been seen by a few people, it is an event that is not commonly observed. The fact that queens mate more than once was not discovered until the 1950's, and the physical position assumed by the sexes was still a question of speculation until the research by Gary was published in 1961.

Though drones fly so high and fast that they are not seen, there is a very definite hum in the air in a drone congregation area. Over the years several people suggested that such areas exist, but scant attention was paid to this suggestion; Gary's discovery of the sex attractant was a necessary precondition for proving the existence of drone congregation areas. In 1963, Cyprian Zmarlicki and Roger A. Morse published their observations, demonstrating that drone congregation areas do exist. They used queens tethered on fishline and suspended from helium-filled balloons. In one long valley near Ithaca, New York, ten areas were studied in detail. There was one primary drone congregation area, two areas to which a lesser number of drones were attracted, three areas where only a few drones could be attracted at any one time, and four areas to which no drones were attracted under any circumstance. George E. Strang, in the period 1965 through 1968, restudied the drone congregation areas discovered by Zmarlicki in 1962. He found that these areas were little changed from year to year despite the fact that males do not survive the winter and that memory could not play an important role in this regard.

The question of drone congregation areas has also been researched in Germany by Friedrich Ruttner (1966), who has likewise found that drone congregation areas remain the same year after year. Ruttner found that drone congregation areas were smaller and better defined in hilly, than in flat, areas. Several people have unsuccessfully attempted to define what constitutes a drone congregation area. Strang (1970) found that he could create an area by saturating it with the synthetic sex attractant; however, after he removed the sex attractant, drones were no longer attracted to the area. Ruttner has suggested that drone congregation areas are a function of the local terrain and are affected by local climatic conditions; this theory has the greatest support and seems most plausible.

Everett Oertel (1971) has called attention to research undertaken by F. W. L. Sladen in 1919 and 1920 which suggests that, although a queen mates with only seven to eight males, drones must be present in greater numbers for successful mating to take place. Sladen worked on an island, and when he had 500 drones in flight, obtained very poor mating results. Even with over 2,000 drones, only 11 of 27 queens were perfectly mated. The question posed as a result of this research is, how do queens find the drone congregation areas? It is possible that they use the same physical mechanisms as do males; it is also possible that there is a male pheromone that first attracts the queens to the area.

7.2. Bees in a natural swarm cluster on this individual's hand because he is holding a cage containing a queen. These bees are engorged and will not sting.

Swarming and swarm orientation

There is one instance in which a beekeeper can play Pied Piper: he can lead a swarm and have most of the bees airborne for long distances. By using the attraction of bees to their queen, several people have made a beard of bees or caused the bees to settle in a desired place. Throughout the process of swarming it is important that the queen be aware of the presence of the swarm and that the swarm be aware of the presence of their queen. If either is separated from the other, both will be lost, or the workers will be forced to return to their parent hive where they may or may not successfully swarm again (fig. 7.2).

In 1963, I determined that if a queen is removed from her swarm cluster and placed nearby, some workers in the swarm will always look for her. These bees find their queen and attract others to her; when a queen is removed from a swarm and placed within about two meters of it, the entire swarm cluster breaks up and will have moved to her usually within about two hours.

Later, in 1970 and 1971, Rolf Boch of the Canada Department of Agriculture and I determined that bees recognize their queen, at least in part, by queen substance. Bees recognize their queen, expose their scent glands,[4] and attract other bees to the swarm. In cooperation with Dietrich Mautz (1972), we observed a back and forth movement of worker bees between the queen and the swarm when we artifically separated the two. We noticed that bees expose their scent gland more on the queen than they do on the swarm cluster and that they are more inclined to break (to perform breaking dances) on the queenless cluster than on the cluster forming on the queen. Thus, both pheromones and physical movements are involved in swarm orientation.

Experimentally, we induced queenless swarms to cluster about synthetic queen substance and synthetic scent gland substances, thus showing that these are important pheromones in swarm orientation.

It has been suggested that bees are able to identify their own queen and can tell the difference between their own queen and a foreign queen when offered a choice between the two. I was able to confirm this in the winter of 1971–1972 in Florida. Bees finding their own queen exposed their scent glands and attracted other bees to the area. The bees finding a foreign queen exposed their sting and alarm odor. However, how workers first identify which queen is their own and which is foreign, and make the decision to expose their scent glands (in the case of their own queen) or their stings (a foreign queen) is unknown.

Alarm pheromones and colony protection

Worker and queen honey bees are armed with stings, but drones

4. For a more thorough discussion of the scent gland, and scenting, see below, The scent gland pheromones.

lack this protection. The queen will rarely use her sting except against another queen. In time of real danger worker honey bees do not hesitate to sting any animal, including other bees, which might try to invade their hive. In the process of stinging the sting is torn from the worker bee's body, and as a result she dies. The worker honey bee's sting is barbed, and it usually remains in the victim, continuing to pump venom and to cause pain and irritation. Leaving the sting behind also serves to mark the enemy, because alarm pheromone will be released from it for about five minutes. Queen stings have very small barbs and the queen usually does not lose her sting in the process of stinging or killing another queen.

Many animals use alarm pheromones to alert others of the same species to danger, and these pheromones have certain characteristics that set them aside from others. First, they must be distinct and carry a very positive message. Second, they must be volatile and act rapidly; alarm pheromones usually have molecular weights of between 80 and 200, whereas pheromones in general have molecular weights ranging from 80 to approximately 300. Last, alarm pheromones must fade rapidly so that a colony is not kept in an undue state of alarm after a danger has passed.

If a worker honey bee encounters a dangerous situation, she protrudes her sting and releases alarm odor, thus alerting nearby bees, which will rush to the scene. If the danger passes, nothing further happens. If the danger persists, other bees release alarm odor, reinforcing the actions of the first bee and arousing still more bees to the point of danger.

In the case of certain wasps, alarm odor is apparently contained in the venom itself. Most wasps have unbarbed stings (though a few are very lightly barbed). Thus, the sting is not left in the victim, and wasps will usually sting two or three times in rapid succession, dragging the stinger behind as they move from one site of injection to another. In this way they leave alarm odor on the surface of the victim's body, marking it so that other wasps (of social species) can follow the victim.

The alarm odor

The alarm odor in the honey bee is iso-pentyl acetate. This was discovered by R. Boch, D. A. Shearer, and B. C. Stone in 1962. It is not in the venom itself but is released from the vicinity of the sting and has the physical characteristics typical of alarm odors. Iso-pentyl acetate is not a new chemical and has been on laboratory shelves for years. Although its presence in certain plant tissues has been known, Boch, Shearer, and Stone were the first to report finding the material in an animal tissue.

Iso-pentyl acetate has a sweet odor that is not at all unpleasant to man. The function of the alarm odor, like that of the sex attractant, can be demonstrated with relative ease. It is only necessary to place a drop of iso-pentyl acetate on an object such as a cork, or a cotton ball, and to put the object at a hive entrance and watch the bees attack it. The observer must be careful for the colony may become sufficiently aroused to sting anything or anyone in the vicinity.

A secondary alarm odor

In 1965, Shearer and Boch discovered that 2-heptanone was present in the mandibular glands of worker honey bees and that it would also alarm bees. Precisely how bees use 2-heptanone in nature is not known, but it is suspected they may use the substance in the field to mark flowers from which the food has been exhausted and perhaps to mark an enemy by biting it. Possibly it is released when bees are biting and holding a queen, not their own. If used in sufficient quantity, it will arouse bees in much the same way as will iso-pentyl acetate.

Although a queen honey bee has a sting and her mandibular glands are somewhat similar to those of worker honey bees, she produces no alarm odor. When two queens are fighting and using their stings and mandibles to attack one another, bees in the vicinity are not disturbed and do not participate in the fracas. In fact, two queens may fight to the death in the midst of thousands of worker honey bees with the workers apparently unaware that anything is taking place.

Defense in winter

Honey bees are cold blooded animals, but in the winter they form a cluster and generate heat. If brood rearing is taking place, the interior of the cluster may be between 27 and 33°C. (approx. 80 and 92°F.) even when the temperature outside is subzero. Bees on the exterior of the cluster become cold and in fact so cold that they cannot move. However, they do not normally die of cold for bees from within the cluster will move outward, pushing the cold bees to the interior where they may warm their bodies.

Although bees on the exterior of a cluster may become so cold that they cannot move, they are apparently never too cold to protrude their stings. If one disturbs a winter cluster (or looks into the top of a hive during a cold fall or spring day) it will be noted that the outside of the cluster reminds one of a porcupine because of hundreds of bees exposing their sting. Any animal which molests or touches the bees on the outside will be stung just as though it were being attacked by the bees.

If one continues to molest a winter cluster, bees from the interior of the cluster will fly out, arcing in all directions and stinging anything on which they light. I have deliberately provoked bees in order to observe this action on subfreezing days. If the provocation is prolonged, many bees will land on the snow or the cold ground and, being unable to return to the hive, they will die.

It is not known if the same alarm odor that alerts bees in the summer also alerts them in the winter cluster; possibly, in the winter only a physical action is necessary. Although the winter cluster is as well protected as is the colony during the summer, during the winter bees cannot protect their food supply as well as they do during warmer weather. If a large animal such as a man or a bear attempts to remove honey from a winter cluster, the vibrations made in the process are usually sufficient to alarm the bees. It is not uncommon for mice to overwinter in beehives, and bees find it difficult to dislodge a mouse once it has constructed its well insulated nest; they will do so in the summer.

An English novel

It is said that truth is stranger than fiction, but in one instance, fiction precedes truth. In a short novel, *A Taste for Honey,* 1941, H. F. Heard wrote about a beekeeper who discovers a chemical substance which arouses bees, in effect, an alarm odor. The beekeeper then breeds a race of bees that is unusually vicious, and using the vicious bees and the alarm odor, arranges to kill his wife in his apiary. The murder occupies only a small portion of the novel, and the remainder of the book is devoted to the discovery of the crime by a self-styled detective, a resident of the village. In the end, the beekeeper's bees turn on their owner and he, himself, is killed.

The interesting fact is that the author suggested that a chemical substance capable of arousing bees might exist. This of course occurred long before 1959, when Karlson and Butenandt coined the term *pheromone,* and long before 1962, when Boch, Shearer, and Stone discovered the alarm odor in honey bees.

The scent gland pheromones

The scent gland, perhaps better known as the Nassanoff gland, is found on the top of the abdomen of worker bees only (figure 7.3). The gland is formed from tissue of the intersegmental membrane between abdominal segments six and seven; the gland is covered by the tip of segment six. When a worker bee exposes her scent gland, she extends the tip of her abdomen and bends it downward. The scent gland is a large mass of cells, estimated to number 500 to 600. The scent gland substance is secreted from the cells and presumably remains on the surface, evaporating when the gland is exposed. Worker bees exposing their scent glands usually fan with their wings, forcing a current of air over the exposed glands that flows in the opposite direction from which the bees are facing. Worker bees receiving the scent gland odor therefore move "upwind."

The scent gland is not exposed in the hive and is used outside of the hive only under specific circumstances. Scout bees mark a

7.3. A scenting worker honey bee. In the process of scenting a worker honey bee fans her wings, forcing the air back over the scent gland (arrow). This indicates to bees in the vicinity to move in the direction that this worker is faced.

food source by exposing their scent glands. They may also scent at a new home site to attract other scouts, and bees from the swarm as well, when the swarm finally moves to the home site. The scent gland is also used by bees in a swarm to indicate the presence of their queen. Experimentally, one may best observe the actions of scenting bees by removing a queen from a settled swarm and placing her, in a cage, a few meters away. Workers from the swarm will find the queen; movement of the bees to the queen will follow, usually taking one to two hours. During this time there will be movement of some workers back and forth between the queen and the queenless swarm; scenting will also take place especially in the vicinity of the queen. If the bees are allowed, or forced, to walk between the swarm and the queen, they will form a line of scenting bees, which in effect builds an odor trail between the two.

A remarkable bit of chemical sleuthing by Boch and Shearer

led to the identification of the components of the scent gland secretion; the results of this difficult research appeared in three papers, published in 1962, 1964, and 1966.

It was found that a worker could be grasped, the tip of the abdomen bent downward and the scent gland wiped with filter paper which then became contaminated with scent gland pheromone. The pheromone could be extracted from the filter paper with a solvent and placed in a gas chromatograph for analysis.

Four chemicals are found in the scent gland secretion. These are geraniol, geranic and nerolic acids, and citral. All of these compounds are easily synthesized, and the synthetic substances may be substituted experimentally for the natural substances. Exposure of synthetic scent gland substance will usually result in the natural exposure of scent glands by worker bees in the vicinity.

Pheromones in food gathering

In the normal course of events, honey bees that are foraging in a field or forest distribute themselves more or less uniformly over the foraging area. There are usually more bees foraging near the hive than there are at some distance from it, but a given area can accommodate only so many bees. The classical experiment on this subject was performed by Bonnier in 1906.[5] Bonnier found that if he made up a bouquet of a given number of branches in water, that this bouquet, no matter how attractive, would be visited by only a given number of bees. If he doubled the size of the bouquet, the number of its honey bee visitors would be more or less doubled. Further proof of the fact that a given population of flowers will support only a certain population of bees is shown when a colony of honey bees is caged with a nectar or pollen-producing plant. A limited number of bees from the hive will visit the flowers, and the remainder of the bees in flight will spend all of their time trying to escape from the cage. Under these circumstances one will note that the foraging bees in the cage are capable of collecting

5. Bonnier's account of his work is translated and quoted at length on pages 128–131 of E. F. Phillips, *Beekeeping*.

pollen, and small pollen balls will form on their legs. This indicates, too, that bees will not forage unless it is profitable for them to do so even under these extreme conditions.

How then do bees distribute themselves so evenly in a field? Casual observation suggests that the bees which first find the flowers mark them and in this way deter other bees from foraging in an area; it has been suggested that 2-heptanone may act as the deterrent in this matter, but there is no proof of this suggestion, except that when 2-heptanone is placed near bees in the field, they will flee from it.

One exception to this unwillingness to forage under crowding occurs when bees are stealing honey from another hive or from recently extracted supers, which the beekeeper may purposely expose to the bees for the purpose of getting the supers clean. One may create a similar circumstance by offering the bees sugar syrup in a tub or barrel exposed in the apiary. However, under these circumstances it will be noted that the bees are extremely flighty and that the slightest disturbance will cause them to take wing. While they are engaged in stealing and robbing, they do not retain the calm disposition that they display while collecting pollen or nectar from natural sources. Their nervous behavior suggests the presence of some marking substance or pheromone.

In contradistinction to the above, bees may expose their Nassanoff glands at food sources and thus attract other bees to the vicinity.

Plant attractants

Although plant attractants are not pheromones, they are odoriferous and act in somewhat the same manner, and for this reason are most appropriately discussed with them. One plant attractant has been identified from pollen at this writing. The data suggest that many plant attractants exist in nature. This subject has been discussed in part in Chapter 3; suffice it to say that a plant attractant is only one of the factors that cause bees to collect pollen. Floral odors, of course, play the same role in the collection of nectar.

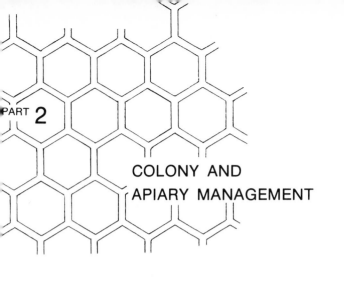

PART 2

COLONY AND
APIARY MANAGEMENT

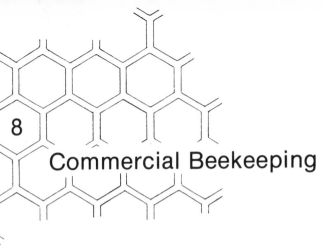

8

Commercial Beekeeping

Keeping bees is one of the oldest agricultural pursuits. It is estimated that nearly 300,000 people keep honey bees in the United States. This figure includes commercial beekeepers who make their living producing honey and beeswax or growing queens and package bees, and semicommercial beekeepers who may have 100, 200, or 300 hives and may rent their bees for pollination or produce honey as a sideline. The majority of beekeepers, however, are hobbyists who keep from one to ten hives of bees. Many of these are experts, but many others are still learning how to keep bees and how to manage them for a profit.

There are over five million colonies in this country, and bees produce approximately 250 million pounds of honey annually, slightly over one pound per person in the United States. World honey production is somewhat over one billion pounds per year.

The number of colonies that may be kept in any one location is limited by the availability of pollen and nectar for the bees. Still, it is difficult to find a location where at least one colony will not survive. While it is scarcely monetarily profitable to keep only a single hive of bees, it is possible for the hobby beekeeper to live almost anywhere and pursue his hobby. In parts of the country where bee forage is limited, one may supplement the colonies' food by feeding sugar syrup and perhaps pollen substitutes.

The honey bee itself can adapt to a wide range of climatic conditions. Generally speaking, bees will live in any location where people can survive, the only exception being the polar regions. Even in extreme latitudes bees sometimes survive during parts of the year.

The commercial beekeepers

The approximately 2,000 to 2,500 commercial beekeepers in the United States are primarily concerned with honey production. For each ton of honey produced the commercial beekeepers harvest from 20 to 40 pounds of beeswax. In the average year beeswax sells for a price of about three to five times that of a pound of honey and is therefore a valuable adjunct to the beekeeper's overall sales.

Some beekeepers specialize in pollination. In many of the western states beekeepers rent hives of bees for the pollination of alfalfa, and in Washington and Oregon for apples and related crops. Thousands of colonies are rented for almond pollination in California. Across the country many colonies are rented for the pollination of squash, cucumbers, and such crops as carrots and onions. In the eastern United States bees are rented for the pollination of special types of citrus fruits in Florida, and apples in Maryland, New York, New Jersey and the New England states. Blueberry growers in Michigan, Maine, and New Jersey rent bees; cranberries are also a special crop for which bees are rented for pollination, both in the East and the West. This is to mention a few of the special circumstances under which bees are valuable.

California is usually the leading honey-producing state, followed by Minnesota and Florida; however, New York, Ohio, Michigan, Illinois, and certain other states also have large numbers of commercial beekeepers. Many beekeepers are migratory. For example, some who live in New York State in the summer have their winter homes in Florida, and in many cases these men move their bees back and forth between the two states. Those who operate in Utah and the Dakotas may very well winter in Texas. California beekeepers move not only within the state but also to neighboring states.

It is said that a commercial beekeeper needs at least 500 colonies of bees to make a full-time living; however, most own or manage a thousand or more, depending upon individual management techniques, location, and market. Since the price of honey is strongly influenced by the quantity of honey available on the world market, the commercial beekeepers must be alert to world as well as local conditions.

A few hobby beekeepers wholesale their honey, some sell to local stores, and others have stands near their homes from which they sell their wares. However, many beekeepers confine their efforts to supplying honey for themselves and their friends.

Like commercial beekeepers, hobbyists may specialize in honey production, pollination, comb honey production, queen rearing, or in other related ventures. Those who live near some of the large fruit producing areas in the country find that at certain times of the year there is always a demand for five, ten, or more hives of bees for pollination. Often orchardists are willing to move the colonies to and from the orchard themselves, relieving the beekeeper of the need for a truck or trailer.

Most beekeepers feel that locally grown queen bees are better than queens bought from afar; however, queen rearing is a specialty and not everyone is adept at it. A beekeeper who builds a reputation as a queen breeder and who always has ten, twenty, or a hundred queens for sale will usually find a good market for them anywhere in the United States, or abroad for that matter.

Why beekeeping is possible

Beekeeping might not be practical were it not for certain physical characteristics of the honey bee nest. It is important to beekeeping that honey bees hoard honey and that honey is a storable product. Pasteurization of liquid honey after it has been removed from the hive is advisable in order to prevent fermentation, but it is not necessary to add preservatives to honey.

Also important is the separation of the brood and the food that occurs in the honey bee colony. In the modern hive the honey is stored above the brood to facilitate beekeeping. In the evolutionary process it was probably the importance of controlling the brood-rearing temperature that encouraged separation of the food from the brood.

In addition to depending upon the natural separation of the brood and the food, some beekeepers use a queen excluder, a grid of wires wide enough so that worker bees can pass through, but the queen, with her broad thorax and abdomen, cannot. This further separates the brood from the food, and in some ways is an advantage. However, many beekeepers believe that queen excluders tend to have an adverse effect on ventilation in the hive and may even contribute to swarming; thus, not all beekeepers use them.

Bee space

Bee space is walking space one-fourth of an inch to three-eighths of an inch wide around and between combs in the hive. If the space between combs is less than one-fourth of an inch, the bees will fill it with propolis or wax or otherwise block it. If the space is much greater than three-eights of an inch, the bees will build burr or brace comb between the combs. Not only is there a space around and between the combs, which are side by side, but when supers [1] of combs are placed one above the other, there must be the proper space between the bottom bars of the combs above and the top bars of the combs below (figure 8.1).

The discovery of bee space made modern beekeeping possible. Before the discovery it was necessary to kill the bees or cut the combs from a hive to harvest the honey. The beekeeper could neither inspect the brood in his hive, nor could he determine if disease was present and whether or not the colony needed re-queening.

The principle of bee space was discovered in 1851 by the Reverend L. L. Langstroth, a hobby beekeeper, at the time living in

1. A super (sometimes called hive body) is the box which holds the combs or frames. The boxes in which the brood nest is located may be called brood nest supers; those holding honey, honey supers.

8.1. A swarm of bees entered this hive body, which was without frames, and built natural comb. The bees respect bee space and leave a space between the combs.

Philadelphia. The discovery was accidental, but Langstroth had a sufficiently keen mind to recognize the importance of what he was seeing. He observed that if he left a space above the top of the fixed frames or combs in his hive, and below the cover, the bees would not attach the cover to the rest of the hive so rigidly, and he could remove the cover, thus facilitating the cutting of the combs from within the hive. In the fall of 1851 he realized that if he used the same space around and between the combs, he could have a movable frame hive. In the spring of 1852 Langstroth made the first movable frame hive and in November of that year he was granted a patent for his discovery. Langstroth wrote a book on bees, *The Hive and the Honeybee,* which first appeared in 1853. Today he is honored as the father of American beekeeping.

Langstroth continued to study the honey bee. He wrote articles for the bee journals and prepared several editions of his book.

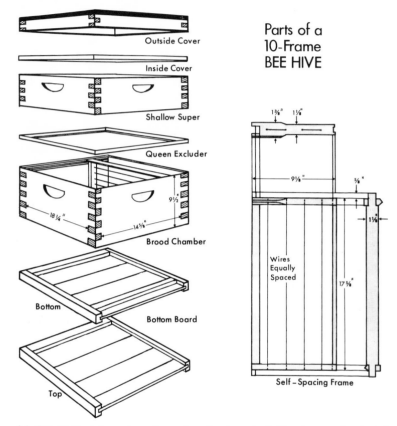

Parts of a
10-Frame
BEE HIVE

Outside Cover

Inside Cover

Shallow Super

Queen Excluder

Brood Chamber

Bottom

Bottom Board

Top

Self-Spacing Frame

8.2. The standard dimensions of a modern day, Langstroth hive. Langstroth selected these dimensions arbitrarily, using what were then standard lumber dimensions to make his first hives. Most beekeeping equipment now in use in North America is of these same dimensions.

Langstroth's discovery made him no money, for his patent was infringed upon by many persons. Nevertheless, no one has ever doubted his ability, nor have others been able to steal his claim to fame. The standard dimensions for Langstroth equipment are shown in figures 8.2 and 8.3.

Special Beekeeping Equipment For 10-Frame Hives

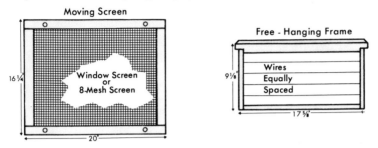

Moving Screen

16¼

Window Screen
or
8-Mesh Screen

20"

Free - Hanging Frame

9⅛

| Wires |
| Equally |
| Spaced |

17⅝"

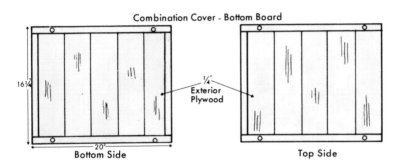

Combination Cover - Bottom Board

16¼

¼"
Exterior
Plywood

20"
Bottom Side

Top Side

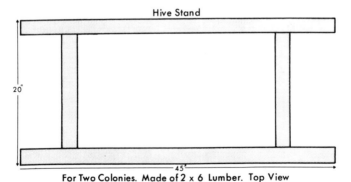

Hive Stand

20"

45"
For Two Colonies. Made of 2 x 6 Lumber. Top View

8.3. Many beekeepers make at least some of their own equipment. Some home-made, special items are illustrated here.

Where bees build nests

The honey bee with which we are familiar in North America and Europe builds its nest in hollow trees or, less frequently, in caves.[2] When men came on the scene, honey bees found that houses, barns, boxes, and other man-made objects also made good nesting sites. Probably the fact that 10,000 years ago a nest of honey bees accidentally swarmed into a man-made object, led to the manufacture of the first bee hive.

A number of years ago I found that light inhibits the comb construction of *Apis mellifera*. One may make an artificial swarm or capture a natural swarm, cage the queen, and place the bees on a stake where they are exposed to sunlight. The bees will attempt to move to a new homesite, but they will not abandon their queen. Even though they are held on a stake in this manner for several weeks, comb building does not occur. Yet these bees continue to secrete wax, and large quantities of wax scales may be found on the ground. Very rarely one will find a nest of *Apis mellifera* out-of-doors in an unprotected area, and an examination of the combs will reveal that the nest was started when there was dense foliage to protect it. The pictures of exposed nests which have been published show, upon close examination, that many of the nests were in apple trees, which are noted for their dense exterior foliage. It seems likely that the nest shown in figure 8.4 was built when leaves were dense and when inclement weather further darkened the area and spurred wax production. Once the bees have started to build a nest and have a large quantity of comb and brood, they will not abandon it even though they cannot survive for long under these circumstances.

2. Two of the four existing species of honey bees do not nest in protected cavities: *Apis dorsata* and *Apis florea,* two of the Asian species, nest in the open and build only a single comb. The fourth honey bee species, *Apis indica,* whose common name is the Indian bee, nests in much the same type of place as does the European species, *Apis mellifera;* however, unlike the latter, it will also nest in the ground (see Chapter 1). Close observation indicates that a ground nest is usually in a rocky area where there is some protection from the elements, and where there is fairly good water drainage.

8.4. Sunlight inhibits comb construction. However, a swarm may settle in a tree when foliage is dense and build its nest, as it has done here, making parallel combs. The swarm which built this comb perished in the fall because of lack of food and protection.

Organization of the hive

In the evolution of the honey bee it is evident that temperature control and, to a lesser extent, humidity control in the brood nest are important. If the nest temperature, especially the brood nest temperature, can be controlled, an animal can rear young in a fixed period of time, but when there is no control over the temperature at which the young are reared, brood development time varies greatly. The control of the brood nest temperature is especially important in areas where the temperature is not uniform all year. In the northern United States and Canada, for example, brood rearing in January, if in limited quantity, is now considered quite normal for honey bees. Rearing brood in the early months of the year, January, February, and March, allows a day-to-day replacement of the older bees and gives the colony a supply of young bees with which to begin the spring.

Brood-rearing temperature control can be accomplished only if the brood is reared in a compact area. Thus, in its evolution, a natural separation of the food and brood developed. In the modern hive, the entrance is usually at the bottom of the nest; the food is stored above and the brood below. This is not always true in nature,

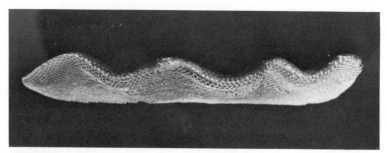

8.5. Natural comb built by bees in a bee tree, not all natural comb is wavy as is this piece. One of the reasons for using comb foundation is to force the bees to construct straight, even combs.

and one will find bee trees where the primary nest entrance is at the middle or above the brood rearing and food storing areas. In such cases the food may be stored below the brood. However, there has been no research to determine how commonly this occurs.

People who have examined natural nests constructed by bees in trees, buildings, and caves have found that bees may successfully nest under a variety of conditions (see figure 8.5). In fact, some of the peculiar nest structures, and the success of bees in them, have led a few people to design a hive radically different from that used commercially. This has resulted in some conflicting theories. Although some people believe that there must be a "perfect" hive or nest for bees, I am inclined to the view that the honey bee is a remarkably adaptable animal, capable of succeeding under a variety of conditions.

While the discovery of bee space in 1851 was of primary importance in establishing a beekeeping industry, three additional discoveries during the next 22 years were almost equally important.

Comb foundation

The first of these was the discovery of comb foundation. Comb foundation is a thin sheet of beeswax with the bases and the beginnings of the cell walls embossed on both sides of the foundation. Worker honey bees will "draw out," or make, the cell walls if given the proper size foundation. While Langstroth had found that he could take a piece of natural honey comb and put a wooden frame around it, he had no good method of forcing the bees to build a comb within one of his wooden frames. It was J. Mehring who found, in 1857, that he could make a wax press out of wood. Later it was found that by pouring hot wax onto plaster of Paris, or some other reasonably hard material, and then lowering an opposite side, somewhat like a waffle iron, one could emboss the cell bases onto the sheet of wax. The bees would accept this comb foundation and make new comb. There were several problems with the wax press, among them being the fact that the comb foundation sheets were often very thick and certain cells might have imperfections. Metal rollers, which somewhat resemble the ringers on an old-fashioned washing machine, with cell bases embossed on them, were first invented in 1873. There were several refinements in these, and by the end of the nineteenth century comb foundation was readily available from several manufacturers. Figures 8.6 to 8.9 illustrate foundation, new and old comb.

The extractor

Prior to the establishment of the Pure Food and Drug Laws in 1906, much of the liquid honey that was on the market was adulterated. For this reason many beekeepers concentrated on the production of comb honey, for it was well known among consumers that comb honey was a pure product. However, commercial beekeepers recognized from the first that liquid honey was easier to produce and that it helped save the bees the effort of building new comb each year. Therefore, the invention of the honey extractor by Franz von Hruschka in 1865 was important. Langstroth immediately recognized the importance of this machine and built an extractor for himself in 1868. The radial extractor is the most popular one in use today among commercial beekeepers; however, there are several other types, including reversible extractors, merry-go-round, and others. All extractors are based on the principle of centrifugal force. They are easy to use though they have a

8.6. An old comb (left) and a new frame with wired foundation (right). Note that bees have started to draw out a few cells in the center of the new comb and have added some burr comb to the top bar.

few shortcomings. For example, it is important for beekeepers to be careful in extracting new comb, since new comb breaks easily. Once a comb has been in use for more than two or three extracting seasons, the bees will have strengthened its weak points, and breakage is less common.

The smoker

The fact that smoke will calm bees was known to the ancients. Many of the early writers on beekeeping from the Greek and Roman times said that burning dung or blowing the smoke from punk wood across the hive would calm the bees. It was not until 1873, however, that Moses Quimby built the first practical bellows smoker. For the first time the beekeeper could direct a large puff of smoke precisely where it was needed; he could, for example,

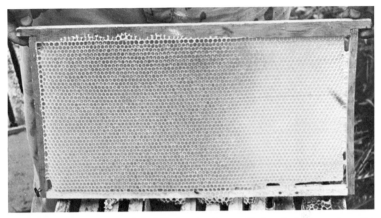

8.7. A newly drawn comb partially full of unripe honey. That part of the comb on the right, where the cells are not completed, was in the front of a hive that tilted forward; bees tend to draw comb and fill cells directly above the brood nest first.

8.8. A frame of partially capped honey. In the process of capping, honey near the top of the frame is normally capped first. Note that as individual cells are capped, the center of the cell is the last portion to be capped.

8.9. A mediocre comb. Some beekeepers would discard this comb because it contains too much drone comb, especially in the lower right hand corner.

use it to calm the bees in the colony he was inspecting. The early smokers had bellows that were too small and firepots that would not hold sufficient fuel. These shortcomings were soon corrected, and within a few years practical smokers had been invented and were readily available.

In the short span of twenty-two years, beekeeping changed from a primitive art to a commercial agricultural system. As far as beekeeping equipment is concerned, there have been few changes, other than standardization, during the last hundred years. The bee escape, the queen excluder, and the division board feeder were important discoveries, but not so important as bee space, foundation, the extractor, and the smoker.

The changes in the beekeeping industry in recent years have been a result of the introduction of gasoline and electric engines, and improved methods of packaging and marketing honey. As long as the bee is not altered through an improved bee breeding program, or until more is known about the biology of the bee, further changes are unlikely.

8.10. A commercial beekeeper moving a stack of extracting supers, filled with honey, into a closed van.

Practical beekeeping

Commercial beekeeping, like many specialized agricultural pursuits, tends to be a family business; however, many beekeeping operations are not family oriented, and beekeepers, like many other agriculturists, are often plagued with labor problems. During parts of the year it is possible for a beekeeper and his helpers to work only a 40 hour week, but when the honey crop is being harvested, or bees are being moved for honey production or pollination, beekeepers are forced to work longer hours and often at night as well as during the daylight hours. Figures 8.10 and 8.11 show a beekeeper removing his honey crop.

As a general statement, a commercial beekeeper usually operates 500 to 1,000 colonies of bees, but if he is producing comb honey (large combs which may be cut into smaller pieces for sale), or rearing queens, he may keep fewer colonies. The commercial

8.11. Removing bees from an extracting super with an air blower. Blowing the bees from the frames of honey does not harm them. The bees which have settled on the beekeeper's shirt are young bees which are lost; they will not sting unless crushed.

beekeeper also has the option of intensive or extensive management; both systems are practiced in the United States. Many beekeepers prefer to have a greater number of colonies and to pay less attention to requeening, swarming, and general management; their per colony production will be much lower than that of a man who practices intensive colony management. The beekeeper who owns many colonies will usually have them spread over a greater area, thus increasing the chance that every year, somewhere within his holdings, a crop will be produced. Crop failures do occur in the beekeeping industry, and every commercial beekeeper is alert to the possibility.

Various choices are open to the beekeeper in marketing his honey. Most commercial beekeepers prefer to sell their honey in large drums or cans, thus minimizing the effort which they put into sales. Others specialize in packing honey for the baking trade,

8.12. A well-protected apiary surrounded by woods but with the colonies themselves exposed to full sunlight. The building in the rear is used for the storage of equipment.

the mail order trade, roadside stands, or local grocery stores. While the per pound price may be greater in certain of these instances, this is achieved at the cost of considerable time devoted to packaging and selling.

A commercial beekeeper has one advantage over the agriculturist who husbands domestic animals. Domestic animals usually require day to day care. Although beekeepers, like those men who tend crops, must at times during the year take steps to maximize their production, at other times they are free from routine tasks. The fact that honey bees are relatively inactive in winter in the North, and in the summer in the South, has led to the development of migratory beekeeping in this country. But since moving colonies of bees requires a great deal of lifting and trucking, many of the beekeepers who move south in the winter and north in the summer have permanent apiaries in both parts of the country (see figures 8.12 and 8.13). This option requires a greater investment in bee-

8.13. A commercial apiary in a Florida orange grove. Finding an isolated location on a good road is a difficult task faced by every beekeeper.

keeping equipment but less in the vehicles necessary to move the bees.

The routine of seasonal management

A beekeeper's seasonal management is dependent upon his interpretation of the cycle of the year (Chapter 4). In the northern states the beekeeper's year is said to begin about August 1, when routine requeening is usually done; however, for the purpose of this discussion, we shall review the routine of seasonal management starting in April. The information below pertains to the State of New York, more especially, central New York. Farther north the season starts later, and farther south, earlier (see figs. 8.14–8.16).

There is not much apiary work that a beekeeper can do until mid-April. Brood rearing usually starts much earlier in the year, and its success depends upon the amount of pollen and honey

8.14. Opening a colony of bees for examination. The beekeeper stands at one side of the hive so as not to block bee flight to and from the entrance. As the inner cover is lifted, a small amount of smoke is forced over the topbars of the frames. The hive cover has been set to the rear, again, so as not to block flight to and from the colony.

8.15. Removing a frame to make a colony examination. The beekeeper holds the smoker between his legs where it is ready for use, his hive tool is in his right hand. The bees have been smoked down off the topbars so as to facilitate removal of the combs. In removing a comb it is usually advisable to take one from the side of the brood nest first, not from the center.

8.16. Examining a brood frame. This beekeeper is standing with the sun behind him so that the light entering the cell enables him to see the cell contents. Note that two frames have been removed from this brood chamber; one has been set aside to make room in the chamber for the beekeeper to examine the next comb.

available in the hive, as well as the number of bees and the ability of the queen as an egg layer. Although most days in April are still too cold for making a thorough colony examination, the beekeeper can check the food supply in the hive, remove dead colonies, and combine weak ones. It is important that dead colonies be given a thorough examination to determine whether they died because of mismanagement or disease.

In late April or early May the beekeeper makes the first thorough inspection of the colony itself. At this time he checks for three things: disease, food (pollen and honey, though most commonly honey) and the brood pattern of the queen. It is not necessary for the beekeeper to find the queen in the colony to determine if she is a good queen; this is determined by checking her brood pattern. Within the brood rearing area, adjacent cells should contain brood of more or less the same age. Thus, there will be large areas of capped brood, areas of glistening white larvae, and areas that contain only eggs. Good queens fill most of the cells in the comb, and only an occasional cell should be empty. If these criteria are not met, the colony is marked for requeening, usually at a later date.

When the first pollen becomes available from spring flowers, brood rearing increases sharply; in crowded, populous colonies, swarming may take place in late May, June or early July. The swarm prevention method favored by most beekeepers involves reversing the supers (hive bodies). This, as has been discussed in Chapter 4, rearranges the brood nest and gives room for the bees to work in an upward direction within the hive. Most beekeepers will reverse their supers three or four times during May and June and at the same time will add others so that, by the first of July, strong colonies will occupy four to seven supers.

Honey flows vary from area to area, but the primary honey flow is said to begin between the twentieth of June and the fifth of July in much of New York State; the dates are approximately the same for the other northern states and Canada. This first honey flow is usually referred to as the clover flow as plants in this family

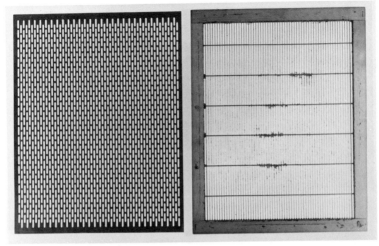

8.17. Two types of queen excluders. On the left is a single sheet of perforated zinc; on the right, a welded-wire, wood-bound excluder.

provide the greatest quantity of nectar during this time. In those areas where beekeepers experience a good clover flow, they usually put queen excluders on their colonies, forcing the queens down into a single super about the first of July (see figure 8.17). At this time also, beekeepers who are making new combs, that is, having new foundation drawn out, put these frames on the hives. The best combs are made during an active honey flow.

In late July or early August, the beekeeper prepares to remove the early crop of honey. He first checks each colony for disease and the same time checks the brood pattern of the queen, marking those colonies which have poor queens so that they may be requeened.

There is no perfect way to remove honey from a colony. Different methods are used in various parts of the country. In order to harvest the crop the bees must be separated or removed from the combs full of honey, and to be anthropomorphic, bees leave their stored hoard reluctantly. In the early days of commercial beekeep-

8.18. Two helpers remove the top three supers full of honey while the beekeeper places an inner cover, with a bee escape in the center hole, just above the brood nest. The bees will vacate the honey supers, through the one-way bee escape, in 24 to 48 hours. The supers of honey may then be removed and extracted.

ing individual combs of honey were removed from the supers, one at a time, and the bees brushed from them. Brushing breaks some of the cells' cappings though little honey is usually lost in this manner; more important, brushed bees become angry and the bee-keeper receives many stings. Still, brushing is a practical method for the beekeeper with only a few hives of bees, or when other methods fail. Bee escapes, devices which allow bees to pass in one direction only, and usually one at a time only, were invented in the late 1800's (see figure 8.18). The chief problem with using bee escapes is that there is a delay of one to three days between the time they are put into place (below the stored honey and above the supers containing brood) and the time when the supers are cleared of bees. This delay means the beekeeper must take two trips to the apiary; if it is some distance from his home, this is a nuisance. Still, I prefer the use of bee escapes to other methods of removing honey. In the 1930's beekeepers learned they could drive bees off combs of honey with repellents; two, which are now popular but not perfect, are benzaldehyde (artificial oil of almonds) and propionic anhydride. The repellents are placed on a cloth which is held with a wooden frame 2 to 5 centimeters (1 to 2 inches) above the combs from which the bees are to be driven; most of the bees will leave in a matter of ten minutes when the temperature is between 70 to 80° F. In the 1960's beekeepers began to experiment with bee blowers, machines which could be used to blow bees off combs of honey. Interestingly, blown bees do not become angry as do brushed bees. The method is popular with many beekeepers; if shallow supers are used, it is usually not necessary to remove the individual combs from the supers but only to put the super on end and to blow the bees out.

During August and September, bees make honey from alfalfa in some parts of the North and goldenrod and aster in other parts; in some areas, colonies may gather nectar from all three of these major plants. Alfalfa is a high-quality, table-grade honey whereas goldenrod and aster honey is usually sold to the baking trade. Honey from these crops is usually removed from the colonies in late September with the beekeeper again making an inspection for disease, checking brood patterns, and combining weak colonies. Sixty to eighty pounds of honey are left in the colonies for winter food.

In October and November, many beekeepers wrap their colonies with black tar paper, a process which is called "packing," [3] and thereby protect them against the elements for the winter. Wrapping colonies in paper serves several purposes. The black paper

3. For details on preparing bees for winter in the northern United States see a bulletin by Dyce and Morse entitled *Wintering Honey Bees in New York State;* the methods described are applicable throughout the northern states and Canada.

helps to warm the colonies on sunny days in the winter, especially during January and February, when they might not otherwise be able to fly. Bees do not normally void their feces in the hive, and it is important that they be able to take an occasional flight to do so. Many bees are lost during winter flights; they become chilled and die in the snow or on the cold ground. However, insofar as the welfare of the colony is concerned, it is better that bees carrying a large quantity of fecal matter fly from the hive and die, rather than remain in the hive for too long a period of time and void their feces in the hive.

Black wrapping paper also helps to melt the snow and ice around colonies on warm winter days, thus freeing colony entrances for flight. Wrapping colonies protects equipment and thereby adds to its life. Many beekeepers do not pack their colonies for winter and find that they can winter bees successfully without any special preparation, but, for the reasons given, I believe it is a worthwhile practice.

In the northern states the beekeeper is active with colony management from mid-April to late October or early November. Most beekeepers visit their apiaries a few times during the winter, checking only for vandalism or wind or animal damage to the paper in which the colonies are wrapped.

It is not unusual for 10 to 20 per cent of honey bee colonies to die every year in the northern states. Probably no other agricultural industry has so high an annual loss of animals. Those beekeepers who have winter losses of less than 10 per cent practice intensive management schemes which usually involve a detailed examination of each colony late in the fall and weighing colonies to make certain they have sufficient food. Supplemental fall feeding is sometimes necessary.

The reason for the high winter loss of colonies is that, in most of the northern states, one cannot effectively determine a colony's condition for about six months, that is, from October through March. Men working with cows, chickens, horses, and other animals have an opportunity to examine them daily throughout the winter months and are thus alerted to the presence of diseases, food shortages, and other situations that require attention. The abnormally high winter losses that beekeepers suffer, as well as the long period of inactivity in the North, have led many of them to migrate with their bees to the southern states where they may remain from October through April or May.

Beekeeping in other parts of the world

For the same reasons that beekeeping is a popular avocation and vocation in the United States, it is popular elsewhere as well. In fact, for the world traveler, one of the fascinations is to observe how the industry is conducted in other countries. As has been indicated earlier, our honey bee is European or Near Eastern in origin and in addition to being present in Europe and Africa has been taken successfully to North and South America, Australia, and New Zealand. While slightly different races of bees are used in different parts of the world, the principles of management remain the same. Thus, there is a similarity in beekeeping equipment and in management techniques around the world.

Not only are there county, state, and countrywide beekeepers' organizations, but there are also two international beekeepers' groups. One, the Bee Research Association, has headquarters in England and has as its primary concern the dissemination of information on research. The Bee Research Association maintains a large library, abstracts current literature, makes translations, arranges international conferences, and publishes three journals: *Bee World, Apicultural Abstracts,* and *Journal of Apicultural Research.*

Apimondia, a second international beekeepers' organization, sponsors an international congress, usually every second year. Congresses have been held in the United States, Canada, Australia, Russia, and in several other European countries. Apimondia now has headquarters in Bucharest, Romania, and Rome, Italy. It publishes an international journal in several languages, *Apiacta.*

As beekeepers travel, they often attend bee meetings in various parts of the world. Meeting notices are posted in local, national, and international journals.

The major honey producing countries

In very general terms, the annual world honey crop may be said to approximate one billion pounds. It is thought that about one-quarter of this is produced in the United States and another one-quarter in Russia.[4] Certain countries are major exporters of honey and others are major importers, and the quantity of honey exchanged between them determines the world price. The major honey exporting countries are Canada, Mexico, Argentina, New Zealand, and Australia; the major importers are Germany, Japan, and England. The crops of each of the five major honey exporting countries range from approximately 30,000,000 to 75,000,000 pounds annually. Fortunately, the crops from these countries come on the market at different times of the year.

Europe

Beekeeping is a popular avocation in Europe, and although Europe (excluding Russia) is densely populated, it has more colonies per unit area than does the United States. At the same time, and more important, the European countries do not have the vast acreages of abandoned and unused land that we have in the United States to provide bees with forage. It is evident to one who travels about the United States that over half of our honey is produced from weed plants, or cultivated plants that have escaped an agricultural system.

While the precise quantities of honey consumed in various parts of the world are not known, it does appear that people in the northern countries consume more honey than do those in the southern countries. Honey production is limited in Europe, but Greece, Italy, France, and Spain contain very small areas that have a long history of being major honey producers. In each of these countries, the quantity of honey produced is small, and under most circumstances few plant species are involved.

4. This figure does not agree with estimates published by the Russians.

Russia

Despite the fact that Russia is one of the major honey-producing countries in the world, we know little about honey production and beekeeping techniques there. It is understood that there are collective farms devoted exclusively to beekeeping, and it is said that certain of these have 25,000 or more colonies under their direction. Since Russia neither imports nor exports honey, little is known about the quality and types of honey produced there. Visitors to Russia say that honey is not a common commodity on store shelves.

Under the Russian political system, the government issues formal statements about the number of bee colonies that one individual should manage on a collective farm. The number is approximately one-fifth (or less than one-fifth) of the number that one commercial beekeeper might operate in the United States. However, I have found, in searching through Russian journals and books, and after attending meetings with persons in Iron Curtain countries, that there is less standardization of equipment and techniques than there is in the United States; while this lack of standardization in itself is not a full explanation of the lower production per individual, it is a contributing factor.

The Russians were hosts to an international beekeeping congress in 1971, and several hundred people from out-of-country attended the meetings and were given further information about beekeeping in Russia. In figures posted at the congress, it was stated that there were 4.5 million colonies of bees on state farms in Russia and 5 million colonies in private hands. Honey production was said to be about one billion pounds per year, a figure much higher than had been published previously. If the number of colonies given is correct, then there are about twice as many colonies in Russia as in the United States, and production per colony is twice that in this country.[5]

5. The discrepancy may also have to do with an accounting system. I have been told that in Russia they count the nucleus colonies and the small queen mating nuclei; we record only the producing colonies of bees. Also, in considering production, the Russians may include the honey that the bees use as winter food in the total production; if this were done in the United States, our production figures would be more than doubled.

Africa

East Africa has been a major source of beeswax for export since the turn of the century. At least as much beeswax is exported from this area as is produced in the United States. The wax is of high quality and commands a good price on the world market. Interestingly, however, honey from that part of the world is unknown on the world market. Most of the honey produced in East Africa is said to be used for the production of honey beer or some other alcoholic drink.

In African countries bordering the Mediterranean, there is some trade with Europe; the bees there resemble those in Europe, and beekeeping techniques are closely aligned with European methods. However, this area is separated from central and southern Africa by the Sahara and other deserts. Not only are beekeeping techniques in central and southern Africa different from those used elsewhere in the world, but there are two races of bees that are quite different from the bees found in Europe even though they are of the same species. African races below the Sahara are said to be good honey gatherers but are thought to be slightly more prone to swarming and to attacking and stinging than are their northern neighbors.[6]

6. African bees have been much in the news since their accidental release in Brazil in 1957. In Africa there are at least five distinct races of honey bees; all are husbanded, some in primitive, some in modern hives. African bees have been extensively studied and written about, and their aggressiveness and ability to defend their nests are well known. Physically they look much like other honey bees; they are slightly smaller, but one cannot positively identify African bees by size alone.

Brazilian authorities, aware of the African's aggressiveness and also of their reputation as honey producers, brought the African bees to Brazil, to cross them with the European races that had been taken to South America earlier and from these crosses to obtain bees that would do well in Brazil. Their plans included breeding out of the crosses the aggressive traits. Unfortunately, a meddler allowed the bees to escape before the experiments were complete. The Africanized bees now in Brazil have retained both their ability to gather nectar and their aggressiveness. I visited Brazil in 1972 and talked with commercial beekeepers who keep and prefer the Africanized bees. The colonies they showed me were more aggressive, on the average than our own (although I have seen a few equally aggressive colonies in the United States). I asked the beekeepers why they did not requeen with

There has been some effort to develop a beekeeping industry in Rhodesia and South Africa, and these ventures appear to be quite successful. Producers in this part of the world benefit from a cheap labor market. The real potential for honey production in Africa, and how increased production there might affect the world market, are unknown.

Asia: its potential for beekeeping

As is discussed in Chapter 1, there are three species of honey bees that are found only in Asia. From the point of view of practical agriculture, these species (especially *Apis florea*) produce too little honey to be desirable, though one of them, *Apis indica,* is husbanded and used in much the same way that *Apis mellifera* is used in this country. *Apis indica* is a small honey bee, and production from a colony is limited to ten or twenty pounds of honey annually. Honey is harvested from the other species, especially *Apis dorsata,* and this honey reaches local markets where it commands a good price.

---

gentler bees, and they replied that the Africanized bees produced more honey and that the beekeepers just put on an extra pair of pants and shirt to avoid excessive stinging. Brazil is now producing more honey than ever before and in areas, especially in the tropics, where bees have never been kept. Many hobby beekeepers have given up their avocation because they do not care to work with agressive bees. I also saw, in Brazil, beekeepers who had requeened their colonies with less agressive races and were successfully keeping colonies of these bees not too far from colonies of Africanized bees. These beekeepers, of course, must watch their colonies closely and requeen again if the old queen is lost. Clearly, the newspapers often blame Africanized bees for the attacks on people that have in fact been made by wasps, bumble bees, and solitary bees.

There is little justification for the concern that the Africanized bees will spread northward and into the United States. Starting in the late 1800's queens from all African races have been shipped to Europe and North America many times (Morse et al, 1973). In fact, some aggressive traits occasionally exhibited by our own bees may be traceable to these introductions. However, work by Woyke (1973) showed that the Africanized bees could not survive in Poland where he took and studied them for many years in the late 1960's. Both African and Africanized bees are tropical races. They will unquestionably continue to prosper in the tropics where European races do not, and in my opinion they pose no threat in the temperate areas of the world.

European and North American bee journals have published many articles on improving beekeeping techniques in Asia and especially in those countries to which we have sent missionaries over the years. The Peace Corps has taken up the same cry, and often articles in newspapers and journals explain how some well-meaning individual has taken bees from the United States or Europe into a part of Asia. Except in China and Japan, these projects have been short lived, for diseases of the Asian bees, especially in the tropical areas, soon bring about the demise of the European bee. Additionally, and most unfortunately, European bees have introduced both American foulbrood and *Acarapis woodi,* the acarine mite, into India. This is an excellent example of why plant and animal introductions into foreign areas should be left in the hands of experts.

Beekeeping in Asia with the European bee, has been unsuccessful largely because of the existence of two mites, *Tropilaelops clareae* and *Varroa jacobsoni.* The biologies of these mites have not been researched; they apparently attack the honey bees in the larval stage, and death occurs in the pupal stage. The Asian mites are discussed further in Chapter 12.

There is unquestionably a great potential for honey and beeswax production in Asia. I observed an industry develop in the Philippines; it was successful until the colonies were weakened beyond recovery by mites; a similar sequence of events also took place in Thailand. If one reviews the success of the beekeeping industry in other tropical areas of the world, the Central Americas and Africa, it is apparent that a thriving industry could be built in parts of Asia. Good honey plants are present throughout Asia, and it is only a question of working out appropriate management techniques for the areas and controlling the mites and perhaps other special diseases that exist there.

9

Package Bees and Queens

The business of packaging bees and producing queens for sale is a fascinating, specialized aspect of the commercial beekeeping industry.[1] Buying a package of bees and a queen is one of the simplest ways to start in beekeeping, although it is neither the cheapest nor the best (see Chapter 13).

Bees are sold in packages of from one to five pounds; a one-pound package contains nearly 4,000 bees. The bees usually come from the same colony, and a small cage containing a newly mated queen, often from a different colony, is added to the larger cage prior to shipment. By the time the bees have been in transit for several days, they accept the new queen as their own.

The first packages of bees were made in the South around 1890 for shipment to the North. The business did not become firmly established, however, until about 1920. Until the 1930's it was usual to include a comb of brood with each package, but it is now illegal to ship packages with combs to some states (including Michigan, Alabama, Hawaii, Louisiana, Nevada, and Connecticut) and to Canada, and most people feel it is either ill advised, because of the danger of transmitting disease, or unnecessary. In the North, after a package has been installed, 21 or 22 days are required before adults emerge from the first eggs laid by the queen

1. For details on installing package bees, see the bulletin by Combs and Morse entitled *Package Bees: Their Installation and Immediate Care;* the methods described are applicable throughout the United States.

and the package population is reinforced by young bees. During these three weeks, the older bees from the package colony die, and the population of a three-pound package, which initially may have been 11,000 to 12,000 bees, may fall to 7,000 to 8,000 bees. One reason the frame of brood was formerly included in packages was to quickly replenish the depleted population. The beekeeper in the northern states can make up for this loss by giving the package a frame of capped brood from one of his own colonies. The chief disadvantage in doing so is that this is one way of spreading disease, but the cautious beekeeper should have little difficulty in this regard.

Practical queen rearing is based on methods designed by Henry Alley and G. M. Doolittle just before the turn of the century. These men were the first to develop techniques and equipment for forcing worker bees to enlarge the cells and lavishly feed certain selected worker larvae which would then grow into queens. In nature, queens are produced under one of three circumstances: swarming, supersedure, or queenlessness. Commercial queen rearers simulate queenless conditions, and by feeding their colonies, are able to stimulate them to produce large numbers of queens.

Where and how package bees are produced

The package bee industry in this country is limited to Georgia, the Gulf States, and California. In general, package bees move in a more or less northerly direction from the state of origin (though there is some east-west movement) and large numbers cross the Canadian border for use in honey production there.

Most shipments of package bees are made by commercial trucks and trains. Air shipments have not proved very successful, but to northern Canada or even the northern United States they would be of great value if one could guarantee that there would be no delays in arrival. Package bees usually arrive in good condition, being handled by postmen with more respect than are many packages. Usually 100 to 1,000 bees die in transit, and the receiver should not be unduly concerned to find this many dead bees in the package. If the number of dead is greater, the bees have been too long in transit or have been mistreated.

Queenless packages are rarely used. At one time they were popular for reinforcing populations in old colonies, but now beekeepers feel that package bees shipped without queens are unsatisfactory, since there may be ovary development in the workers in the package (see Chapter 7). The queen shipped with the package is almost always caged separately so that the beekeeper can easily determine whether she is alive upon arrival.

Southern producers as a rule use one of three techniques to collect the bees to place in the package. (1) They find the queen in the colony and shake the remaining bees, or most of the remaining bees, from the hive into the package. (2) They take only those bees that are above a queen excluder to make up a package; so doing requires using colonies that have larger populations of worker bees than are necessary with the first technique. (3) They drum the bees through an excluder, leaving the queen with the brood below. Drumming is an old technique for removing bees from a hive, dating back to the 1400's or earlier. If one beats on a hive rhythmically with his hands or a rubber mallet, the bees will move in an upward direction, and most of them will abandon their brood and the nest, clustering at the highest point in the hive. Drumming is discussed further in Chapter 13.

In several southern states, colonies of bees are used almost exclusively for package bee production. Under some circumstances, for example, when there is a long pollen and nectar flow, a single-story colony may produce enough bees during the season for two or three packages. The package bee season usually lasts from the first of April to late June.

A package in which bees are shipped usually has a hole in the top board, three to four inches in diameter, which will hold a funnel used in shaking the bees into the package. Frames covered with bees are removed, one at a time, and given a hard shake into the funnel, or bees are drummed into empty shallow supers, and then the entire mass of bees is shaken into the funnel.

Most package bee producers add slightly more than the required weight of bees. After every package has been filled with bees, the funnel is replaced with a feeder pail which holds approximately a quart of sugar syrup so that the bees will have sufficient food while in transit. (The pail has small holes in the bottom.) The queen is added, and the package is sent on its way as rapidly as possible.

Growing queens

Of the various specializations in beekeeping it is hard to say whether raising queens or producing comb honey is the more difficult. Certainly both specialties require attention to detail, and only persons well versed in bee behavior are successful in either venture. Comb honey production is much less popular than it was years ago largely because liquid honey is easier to produce, and the public does not care to pay the price which a section of comb honey should command. Queen rearing, on the other hand, continues to be popular, especially in the southern states. Unquestionably, it could be undertaken more extensively in the northern states, on either a large or a small scale.[2]

Most queen breeders use beeswax cell cups made by dipping rounded wooden pegs into molten wax, but in recent years plastic queen cups have become popular. The process of placing one-day-old worker larvae into the wax or plastic cups is called "grafting." The queen cups are usually fitted into wooden cell bases, and the finished queen cells are grasped by these wooden bases to prevent the cells themselves from being damaged.

Queen rearing methods vary, but usually the newly grafted cells are placed in queenless swarm boxes. A swarm box usually has a screen bottom but no entrance. It is filled with bees of all ages,

2. At least three good books on queen rearing have been published in the United States, two of which are out of print and available only through libraries or second-hand book dealers. It is suggested, however, that anyone who cares to pursue the art of queen rearing read these books carefully. The out-of-print books are *Queen Rearing Simplified* by Jay Smith and *How to Grow Queens* by Walter T. Kelley. *Queen Rearing* by Harry H. Laidlaw, Jr., and J. E. Eckert, which is still available, was first published in 1950 and revised in 1962.

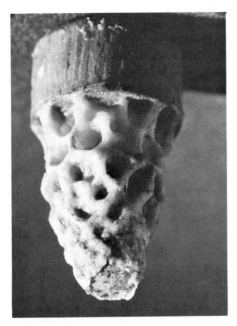

9.1. A queen cell. The queen in this cell is about to emerge; the bees have removed the wax from the tip of the cell, exposing the cocoon and thus facilitating her release from within. In the hive, the queen cell hangs in the position shown. (Photo by New York State College of Agriculture and Life Sciences, Cornell University.)

especially young bees that have been feeding larvae. The new queen cups, which are rapidly being built into queen cells (see figure 9.1), are left in the swarm box for only 24 hours, and during this time the bees feed the young larvae lavishly. The cells are then moved to cell-building colonies, which may be either queenless or queenright. In queenright cell-building colonies, a queen excluder is used, the queen is kept in the hive body below, and the cells in the hive body above. Cell-building colonies should be well populated, and it is often necessary to add frames of emerging brood to them. In addition, frames containing young larvae should be placed on either side of the frames containing the queen cells so as to attract nurse bees to the area which are producing royal jelly in large quantity.

Almost immediately upon emergence, virgin queens will fight each other, and they will also destroy other queen cells. Therefore,

9.2. A queen breeder examining a mating nucleus in a Florida apiary. Queen cells are placed in nucleus colonies a day or two before the queens emerge. After they mate the queens are transferred to larger colonies.

about one day before the young queens are to emerge, the ripe queen cells are taken from the cell-building colony and placed individually in queen-mating nuclei (see figure 9.2). These are small colonies usually containing 500 to 1,000 worker bees and a small quantity of food. The queens emerge in these colonies and fly from them to mate when they are of proper age. About two days after mating, the queens will begin to lay eggs, and it is usually one to two days after this that the young mated queens are removed, placed in special queen cages, and sold. Five or six worker bees are added to the queen cage to care for the young queen while she is being shipped. If there is no immediate need for the queens, they may be left in the queen mating nuclei for longer periods of time.

Installing packages

A package of bees is usually enroute for two to four days and during this time may exhaust its food supply. It is best to place package bees in hives soon after they arrive, but installation may be delayed for a day or two if necessary. When there is a delay, the bees should be stored in a cool, dry, dark place and fed generously with sugar syrup. A three-pound package of bees will often consume a pint or more of sugar syrup within the first five or six hours after arrival.

A package should be installed in a single ten-frame standard Langstroth hive body. Most packages will need no more room than this for the first six to eight weeks, unless they are given additional brood to strengthen them. The colony entrance should be reduced and should be kept reduced for five or six weeks after installation, depending upon temperature. It is easiest to feed the newly installed bees by giving three or four full frames of honey, but the beekeeper who has no honey on hand must feed the bees sugar syrup. This is usually done using a five- or ten-pound pail or a gallon-sized glass jug which is filled and inverted on top of the frames, or by using a division board feeder. A new package of bees will consume 25 or 30 pounds of sugar (as a syrup) within the first month.

Before the package is actually installed, one should make sure that the bees are well fed, taking several hours to allow the bees to consume up to about a pint of sugar syrup. The best way to feed the bees in the package is to paint the sugar syrup onto the wire screen of the cage with a small paint brush.

Package bees should be installed in the evening when the bees are not likely to fly. Package bees do not accept the package itself as a hive, and when given an opportunity for flight, they behave like lost bees, drifting into any nearby colony. Drifting can be a serious problem when two or more packages are installed in the same apiary as bees in one package may attract bees from another package. Packages may be installed during cool weather or a light rain; placing the bees in a hive at this time may diminish the drifting problem.

The little cage within a package, which holds the queen, usually contains a small quantity of soft sugar candy that blocks the exit and serves as food for the queen and her attendants in transit.

Releasing the queen immediately upon installing the package is a bad practice; in the first few hours after installation the bees may still not recognize her as their own and may kill her. The beekeeper should remove a sufficient amount of the soft candy plugging the exit hole in the queen cage so that bees may consume the rest within 12 to 18 hours, thus freeing the queen and allowing her to begin egg laying. Any delay longer than this is not necessary.

Two or three days after the package of bees is installed in its hive, the new colony should be inspected to make sure that the queen has been released and is laying eggs. It is necessary, usually, to check only a single frame in a hive, the one where there appears to be the most activity. So long as cells contain single eggs, deposited more or less in the bottom center of the cell, one knows that the queen is free and laying, and no further manipulations are needed for the next two or three weeks, except to make certain that the colony has ample food.

In most northern states the best time to install a package of bees is mid-April. If the package is given no additional help, that is to say, additional bees or brood, it will probably grow so that by fall it occupies two Langstroth hive bodies. By this time it should have stored 60 to 80 pounds of honey, which is enough for winter. In very few areas in the northern states are there sufficiently good honey flows so that a colony started from package bees can produce a surplus the first year. In certain parts of Canada, and to a lesser extent in some northern states where there are unusually good nectar flows during the year, package bees are used for honey production, being killed in the fall by the beekeeper, who harvests 100 or more pounds of honey per hive. It should be emphasized, however, that this is only possible in limited areas. For most beekeepers, it is not until the second year that a package of bees produces a surplus of honey which may be harvested.

Requeening and making new colonies

Bees in a colony recognize their own queen and are prone to attack and sometimes kill a foreign queen. Thus, requeening a colony, especially a large one, is difficult and sometimes seemingly impossible. From time to time new techniques for introducing queens are described in the bee journals; most of these are based on somehow disrupting normal colony order so that the bees remain confused for some time, and after a state of confusion may accept a new queen. One method even suggests that most of the bees in the colony be driven out of the colony with a bee repellent such as benzaldehyde or carbolic acid. The queen is then released in the mass of confused bees, the old queen having first been found and killed, with the hope that the new queen will be accepted. Other people have suggested heavy smoking of a colony about to be requeened; still another technique is to dip the queen in honey so that it takes some time for the bees to clean her. None of these methods is perfect and none is especially recommended.

Small colonies, that is, colonies containing only two, three, or four pounds of bees, are relatively easy to requeen. It is only necessary to find the old queen and remove her, and to place the new queen, still in her cage, in the colony, giving the bees in the colony the opportunity of eating away the soft sugar candy in the queen cage and releasing the queen in a day or two. After a period of 24 to 48 hours the foreignness of a new queen will have been dissipated, and she can be safely introduced into a small colony of bees.

Probably the best way to requeen a large colony is to unite it with a small nucleus colony. Commercial beekeepers have observed that during the course of the year they find it necessary to requeen 10 to 20 per cent of their colonies because of old, failing queens. To do so, many beekeepers keep several small nucleus colonies in the apiary, usually amounting to about 10 per cent of the total number of colonies in the apiary. When a queen is obviously failing, she may be killed and the nucleus colony positioned on top of the colony, placing a single sheet of newspaper between the two. This method of requeening almost never fails and there is little fighting of the bees between the two units. By the time the newspaper has been chewed away and removed there has been a considerable mixing and mingling of bees, and we presume, of colony odor.

The chief disadvantage of requeening in this manner is that the queen is usually in the third or fourth super after such a combination. The requeening effort is more likely to be successful if the new queen is placed above rather than below the old unit. Several days after the new queen is accepted it is possible to place her in the bottom hive body or to drive her and the other bees down into the lower super with a bee repellent and then to keep her in that position using a queen excluder.

In addition to nucleus colonies which may be used to requeen producing colonies headed by old and failing queens, a small number of colonies are customarily started to replace those lost during winter, or for other reasons. The easiest way to build new colonies is to start in May or June with small nucleus colonies which are treated much in the same way as are colonies of bees started with packages. Usually, with a little care and attention, such colonies will build to a sufficient population by August to gather the 60 to 80 pounds of honey needed to overwinter. The following year they are productive colonies.

To make replacement colonies, many beekeepers select those colonies that show signs of swarming early in the season. Such colonies usually have old or failing queens but are sufficiently strong to be split into four, five, or six units. Some beekeepers allow these small colonies to rear their own queens, but it is far more efficient to give the colonies new, young queens, purchased from one of the southern states. If populous colonies of bees show signs of swarming in the early spring, they probably contain old queens that will soon need replacement anyway. Unless such colonies receive intense management, they are prone to swarm, an event which would be unprofitable for the beekeeper.

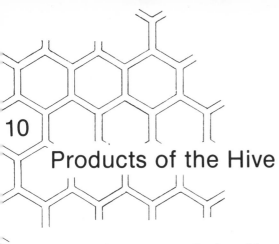

10

Products of the Hive

A bee hive is a box or a collection of boxes in which bees live, store food, and rear their brood. While the chief product of the hive is honey, inventive men have found other ways to exploit the bee hive. Very few people eat the bees themselves, and those who do usually consume only the larvae.

What is honey?

How honey is defined depends upon who defines it. Most people think of honey as simply an excellent food, but some consider it an elixer, others a medicine. Its long and successful use as an ingredient in certain cough medicines testifies to its effectiveness in relieving minor irritations of the throat, especially when mixed with lemon juice or some other fruit juice. True, it is less effective than many of the modern drugs on the market, but in the case of certain minor ailments it is a simple home remedy on which one may depend. Because of its ability to cover up the objectionable taste of certain drugs, honey has been an important ingredient in many medicines, and will undoubtedly continue to function in this role for some years.

Of special interest is the use of honey by overweight people. The average American, who consumes over 100 pounds of sugar per year, cannot easily satisfy his sweet tooth. Honey contains dextrose and levulose, an especially sweet sugar, and has a low pH. A synergism occurs between the high acidity and the intense sweetness of the honey; thus one may eat a small quantity and obtain as much satisfaction as though much more common sugar or candy were eaten. For the person who cannot resist sweets, honey can provide some minor relief.

And so, what is honey? It is a supersaturated sugar solution containing a small quantity of vitamins, minerals, and nutrients. The quantity of the minor constituents varies from one honey to another, and no two are the same. Honey is formed from nectar, a natural secretion of the nectary glands of flowers, whose function is to attract pollinators. Because honey is the chief food of adult bees, they hoard it. Men keep bees for the express purpose of taking honey from them, and whether honey is really an elixer, a medicine, just a good food, or all three, is a question of personal philosophy.

Honey in ancient times

Reliefs in the Egyptian pyramids and tombs depict a few bee-keeping scenes, and from these we have learned that the Egyptians kept bees and moved them up and down the Nile River between 2000 and 5000 years ago. Aristotle (384-322 B.C.), the Greek philosopher and naturalist, wrote on a great variety of animals, including the honey bee. We know from his writings and those of other Greeks that they too kept bees. Little was known about biology in those days, and although parts of Aristotle's writings on biology are accurate, he made an error in thinking that the queen was a male; Aristotle probably could not think in terms of a female occupying an important position in the community.

There are also many references in the Bible to honey and its role in daily life. The Romans had little interest in medicine, biology, or agriculture, and these studies were given over to the poets, who wrote more from imagination than from first-hand knowledge. Still, we know that the Romans had extensive apiaries in Spain and that parts of Italy produced some surplus honey. Even today the environs of the city of Rome are a moderately good honey-producing area.

We may reasonably presume that the beekeeping techniques

popular in the dark ages had survived from earlier times, and there is no indication that the Romans and their predecessors, even at the height of their civilization, were any better than their successors at practical beekeeping. If this is true, we may reasonably presume that the amount of honey produced was very small and the number of people who enjoyed it were very few. Probably only the rulers had honey in any abundance, and whether they had as much as is available to individuals today is questionable. Still, even the common man probably had an opportunity to taste honey once or twice during his lifetime, and once he tasted it, he no doubt came to revere it, for his only other source of sweets might have been a few fruits. We know, too, that the ancients did not have the great variety of fruits which we enjoy today.

Throughout history, honey has been a highly prized agricultural product. Beekeepers have been held in high esteem, and an English king is known to have appointed one to his court. The appointment however, was no doubt for the purpose of securing honey to produce honey wine since people then not only had no sugar, they had few other ingredients for making wine, especially in the northern climates where sweet fruits were not plentiful.

Sugar in ancient times

Sugar cane was discovered in the South Pacific Islands and transported from there to China. It is recorded that the Chinese built the first sugar mill in about 200 B.C. At that time there was very little travel, and several hundred years elapsed before sugar cane was taken as far west as India.

During the Islamic invasion of the Mediterranean area, in the eighth century A.D., sugar cane was introduced to Egypt for the first time. It soon spread throughout the Mediterranean area, but because it is a tropical plant, it was never taken any farther north into Europe. Even after the introduction of sugar cane, honey remained a highly prized item because little was known about efficient methods of growing, harvesting, and extracting the sugar from the sweet cane.

Soon after the discovery of the Americas, a sugar cane industry developed on many of the islands in the Caribbean. It was not until about 1800 that sugar cane was first grown in Louisiana. Even with modern technology and new strains of cane, sugar production from cane is still limited (in this country) to the Gulf states.

The fact that sugar could be recovered from beets was not discovered until the late 1700's, and the first sugar beet mill was built in Silesia in 1801. Compared with sugar cane and honey, sugar beets are a recent source of sweetener.

Modern honey and sugar consumption

The average American or European consumes approximately 135 pounds of sugar a year. In the United States, only about one-third of this is purchased directly as sugar, and the other two-thirds in the form of soft drinks, cakes, candies and other commercially prepared items. Our annual per capita consumption of honey is slightly over one pound per person. There is clearly much room for the expansion of honey consumption.

With the exception of Asia, few honey-producing areas in the world remain to be exploited. It is true that we might be able to harvest slightly more honey from some of our better producing areas, but there appear to be limits. Increasing the acreage of nectar-producing plants cannot be done economically.

Only since 1900 has our per capita consumption of sugar been high. In 1700, the annual consumption was about four pounds per person, and this was much greater than it had been previously. In terms of cash or barter, honey commanded a very high price. By the time of the Revolutionary War, the per capita consumption of sugar had risen to about 12 to 15 pounds, and by the time of the Civil War it was approximately 50 pounds.

Organic honey

For many years certain beekeepers and honey packers have sold what they call "organic honey," a label that is often misleading, depending upon one's definition of the word *organic*. Most dictionaries state that the term, when used to define or describe a food product, refers to something of plant or animal origin. Thus, in a strict sense, all foods are organic.

Some people, however, define organic honey as honey harvested from flowers that have not been sprayed with toxic compounds or pesticides, or from plants that have not been treated with chemical fertilizer. When a toxic pesticide is used, foraging bees are usually killed, and for this reason the governmental agencies that inspect foods for pesticide residues are little concerned about the contamination of honey and honey products by insecticide chemicals. About half the honey produced in this country and in most of the world comes from nonagricultural crops that have never been treated with chemicals, and no major differences except in flavor can be detected in honeys from different sources. But the idea of natural food and the concept of "back to nature" have great appeal to many people today whose families for several generations now have been removed from the land and who have no first-hand knowledge of farming. They are attracted by a romantic vision of living off the land but have no conception of the hard work, material sacrifice, and small rewards farming involves. One can only point to the fact that many people take up beekeeping to derive pleasure from keeping bees and producing a natural food. The very fact that some honey is labeled and sold as organic is further testimony to the role this romantic sentiment plays in our existence.

Liquid honey

Liquid honey, as its name indicates, is honey that has been separated from the wax comb in which it was placed by worker honey bees and put into a jar or can by man. Bees store honey in both worker and drone cells, which are one-fifth and one-quarter of an inch in diameter respectively, but never in queen cells, which are used exclusively for queen rearing.

In the 1860's it was discovered that honey could be recovered from a comb with an extractor or centrifuge. To remove the honey from the cells of the comb, the wax cappings are cut off with a hot knife and the combs are placed in the centrifuge, which throws the honey from the cells when it revolves.

On the American market most honey is sold as a liquid, not in the comb, for the simple reason that many pounds of honey are required to produce the wax, and the bees can be saved much effort if the wax cells are salvaged and used over and over again.

The major problem with liquid honey is that, being a super-saturated sugar solution, it may crystallize; the time required for crystallization to take place varies depending upon the dextrose-levulose ratio in the honey. Unheated honey usually crystallizes rapidly, normally forming large crystals which most people find less palatable than fine crystals or liquid honey. Because heating melts the crystal nuclei on which crystals might grow, most honey that is to be marketed as a liquid is heated to a temperature of 60°C (140°F) for thirty minutes or 71°C (160°F) for one minute, or some combination in between, which will give the honey a shelf life of approximately three or four months. Heating does destroy the enzymes in honey, and may have an adverse effect on its flavor, especially with the darker honeys; for this reason some beekeepers disapprove of it. However, beekeepers and honey packers also heat honey to kill the yeasts which it contains, and which may cause the honey to ferment and be destroyed (see Chapter 12).

About half of the honey produced in this country, and in most of the world, comes from nonagricultural crops. Among the important nectar-producing agricultural crops are citrus, alfalfa, cotton, soybeans, and some clovers. Important weed and woodland nectar-producing crops include basswood, tupelo, goldenrod, and aster.

Crystallized honey

Crystallized honey is basically of two types: one crystallizes naturally, and the other is forced to crystallize by a procedure known as the Dyce process. The naturally crystallized honeys usually have large crystals, but a few may form small, fine crystals, and these honeys, it has been observed, have an especially fine flavor.

Many honeys granulate slowly. As the crystals form, only a small portion of the water present in the honey becomes part of the crystal. Thus, the remaining liquid phase has a higher water content than it had previously. The higher the water content of the honey, the more it is subject to fermentation. The natural yeasts in honey, which cause fermentation when the moisture content is at the right level, produce alcohol and carbon dioxide as do the yeasts used in the alcoholic beverage industry. The result, however, is not a good alcoholic beverage, and for practical purposes the honey is ruined.

In the early 1930's, E. J. Dyce, working at Cornell University, found that honey crystallized most rapidly at 14°C (57°F), and he observed that it could be "seeded" and forced to crystallize in just a few days. Finely granulated honey was already known to have a finer flavor than that which is coarsely granulated. The Dyce patent combined pasteurization, temperature control, and the addition of crystal nuclei to produce the high quality product well known on the market today. Crystallized honey does not drip or run as does liquid honey and is therefore easier to use. For these reasons many people prefer crystallized honey.

Since Dyce was a Canadian citizen at the time, the patent that he obtained for his process was given to the Ontario government in Canada; however, in the United States the patent was donated to Cornell University. The royalties which accrued were used to build the Dyce Laboratory at Cornell and to endow further research on bees and honey.

Comb honey

Very little comb honey is available on the American market today. Not only is it less profitable to produce than liquid honey, but its production is much more complicated and requires a greater knowledge of beekeeping. It is not easy to force the bees to build a comb and store honey in such a small area as a comb honey section for the bees must work harder moving from section to section. The special furniture used in comb honey production occupies a great deal of space, making ventilation a problem. In addition, the whole hive space must be crowded, and under these conditions swarming is encouraged, causing colonies to lose a large portion of their field force. Since their population is reduced, they produce less honey.

Comb honey can be produced only when there is a good nectar flow so that the bees are not only stimulated to collect nectar, but also to produce beeswax. A section of comb honey usually contains honey from only one floral source. Thus, unlike most liquid honeys on the market, it is not blended. While comb honey will change character over a period of time, and the wax cappings on the cell are not impervious, the cappings do help to retain the delicate flavor of the honey. If comb honey is stored in a freezer it will retain its flavor and will not crystallize; however, the wax cells fracture easily when frozen and the combs must be handled with care.

A popular substitute for comb honey today is chunk honey (sometimes called cut comb honey). Chunk comb honey consists of pieces of honey in the comb, usually varying in weight from two ounces to a pound or more. Chunk honey is usually produced in a shallow frame, that is, a frame four or five inches deep; the large comb is cut into the desired sizes for sale. Chunk comb honey is easier to produce, yet has the flavor advantages of comb honey. It is more difficult to produce chunk comb honey than liquid honey for, as in the production of comb honey, the colony of bees must be crowded and forced to work in a smaller area. But bees are less crowded and there is better ventilation in a chunk honey super than in a comb honey super even though both may be approximately the same depth.

A popular variation in chunk honey, especially in the southern states, is made by placing chunks of comb honey in a jar and surrounding them with liquid honey. This combination of liquid and comb honey is a favorite with many purchasers. Chunk honey packs are little used in the North for, generally speaking, northern honeys tend to granulate too rapidly and it is not possible to liquify honey in the comb. Most of the honeys produced in the southern states do not granulate rapidly, but the beginner should check carefully with neighboring beekeepers about this matter. Even though southern honeys tend to granulate less rapidly, the liquid honey used in the chunk honey pack is usually heated prior to being placed in the jar to deter its granulation.

The history of comb honey

Before the discovery of bee space in 1851, honey was a scarce commodity. However, most persons knew that bees made honey comb and placed honey in it, and many were familiar with "virgin" honey, that is, honey in new, white comb. Only new, white wax can be eaten palatably with honey; old, dark or brown comb has a bitter taste imparted to it by pollen, propolis, and pupal cases. Thus, when beekeepers began to produce honey in quantity, they sought to duplicate the most popular form of honey, that is, the virgin honey in the comb. Comb honey has been known by that name, but it has also been called "section honey" and "card honey."

The history of the comb honey industry is outlined by Frank C. Pellett in his *History of American Beekeeping*. He gives credit to J. S. Harbison of California for originating, in 1857, the idea of forcing bees to build honey comb in a small box or section. Harbison was an early California beekeeper who was later to send carloads of honey from California to the eastern market. Sections of various sizes and depths were used by beekeepers soon thereafter. While beekeepers were familiar with the principle of bee space, most beekeeping equipment was homemade; perusal of the literature of the time shows that a great many sizes and shapes of hives were popular. Comb honey sections weighing approximately a pound were apparently most popular, but some contained less, and some had two pounds of honey per section.

Bee supply manufacturers soon learned to make one-piece comb honey sections, that is, pieces of thin basswood that could be folded into a square or rectangular shape. Today most beekeepers prefer a comb honey section that is $4\frac{1}{4}''$ x $4\frac{1}{4}''$, a square section. The author and certain other comb honey producers prefer a rectangular section, usually about 4″ x 5″, the sections being placed upright in the super on one of the shorter sides. The 4″ x 5″ comb honey sections are preferred because they can be better centered over the brood nest. In drawing new combs of foundation, either full frames or comb honey sections, the best comb is made immediately over the brood nest, and in the production of comb honey, a small change, such as using 4″ x 5″ sections instead of $4\frac{1}{4}''$ x $4\frac{1}{4}''$ sections, can make a profound difference, especially in years when the honey flow is not good.

In retrospect, it is perhaps important and fortunate that beekeepers first devoted their attention to the production of comb honey rather than liquid honey. One way to prevent swarming is to give the colony of bees a great deal of room, and this can be accomplished in liquid honey production merely by adding extra supers. In producing comb honey, the beekeeper must crowd the brood nest and the honey storage area, thus encouraging swarming. The early commercial beekeepers developed good management systems. The successful comb honey producer must have a good knowledge of bee behavior and understand how to implement swarm control measures. Thus, it was during the early comb honey era that the basic management techniques used by all beekeepers today were developed.

The future of comb honey

Many of the students in my elementary beekeeping course at Cornell taste comb honey for the first time in my class. While this may be a sad commentary on our way of life, it is a fact that many people today are not familiar with old fashion methods of preparing, packing, and preserving foods. Although most of our foods today are better packed and processed, taste better, have more food value and are safer from harmful microorganisms than they were some time ago, certain delightful products such as comb honey are no longer known or popular.

Today, for example, there is no commercial beekeeper who

makes a full-time living producing comb honey in New York State, or in fact who devotes even 10 per cent of his time to the production of comb honey. As late as 1950, there were three men in New York State who produced comb honey exclusively, and several decades earlier there were many more than this number.

Still, today there is a small demand for comb honey just as there is for maple syrup and a few other natural products that are preferred by some people. Some hobby beekeepers have learned that a few people will pay a good price for comb honey and that it is worth their effort to produce enough to supply the local demand. The introduction of the Cobana comb honey section in the 1950's, a round plastic section, has made inroads on the market for the standard square or rectangular wooden section. The production of Cobana comb honey sections requires less attention to detail. Although this section weighs less than the average comb honey section, it is more evenly filled and has a good eye appeal.

We can predict that the production of comb honey will continue to decline.

Management for comb honey production

There are three outstanding references on comb honey production, all of which are out of print. Some of these may be available from second-hand book dealers or a library and should be consulted by anyone who is seriously thinking of comb honey production. Most recent is a book by Karl E. Killion, entitled *Honey in the Comb,* published in 1951. Killion's methods are similar to those of C. C. Miller, mentioned below. The second reference is a U.S. Department of Agriculture bulletin, *Comb-Honey Production,* by George S. Demuth [1] published in 1919. The third reference is a book by C. C. Miller, entitled *Fifty Years Among the Bees,*

1. Demuth was a practical beekeeper brought into the U.S. Department of Agriculture by E. F. Phillips to assist him in his research; this was at the time when Phillips was head of the U.S. Department of Agriculture bee culture laboratory. Demuth served later (1920–1934) as editor of the trade journal, *Gleanings in Bee Culture.* His forte was the application of our knowledge of bee behavior. In 1921 Demuth wrote *Swarm Control,* a widely quoted bulletin which still has application today.

published in 1911. A 1920 edition of *Fifty Years Among the Bees,* contains tributes to Miller, by both E. R. Root and E. F. Phillips; it is known as the memorial edition, and the tributes make the book more interesting reading and more valuable to book collectors. C. C. Miller also wrote *Forty Years Among the Bees* and *A Year Among the Bees,* both of which contain much information concerning comb honey production, though neither is so complete as his last book.

It is possible to give only a brief summary of comb honey production techniques here. The management system is intense, and attention to detail is required.

To produce comb honey, the colonies of bees are wintered in the normal fashion. In the spring they are allowed to grow and may occupy three or perhaps four supers prior to the start of the first honey flow. It is difficult to produce comb honey in an area which does not have an intense honey flow. During the swarming season the supers may be reversed or other usual swarm control measures taken.

The first comb honey supers are usually not placed on the colony until the honey flow has been in progress for one or two days. At this time the queen is found, and the queen and the capped brood are placed in a single hive body, together with the remaining bees in the colony. The reason for placing capped brood in the colony is two-fold: first, the brood will add as many bees as possible to the colony population as rapidly as possible; and second, the hatching brood will provide more space for the queen to lay within a short period of time. Usually, two comb honey supers are added at this time and the third super is not added until one of the first two comb honey supers is almost filled. In comb honey production, beekeepers "bottom" super, that is to say, add new supers under already filled ones. In liquid honey production, most beekeepers "top" super, that is, they add supers on top of the already existing unit.

Crowding a colony in this manner encourages the production of queen cells, and swarming. Not all colonies will produce queen cells under these circumstances, but many will do so. Swarming must be prevented, and the only method of doing so is to remove the queen cells. Removing queen cells does not always prevent swarming but does slow it, and the hope is that by the fourth time the cells have been removed, the honey flow will have ended, or nearly so.

In areas where beekeepers experience only a single honey flow, it is necessary to use a given number of colonies to produce the honey that the comb-honey-producing colonies need for winter. Beekeepers in areas which have a good fall flow may depend upon this honey for winter stores.

If a colony swarms during the season of comb honey production, the supers must be removed and given to other colonies. As has been indicated elsewhere, the physical presence of a queen is necessary to stimulate honey production. If a colony swarms, leaving a virgin queen, it will be weak in bees and brood, and will not be stimulated to gather as much honey as will a colony with a laying queen. Furthermore, a virgin queen in the colony will not lay for several days, and bees will store collected honey in the brood nest, not in the comb honey sections where it should be stored. Since it is known that colonies with young queens are much less inclined to swarm than are colonies with old queens, comb honey producers are likely to requeen colonies annually.

In some beekeeping territories the honey flow may be so intense that a strong colony may fill one super of comb honey sections which is mixed in with regular extracting supers. The beekeeper who attempts to produce a few comb honey sections under these circumstances is taking some risk, as not all the sections may be properly filled. These, of course, can be retained for home use and the others sold or given to friends.

Another technique used by a few beekeepers to produce a limited number of comb honey sections is to build a special frame for a full-depth, ten-frame Langstroth super, which will hold eight comb honey sections. If such a frame is placed between two standard frames and immediately above the brood nest, in a good honey flow, the sections will usually be filled. Comb honey sections produced under these methods will usually be a little more travel stained from the adjacent frames than are comb honey sections in normal colonies.

As has been noted, bees are more likely to fill Cobana comb honey sections than they are standard wooden sections. At the same time, producing chunk comb honey, that is to say, using shallow frames with new sheets of thin foundation made for comb honey production, is also a method that works reasonably well and does not require such crowding of the colony. Those parts of the chunk comb which are not filled to the beekeeper's satisfaction may be crushed and the honey treated as liquid honey, or the comb may be retained for home use.

Comb honey storage

Wax moths will attack unprotected comb honey, laying their eggs on or near the comb surface. When the larvae hatch they will burrow through the cappings, usually just under the surface, eating mostly wax but probably a small amount of honey. The result is an unsightly product, and the honey is good only to feed back to the bees.

There are several good fumigants which will kill wax moths, but none of these is approved for use with combs containing honey by the government agencies which regulate the use of pesticides. Certain fumigants which we use to fumigate stored combs have an offensive odor. Thus, the beekeeper who produces a large quantity of comb honey is faced with a serious problem as to how to store it. Hobby beekeepers and beekeepers with only a small amount of comb honey find that it stores very well in a freezer.

Honey butter

Honey butter is a combination of finely granulated honey and pure creamery butter. The result is a spread of unusually fine quality and flavor, although it is of high caloric value.

The commercial process for making honey butter has remained

a secret since its discovery in the late 1930's. This does not, however, prevent one from making a mixture at home for one's own gastronomical pleasure. A fairly small proportion of butter (or heavy cream) may be used; people have had success using as little as 5 percent or as much as 25 per cent butter. Honey butter made by other than the secret process has a shelf life of only one or two weeks, but if refrigerated, it may be used over a period of two or three weeks before it will become rancid.

Several companies have attempted to imitate and market honey butter, and several laboratories have expended considerable effort in trying to find why the present process is so successful and others are not. The obvious success of the honey butter on the market, and the test marketing of those materials which have been tried, indicate that if the secret could be learned it would be a profitable discovery. The process for making honey butter was first discovered by a firm in the Province of Ontario, Canada. This company licensed a firm in New York State, which subsequently licensed another firm in California. The production by these independent companies is limited, and throughout the years they have insisted on making only a high quality product, paying close attention to the quality of both the honey and the butter which are used.

Honey wine

A fine quality wine, light or dark in color, depending upon the honey used, may be made from honey. Honey wine was man's first alcoholic beverage which he learned to make before wine was made from fruit juices. Its alcoholic content is usually 12 to 14 per cent. A sparkling honey wine has been placed on the market in some European countries from time to time, and one that resembles a high quality champagne can be made at home.

Recipes for making honey wine abound. They fall into roughly three categories: honey wine, spiced honey wine, and honey-fruit wine. Most of the European honey wines (meads) are made by first boiling a honey-water mixture for 30 to 60 minutes, meanwhile skimming the surface to remove material which rises to the top. The honey-water mixture is usually about 25 per cent sugar. For some of the European-type honey wines, spices such as cloves or nutmeg are added either before or, more often, after the boiling. The mixture to be fermented needs additional nutrients, which may be added in the form of fruit juice or sometimes just yeast food, especially ammonium phosphate. A high quality wine yeast is used for the fermentation. Aging for two or three years, as in the case with most wines, improves the product. In fact, honey wines aged for five or six years are usually superior to those aged for shorter periods.

Boiling the honey-water mixture is not really necessary though it may aid in the clarification and stability of the product. In North America, the honey is diluted with water to obtain a 25 per cent sugar solution. Ammonium phosphate, cream of tarter, urea, and citric acid, usually about 4 grams of each per gallon of honey-water mixture, are added to provide additional food for the yeasts. The fermentation is usually complete within three or four weeks, after which time the wine is allowed to clear and is bottled and aged in the normal way. Formulas which recommend the use of various fruit juices, including apple juice, cherry juice, or juice from wild fruits such as elderberries and wild grapes, are common. The fruit juice constitutes from 10 per cent to about 25 per cent of the total volume, depending upon its astringency; less juice is needed when elderberries or wild grapes are used than when apple juice is used. When apple juice is used, a small quantity of lemon juice is often added to the honey-water mixture. Depending upon the amount of sugar in the juice, the final sugar content of the material to be fermented is adjusted to about 20 to 24 per cent, and the fermentation is allowed to proceed.

A sparkling honey wine is more difficult to make. Two fermentations are required. The first is conducted in the normal manner but using less sugar to produce 10 or 11 per cent alcohol. Following this primary fermentation, more nutrients and yeast are added, and the new, low alcohol wine is placed in a special champagne-type bottle which will withstand the three to four atmospheres (45 to 60 lbs. pressure) that develop. The second fermentation which takes place in the bottle, results in the deposit of a certain quantity of dead yeast cells and the additional production of about 2 per cent alcohol and gaseous carbon dioxide. When commercial champagne-type beverages are made, before the wine is sold, the yeast cells are removed by a process called disgorging, but when honey wine is made at home, it is only necessary to allow these to settle to the bottom of the bottle where they will remain if the sparkling honey wine is poured from the bottle with care.

Making wine is a specialty unto itself. Within recent years, however, it has become a popular avocation for many commercial and hobby beekeepers. But one should not expect immediate success in beekeeping or any other venture, and practice is often needed to produce a good quality mead.

Honey in baking and cooking

Slightly over half of the honey produced in the United States is sold to the baking trade for the production of a variety of cakes, cookies, and breads. A large quantity is required for cakes prepared especially for the Jewish trade to be used during certain religious holidays.

Honey has several qualities that make it an important ingredient in cooking and baking. Its hygroscopic nature survives in some baked products and aids in moisture retention. Honey serves as a flavoring ingredient in some recipes, and in others it improves the browning qualities of the final product. The subject of honey in baked products is reviewed by Johnson, Nordin, and Miller (1957), who refer to several earlier papers on the same topic. Anderson, in 1958, treated the subject of honey in candies, where its use has also been popular.

Other honey products

Several papers in the literature describe honey products (in which honey is the primary ingredient) and honey in combination with other foods. Although many of these products have appeared on the market from time to time and would appear to have an appeal to the public, few have met with any great success. In certain cases honey combinations pose chemical or physical problems, and in other instances a product has simply not been accepted, possibly because of inadequate promotion.

Honey is an excellent topping for ice cream, but when the two are mixed, the freezing point is depressed so that the ice cream must be held under special refrigeration at a lower temperature than usual. Likewise, ice cream in which honey has been used as a substitute for sugar is too soft when stored at the ordinary temperature. Research at the University of Florida has shown that a variegated honey ice cream which requires normal refrigeration can be made. The process is somewhat similar to using honey as a topping on ice cream.

Honey jelly was marketed by at least one firm over a fairly long period of time. The honey is diluted to about 67.5 per cent solids, the pH is adjusted to about 3.0, and pectin is added. The product evidently has some appeal although it is no longer on the market.

Honey peanut butter was also marketed for some time; the mixture was predominantly honey with about 10 to 20 per cent peanut butter. After storage on a store shelf for one or two months, the product took on a rubbery consistency and lost its taste appeal. However, several firms add a small amount of honey to peanut butter as a sweetening agent, and the marketing of this product has been quite satisfactory.

Tests were undertaken at Cornell University by Brown and Kosikowski in 1970 which showed that a very fine honey yogurt could be manufactured. Initially, it was suggested that a light, mild flavored honey should be used in combination with yogurt, but later tests show that buckwheat honey, one of the stronger, darker honeys, better complements the highly-acid, strong-tasting yogurt. A paper was published on the product, and several firms have shown an interest in marketing it.

A honey cream was introduced in the later 1920's. Honey cream is a very costly product and is, of course, very high in caloric value. It has not been test marketed in many years, and it has probably never been made outside of a test kitchen or laboratory, but for those who enjoy rich dairy products it is a special delight.

Honey vinegar has been made by several people. It is relatively cheap to make, but apple cider vinegar is much cheaper, and there is no special taste appeal in the honey vinegar that makes it superior to other vinegars.

Honey products and various combinations of honey with foods offer great commercial possibilities which are as yet unexplored. Most information about how these products are made rests in the hands of a few beekeepers or specialists who make them for their own use. Perhaps an advertising program might change this, but at present there is no effort to make any major changes. Thus, most honey in the United States is marketed as a liquid. Probably about 10 per cent is marketed in crystalline form and less than 1 per cent is marketed as honey butter. Much less than 1 per cent is sold as comb honey, and less than 1 per cent of the honey produced is used in all other honey products.

Beeswax

Beeswax is secreted from four pairs of glands on the underside of the worker honey bee's abdomen (queens and drones do not have wax glands). Apparently bees need only sugar to produce beeswax though it is possible they draw on body reserves when there is a shortage of fat and protein. Bees can secrete wax at any time of the year, but they make it in quantity only during a good honey flow when it is needed for building additional comb and for the cell cappings.

Beeswax is white when secreted by the honey bee, but since the gums, resins, and pollens that bees collect soon stain it, the public has the mistaken notion that in its natural form it is yellow. Beeswax has a characteristic odor which it acquires from the honey, pollen, propolis, and other materials with which it comes in contact. Its melting point is about 63°C (145°F).

Throughout history beeswax has always commanded a fairly high price. As the first plastic it had multiple uses, and for this reason it commonly served as a medium of exchange in bartering.

Comb foundation

Comb foundation is a sheet of beeswax on which are embossed the three-faced bases of cells of the honey comb. The fact that man can make the foundation, or the midrib, of a comb, was discovered in the 1850's. Man-made comb foundation has several advantages for the beekeeper. First, if a piece of comb foundation is put into a wooden framework, commonly called a frame, the bees will make a comb in that plane. Parallel combs, side by side, are much easier to manipulate than are those that are not in the same plane (see Chapter 8).

Since worker and drone cells vary in size, their bases, which may be embossed on the foundation, do likewise.

By using comb foundation with the bases of worker cells, the beekeeper may control the size of the cells in a frame. For many years, beekeepers have worked hard to discourage the production of drones in their colonies. They have preferred to have worker-size cells in the combs in their brood nest. It is known that, if drone comb is substituted for worker comb in the brood nest, the colony cannot survive since only drones would be produced; however, a small percentage of drone cells in the brood nest probably does much less harm than has been suspected.

In some of the southwestern states, where the low moisture content of the honey makes extraction of the honey difficult, bee-keepers use comb foundation with drone cell bases so as to make a larger cell from which the honey may be more easily extracted. This procedure is little known in the eastern United States, but to a beekeeper in a warm, dry climate, such as Arizona, it can be extremely important.

From time to time there has been an effort to substitute aluminum, plastic, zinc, and other materials for comb foundation, but bees accept the comb foundation made from beeswax more readily than any other. Thus, despite all of our modern inventions, a great quantity of beeswax is still used to make the comb foundation that is purchased by beekeepers.

Candles

It is probable that the principal use of beeswax, one that dates back to antiquity, is the making of candles for churches, especially for the Roman Catholic Church. In the beginning beeswax may have been used for a tithe. It is especially suitable for candles because it burns with less smoke and odor than do animal fats and tallows; in fact, burning beeswax has a rather pleasant odor. Certain church liturgy suggests that, since the honey bee is a virgin, the wax produced by her is symbolic of purity. In further mystical doctrine, the wick of the candle is thought to represent the soul of Christ, and the flame, the concept of divinity which envelops the purity of both Christ and the Virgin Mary.

The demand for pure beeswax in the United States is so great that it cannot be filled at a reasonable price from domestic sources; thus wax is imported, especially from East Africa. Although many church groups prefer pure beeswax candles on their altars, it will be noted, upon examination, that many church candles are only 51 per cent beeswax, depending upon the importance of the ceremony. During the year candles may be 66 2/3 per cent beeswax, 75 per cent, or 100 per cent, again depending upon the event and season. Manufacturers of beeswax candles stamp the percentage of beeswax on the candle.

Historically, a pound of beeswax has always sold for more than a pound of honey. The price varies greatly, and until recently a pound of beeswax has been worth about five times as much as a pound of honey. Needless to say, beekeepers watch changes in church philosophy and the use of candles by churches with considerable interest.

Other uses for beeswax

Fifty years ago a woman's sewing kit would not have been complete without a piece of light-brown or straw-colored beeswax, usually a lump about half the size of a hen's egg. The wax was used to weld together the loose ends of thread or to make a needle more slippery.

Several authors have compiled long lists of uses for beeswax. Today, however, because of the shortage and high price, beeswax is used only by a few select companies for very special purposes. It is still popularly used as a dental impression wax; for this purpose it has a pleasant taste and odor and the correct melting and molding points. The pharmaceutical industry uses beeswax in certain ointments and pomades. It holds color well. Several beekeepers have invented formulas for floor and furniture waxes including the use of beeswax, but cheaper waxes are now available for these purposes. At one time beeswax was used as an insulator in the electrical field, but again other resins and waxes which are less expensive are now favored.

Beekeepers who operate stands to dispose of their honey find it profitable to keep a small quantity of beeswax on hand for sale to special customers who will usually want the wax in one-quarter, one-half, or one-pound lots. Some archers prefer pure beeswax for their bowstrings. Occasionally, a carpenter has his own formula for a varnish or special finish that includes beeswax. Boat owners have sometimes sought out beeswax to use on parts of their vessels to protect them against saltwater corrosion. Beeswax has been a favorite ingredient in mustache wax. And it should be remembered that beeswax, man's first plastic, was originally a favorite material for making metal castings. In recent years, as winter sports have been increasing in popularity, beeswax has been used as an ingredient in ski wax and snowshoe wax.

The list of uses to which beeswax has been put is almost endless, indicating the uniqueness of the material and its important role in history.

Royal jelly

One of the great fascinations in honey bee biology is that the same egg may produce either a queen or a worker bee, depending on how the larva is reared. The hundreds of thousands of queen bees that are reared by professional queen breeders and sold to other beekeepers in the country each year substantiate this. The method of rearing queens is relatively simple, and several books have been devoted to the subject. To grow a queen, one removes a one-day old worker larva from her cell and places it in a larger cell, called a queen cell. The queen cell is then placed in a position parallel with the worker cells, with the mouth downward. If queen cells containing young larvae are placed in queenless colonies, the bees will begin to feed them special food, and the larvae will all become queens. There is no question that either a queen or a worker may be developed from the same egg. How all of this comes about, however, is a question that has attracted the attention of many researchers, all of whom have failed to come up with a definitive answer.

When a queen lays a fertilized egg, the embryo within the egg develops and hatches three days later, producing the larva. If the larva is destined to become a queen, larval development takes only five and one-half days. If the larva is destined to become a worker bee, larval development takes six days, drone larvae spend six and one-half days in the larval stage. At the end of the larval stage, the animal passes on to the pupal stage. In the case of workers and queens, the determination of which is to develop is made in the second or third day of larval life.

The difference in larval development time is not all that distinguishes a worker from a queen. Total development of a worker bee takes 21 days whereas only 16 days are required to produce a queen. A queen bee weighs approximately 0.2 grams whereas a worker is about half that weight. During the active season the worker bee lives for only six weeks whereas queens live on the average of two to three years and a few have been known to live as long as five years. Queen honey bees and workers have two ovaries each, but queens have 100 to 200 ovarioles per ovary whereas worker honey bees have only four to eight underdeveloped ovarioles per ovary. The sting of a worker bee is straight and heavily barbed while that of a queen is curved and only lightly barbed. Queen honey bees can mate, worker honey bees cannot. Queen honey bees have no wax glands while workers do. The active glands in the head of the queen are quite different from those in the heads of workers and produce markedly different substances. Worker honey bees have a pollen-carrying apparatus on their hind legs, which is absent from the legs of queens. These are only a few of the many differences between a queen and a worker.

The substance that is fed to the larvae and is responsible for the great differences between the development of a worker and a queen is called royal jelly. It is a secretion produced by the pharyngeal and the mandibular glands in the heads of relatively young worker honey bees.[2] Honey bees feed all their larvae lavishly, and royal jelly may be collected from the cells of young worker bees though it is present in greater quantity in the cells in which queens are produced. Worker bees do not feed larvae directly but rather place the food next to the larvae in their cells. The larvae turn round and round in their cells, consuming food as they move. There is always a surplus of royal jelly in queen cells; thus, the problem in determining why royal jelly makes the great difference between a queen and a worker is not a lack of material available for study. The difficulty appears to be that the chemical substances responsible for the changes are unstable and break down very rapidly during the process of collection and storage. A few bees which are intermediate between queens and workers have been reared in the laboratory; however, it is not possible to predict which will be produced.

Obviously, royal jelly has remarkable qualities that are not yet fully understood. This fact led to one of the most magnificent

2. The pharyngeal glands probably produce the bulk of royal jelly. The 10-hydroxy-*trans*-2-decenoic acid and perhaps some of the lipid components are produced in the mandibular glands. Whether or not the thoracic glands are involved in royal jelly production is not known.

hoaxes in which the beekeeping industry has ever been involved.

The story is told of a Pope who lay on his death bed. His doctors fed him royal jelly thinking that this remarkable bee food might possibly benefit him, and that in any event it could do no harm. Unexpectedly, the Pope lived for several more months, and who could say that the royal jelly had not prolonged his life. Shortly thereafter, one could buy royal jelly tablets, royal jelly capsules, royal jelly in injection form, and royal jelly in combination with honey. It became a favorite ingredient in such items as face creams and other cosmetics. Successful queen breeders in the United States, who knew how to produce royal jelly in quantity, reaped a profit. It was found that royal jelly could be produced in countries where labor was cheaper. The price, which at one time had risen as high as $500 a pound in this country, soon fell to $100 and less when people outside the United States learned there was a good market for it.

The claims made for the royal jelly products were of the usual type. The ads pointed out that the queens were fully developed sexually and lived for long periods of time whereas the workers were sexually underdeveloped and lived for only a few weeks in the summer. The ads did not emphasize that the queen was an egg-laying machine, and perhaps people using the material were not interested in that attribute. In the late 1950's and early 1960's royal jelly cosmetics could be bought in the most fashionable stores in New York City; the products were expensive, and there was never any effort to put a low-priced product on the market.

The widespread sale and use of royal jelly, stimulated many researchers to work even harder to find out why this material was so crucial in the development of bees. Scientists suggested that a hormone was probably present, and statements to this effect appearing in the press added to the glamour and mystery that surrounded the product.

However, calm prevailed in some minds, and people were slow but sure to point out that, while royal jelly was good bee food and a rich source of protein, vitamins, and other nutrients, necessary for the growth of any animal, there was no proof that it could benefit man. Nevertheless, thousands of people were bilked of millions of dollars before the royal jelly fad waned.

The royal jelly hoax is not completely dead. Even in certain journals and publications today one will find advertisements stating that royal jelly may be bought packaged in various forms. Fortunately, the Food and Drug Administration of the federal government is becoming increasingly alert to the problem of false advertising claims; there are greater restrictions than ever before on what may be said in an advertising campaign.

Pollen

Pollen is the honey bee's source of fat and particularly of protein. Nectar or honey, of course, is their source of carbohydrate. Pollen is especially important for brood rearing since without an ample supply bees cannot produce young. Beekeepers have noted that during inclement weather in the spring, if bees have no pollen reserves in the hive, they may remove brood from the hive and discard the larvae.

There has been a long search for materials that could be used as pollen substitutes and supplements. Just as in other agricultural industries, rearing animals for production purposes, in this case, pollination or honey production, requires great quantities of food. It has been determined that one may use soybean flour and certain distillery by-products as pollen substitutes, but even though these materials are nutritious, honey bees do not find them very attractive and do not consume them readily.

Flowers produce pollen in greater quantity than is needed for cross-pollination. However, this is merely part of the cooperation that appears to exist between flowering plants and bees. Since plants, speaking anthropomorphically, want bees exclusively for themselves, they provide them with an abundant supply of food.[3]

3. This statement can be misunderstood. An individual flower usually provides a bee with only a small portion of the pollen or nectar needed to make a load. Thus, a bee must visit several flowers of the same species for cross-pollination, or the accidental carrying of pollen from one flower to another, to take place. In order that this be accomplished the plant must provide sufficient nectar, or pollen, distinctively marked, so that a bee is not attracted to flowers of another plant species.

In fact, some people have gone so far as to suggest there may be collusion in the evolution of plants in this regard. The idea needs researching. It has been suggested that spring plants produce more pollen than nectar and that indeed, in the early spring, bees need more pollen since they presumably already have honey reserves from the previous year. During the summer and fall it would appear that plants produce more nectar than pollen because bees must have an abundant supply of honey in order to survive the winter. Furthermore, not all pollens are of equal nutritive value; but, since bees collect pollen from several flowers, deficiencies which any pollens may have are compensated for.

In some areas of the country, Arizona for example, a shortage of pollen makes it difficult to rear bees in the spring. Beekeepers in some parts of the country, where pollen is in great surplus, have found it possible to collect pollen which bees have stored and attempt to sell it to others. Bee-collected pollen is too expensive to make this a widely accepted practice. However, if a pollen which is strongly attractive to bees is collected, it can be mixed with a pollen substitute, thereby making that material more attractive to the bees.

Men are willing to exploit almost any idea. Because pollen is the male germ cell of the plant, it has been relatively simple to dream up a sales promotion program which suggests that pollen might be of benefit in the diet of men. Just as there are people to dream up such ideas there are always others who are looking for elixers. Thus, for several years there has been a small trade involving the sale of pollen as a food supplement. Since most pollens have a rather bitter taste, it is necessary to combine them with something to cover up the taste, and what could be more logical than to use honey. Pollen is a rich source of protein, and protein is certainly required in human nutrition, but whether pollen is necessary is another question.

Propolis

Propolis is the name given to the plant gums and resins, often found around buds and wounds of trees, that bees collect and use in the hive to seal holes and cracks and to strengthen cells of the honey comb. Propolis is most often reddish though it may be yellow, orange, brown, and sometimes almost black, the color depending upon the source. Alfonsus (1933) records that bees gather propolis from several sources. In Wisconsin he observed collections from pine and poplar trees; however, there were two other sources he could not identify. The material may also be used to reduce a colony's entrance and as a varnish to cover cracks, crevices, and dead animal bodies which are too large for the bees to remove from the hive. Just as these plant saps give tree wounds protection from insect and microbe invaders, so they protect the interior of the bees' hive. This is discussed further in Chapter 12.

Several papers have appeared suggesting that propolis may contain natural antibiotics and so have medicinal value. Most of these papers have originated in Russia though a few have come from other European countries. The subject of the antimicrobial effect of propolis has been studied by Lindenfelzer (1967, 1968). He showed that a strong bactericidal effect was present and that propolis even has an effect against the causative organism of the most serious honey bee disease, American foulbrood. More recently, Crane (1973) has reviewed the worldwide interest in propolis that has been stimulated by its antibiotic properties.

Although propolis is obviously important in the biology of the honey bee, the researchers who have studied it have avoided the question of whether the bactericidal activity of propolis originates in the natural gums and resins collected by bees or whether honey bees add something to propolis which gives it additional activity. Our present information suggests that bees add little or nothing to propolis, but there are no precise data to back up this statement.

Propolis can be easily collected in large quantities, and some people have suggested doing this in order to study further the possibility of its use in medicine. However, until the questions of the source of unusual properties of propolis are resolved, propolis is not likely to be a marketable by-product of the hive.

The pure food and drug laws and hive products

The comb honey era lasted from about 1880 to 1915. A sharp demand during World War I and World War II encouraged bee-keepers to produce more honey, and predominately liquid honey, which they could produce in greater quantity at a higher total profit. However, it was the Pure Food and Drug Laws that had the greatest effect on the beekeeping industry and brought about the change from comb honey to liquid honey production.

In the early days of the beekeeping industry in the United States, honey commanded a far better price than it has subsequently. In fact, beekeepers in the 1870's and 1880's stated that a pound of honey was equal in value to a pound of butter, and in many markets it was the price of butter that set the price of honey. Sugar was still in too scarce supply to satisfy man's craving for sweets, but honey sold for a much higher price than sugar. There was much adulteration of honey and although beekeepers complained about it, there was little they could do. The public, however, was aware that comb honey was a natural product that could not be adulterated. Therefore, the buying public had confidence in comb honey.

One of the prized pieces of literature in the E. F. Phillip's Bee-keeping Library at Cornell University is a copy of a petition, which was signed by over 10,000 beekeepers in the country and sent to the United States Congress in 1878, asking for the establishment of pure food and drug laws to deter adulteration of honey. While this request was not acted upon favorably at the time, beekeepers continued to pressure the Congress and, together with other agricultural and medical groups, were successful in having the Congress write the first pure food and drug laws in 1906.

The extent to which the public was being deceived, before and at the turn of the century, may be documented by examining some of the patent medicines then on the market. One patent medicine for consumption (tuberculosis), which contained chloroform and morphine, was sold under the name of *Dr. King's Cure for Con-*

sumption. There was another concoction for sick children, labeled *Mrs. Winslow's Soothing Syrup,* which contained heroin; presumably this syrup was to help the child sleep. Elixers containing alcohol were common and were popular with many people. Of course, at that time it was not required that the ingredients in a mixture be printed on the bottle's label. Malaria, typhoid, tuberculosis, whooping cough, scarlet fever, and a great multitude of diseases, which are of little concern to us today, were major killers throughout the country. Medicine was still more of an art than a science, and while many medical practitioners were reasonable and honest men who had come to understand their practice through experience, there were an equal number of charlatans and medicine men who bilked an unwitting public. The death rate among people was high, and a person who lived to see his grandchildren was indeed fortunate. Religious demagogues dominated much of the thinking. Although people had ceased to burn witches, there were many who still believed in witchcraft, fountains of youth, and compounds that would deliver them from evil. Thus, while it is simple for us today to see why we must have pure food and drug laws, the need for them was not so obvious to the people before and at the turn of the century.

There have been very few cases of honey adulteration in the United States since 1906, in part, because honey adulteration is easily detected, both by a good palate and with simple chemical tests in the laboratory. At the same time, world sugar production has increased to a point where the average man's craving for sweets can be satisfied, and while honey remains a luxury item, the incentive to adulterate it for a profit is less than it was a hundred or so years ago.

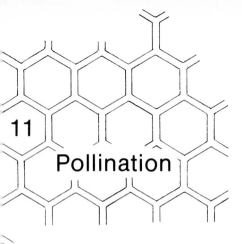

11
Pollination

There are more than 20 fruit and 30 seed crops of commercial value in the United States that require or benefit from cross-pollination [1] by insects. The honey bee is not the only insect of value in pollination, but it is the most abundant, the most commonly used and, generally speaking, the easiest for men to manipulate.

While bees are dependent upon plants for a livelihood, not all flowering plants are dependent upon bees for cross-pollination. Many plants are self-fertile; others use various means of accomplishing cross-pollination including wind, water, birds, and so forth.

At the same time, many plants have evolved mechanisms to avoid self-fertilization. Some plants have separate male and female flowers or parts; examples include corn and cucumbers. In other plants, the male and female parts mature at different times. The positions of the male and female parts in the same flower may vary, as they do in the apple, where the male and female parts are sometimes separated by as much as half an inch. A few plants show an even more curious specialization: hollies and dates have male and female plants.

1. Cross-pollination is the transfer of pollen from the flower of one plant to the flower of another plant of the same species. If the pollen from the anthers of a flower is transferred to the stigma of the same flower, then self-pollination occurs. If pollen is transferred from the anthers of a flower to the stigma of another flower on the same plant, this is again self-pollination.

Different plants have their special pollination problems. In clovers, for example, the number of flowers per acre and the number of seeds produced per flower may vary considerably. Alsike clover and red clover both have many individual flowers, called florets, in a single head; in the case of alsike clover, there may be 400,000,000 florets per acre whereas an equivalent field of red clover would have about 200,000,000 florets per acre. Red clover produces an average of two to four seeds per floret. Another legume, birdsfoot trefoil, has several individual flowers in a cluster instead of florets in a flowering head. In a birdsfoot trefoil field there are usually only about ten million flowers per acre, but each flower is capable of producing ten, twenty, or more seeds in a single pod.

Because of the great variation in the number of flowers per acre, one cannot state that a specific number of colonies or individual bees is needed per acre to pollinate all crops. Each crop must be considered individually. In addition to considering the number of flowers that bees must visit to set a seed or fruit crop, one must also be alert to the distance the bees must fly, the weather conditions, competition, the bees already present, and so forth. These factors are discussed below.

Our changing agriculture

Specialization in agriculture, which has included the selection and breeding of plants for high yields and effective human and animal nutrition, has affected the beekeeping industry as well as all other aspects of agriculture. While approximately half of our honey is produced from weed plants or plants growing on abandoned or unused soil, a certain quantity of our honey is produced from agriculturally important plants. In areas where land is no longer farmed, weed plants have become increasingly important to the beekeeper.

Buckwheat, a common grain in the Northeast for many years, can be grown on wet, poor soils, and at high elevations. Since a crop can be harvested from seed planted in late June or July, farmers

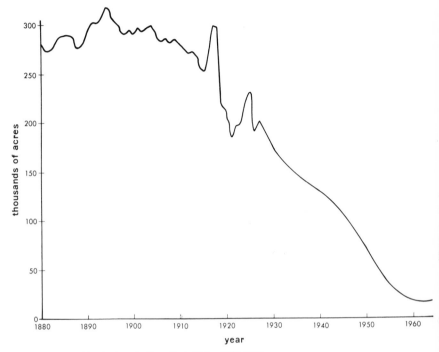

11.1. Acreage of buckwheat in New York State, 1880–1964.

can plant a cash crop even in wet years or after they have planted the earlier crops. However, buckwheat grain is high in fiber and low in protein, and has been replaced by corn and wheat as feed grains. The decline of buckwheat acreage, which is shown in figure 11.1, has been accompanied by a decline in buckwheat honey production. At one time millions of pounds of buckwheat honey were produced in the northeastern United States; today buckwheat honey is a rare commodity, and even though it is dark colored and strong flavored, it is preferred by some people and commands a high price.

Alfalfa and citrus, on the other hand, are grown in ever increas-

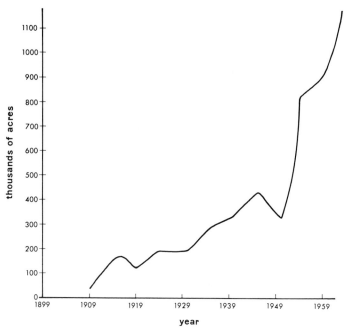

11.2. Acreage of alfalfa in New York State, 1899–1964.

ing quantitites. Alfalfa is an excellent forage plant, especially for dairy cattle. The increase in acreage of alfalfa in New York State, which is typical for many dairy states, is depicted in figure 11.2. Starting in the late 1950's alfalfa became a major nectar-producing plant in New York State, and today it provides a large percentage of the honey crop in the State.

At the same time, the growing demand for citrus fruits has led to an expansion in production; the changing situation in Florida is shown in figure 11.3. As the acreage devoted to citrus production increases, so does the production of citrus honey. Citrus honey, even though it may be gathered from the flowers of grapefruit, tangerine, or tangelo trees, is usually sold under the name of

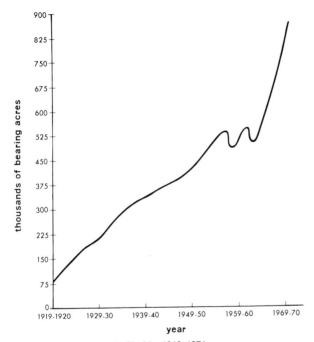

11.3. Acreage of citrus in Florida, 1919–1971.

orange blossom honey; it is popular and commands a good price. The number of colonies of bees kept in the State of Florida continues to increase with the increase in citrus acreage. Many beekeepers from other states have moved to Florida.

The three examples cited here illustrate the changing patterns of land use which must be faced by commercial beekeepers and, to a lesser extent, hobbyists as well. Beekeepers must be alert to cropping and other land-use changes in their area and, if necessary, be prepared to move colonies and apiaries to improve bee pasture.

The behavior of moved bees

If a colony of bees is moved a few miles or several thousand

11.4. A moving screen made with 8-mesh hardware cloth. The screen is held on the hive with four nails and is removed after the colonies have reached their destination.

miles, upon arrival at the new location the bees will commence work immediately, collecting pollen and nectar, provided the season is favorable. It is necessary to move a colony more than two or three miles lest certain of the foraging bees find orientation markers that guide them back to their old location. In fact, for the beekeeper, one of the most difficult things is to move a colony of bees only a short distance. Such a move creates great confusion, and his colony may lose its field force to another closer to the old location than the hive that is moved.

An informative paper on the behavior of field bees moved to a new location has been written by J. B. Free and M. V. Smith (1961). They studied the foraging behavior of bees which were moved into a pear orchard in full flower. Although they were interested mainly in the behavior of bees on pear flowers, the activity they observed also tells us much about the behavior of recently moved bees in general.

The colonies were moved into the pear orchard at 11:00 A.M., at a time when the temperature was above 27°C (80°F). The first pollen-collecting bee returned to her hive 13 minutes after the colony entrance was opened in the new location. During the next minute, six pollen-collecting bees returned to their hive laden with pollen. The fact that such short periods of time were involved points to the ease with which bees reorient in a new location. The observations made by Free and Smith are generally accepted as typical of bee behavior on other crops.

For the commercial beekeeper the greatest danger in moving bees is that the colonies may overheat in transit. This may occur if the colonies have a great deal of brood, are crowded, and have too small openings for ventilation. While moving bees, commercial beekeepers worry more about overheating than they do about chilling the brood, for chilling of the brood occurs very rarely under these circumstances. Beekeepers prefer to move colonies of bees at night when it is cooler; when they move during the day they usually make short stops of only a few minutes, thus keeping a constant flow of air over the hives.

During very warm weather they may wet the hives with water, actually wetting the interior of the hive. Knowing when a hive should be wetted and how much water to use is part of the art of beekeeping and may spell success or failure for the commercial beekeeper who moves large numbers of colonies, especially in the warmer parts of the country (figs. 11.5, 11.6).

Special pollination problems

The question of pollination is often oversimplified, the general thought being that it is only necessary to place colonies in the vicinity of the crop to be pollinated to accomplish cross-pollination satisfactorily. Such is not the case, and some peculiar problems have arisen from time to time. Certain of these have to do with the threshholds of perception and acceptance which honey bees are known to have. Other problems involve the field behavior of honey bees and the fact that, generally speaking, individual honey bees

11.5. Loading bees in New York State in the fall for Florida. The approximately 1,400 mile trip, made in about 26 hours nonstop, has no adverse effect on the bees.

forage in a relatively small area. Still other problems concern the biology of the plant itself, the existence of male and female plants and male and female flowers. Some of the more interesting of these problems are discussed below.

The Orlando tangelo

Citrus, including oranges, tangerines, grapefruit, and others, are all excellent producers of nectar, and, the honey from these plants, collectively called orange honey (sometimes orange blossom honey), has a major place on the United States market. It is produced in Florida, Arizona, and California. Interestingly, however, most citrus trees do not require cross-pollination, and the fact that they produce so much nectar is a paradox. Until 1962, it was thought that no citrus required cross-pollination, though it has been suggested that flowers visited by bees may produce fruit with more seeds and that the juice from fruit with more seeds may be sweeter; however, these suggestions have not been confirmed, so far as I am aware.

11.6. These single story colonies have been stripped of all but 10 to 15 pounds of honey before being moved South in the fall. They will be brought north again in May or June after the orange honey flow.

In what is now referred to as a classic paper on pollination, F. A. Robinson and A. H. Krezdorn (1962) of the University of Florida showed that the Orlando tangelo, as well as other tangelos, must be cross-pollinated to set fruit. Tangelos, though relatively new varieties of citrus, are out-of-hand fruits of excellent quality, which for a number of years were sold on the local market only, being unknown elsewhere. In the study described in their paper, Robinson and Krezdorn harvested the fruit in an Orlando tangelo grove where there were eleven rows of Orlando tangelos side by side. The tangelos were flanked on one side by a grove of temple orange trees and on the other by a grove of valencia orange trees. It was observed that the row of Orlando tangelos adjacent to the row of temple oranges had slightly over 120 fruits per tree and slightly over 20 seeds per fruit. As one moved into the grove of Orlando tangelos, away from the grove of temple oranges, the number of fruits per tree and the number of seeds per fruit decreased. The Orlando tangelo trees six to ten rows away from the temple orange trees produced only 17 to 28 fruits per tree. The row of Orlando tangelos adjacent to the valencia grove produced 44 fruits per tree, much less than half the number of fruits produced by the trees adjacent to the temple grove. Thus, Robinson and Krezdorn concluded that pollen from temple oranges is more effective for cross-pollinating Orlando tangelos than is pollen from valencia trees.

At the time of this discovery in Florida there were fairly large numbers of Orlando tangelos, planted in solid groves, as is the usual technique with most citrus. Although the trees were of bearing age, production of tangelos was low. As soon as these data were made available, Orlando tangelo growers in Florida interplanted, grafted in other varieties, and took other steps to provide pollen so that the trees might set a better crop of fruit.

In the management of most fruit trees, as in the management of many agricultural crops, planting like trees adjacent to like trees or like crops adjacent to like crops facilitates fertilizing, pruning, spraying, picking, and other growing practices. If different types of oranges, for example, require a different fertilizer level, or if certain varieties are more susceptible than others to certain insect pests, growers must undertake special programs for the protection of their crops. Picking is especially a problem, for not all pickers of agricultural crops are fully aware of the differences between varieties of fruit, vegetables, seeds, and so forth. Mixing varieties can be disastrous, for certain of these may have much better storage potential than others.

One might logically ask how it has come to be that citrus produces great supplies of nectar when presumably nectar is for the explicit purpose of attracting insects so that cross-pollination can be accomplished. The answer probably lies in the fact that citrus is a man-manipulated plant which has been bred over a long period. Our knowledge of methods of breeding agricultural crops suggests that in the beginning either nectar production was necessary for the original oranges from which men bred the stock now in use, or, in their unnatural process of plant selection, men unwittingly selected plants which produced large supplies of nectar but which either did not require seeds to set fruit or which had pollen that was compatible and could fertilize its own kind. It is also possible that growing practices make the difference; not all citrus plantings produce a surplus of nectar every year.

The Orlando tangelo is an example of what can happen as men continue to make varieties for their own benefit, without regard for certain natural processes.

Pollination problems

The sugar content of pear nectar is low. Most pears have nectar with a total solids content of ten to fifteen per cent, most of which is sugar. At the time pears are in flower they must compete with apples, dandelions, and yellow rocket, all of which have nectar with a sugar concentration averaging about 40 per cent. Since bees are able to determine the amount of sugar in a nectar, those visiting pears soon leave and search for better food. As a result, in those years when the weather during fruit bloom is not favorable for bee flight, the set of pears may be low in comparison with other fruits in an orchard. Pears are not the only fruits with a low sugar concentration in the nectar, but they are one of the prime examples of the type of problem which may occur. The problem is accentuated by the fact that pears are usually grown in locations where other, competing fruit trees are nearby.

As described in a paper already cited, J. B. Free and M. V. Smith moved colonies of bees into a pear orchard at 11:00 A.M. on a day when the temperature was above 80°F; they subsequently collected pollen from the foraging bees. The pollen was examined to determine its source. It was found that 91.3 per cent of the pollen collected during the first 30 minutes after the bees were liberated in the pear orchard, was pear pollen. However, six hours later, only 47.5 per cent of the bees returning to the hive with pollen had been working on pear blossoms. Thus, during a matter of six hours, over half of the bees which had been liberated in the new area had found alternate food sources even though they were farther from the hive than were the pear trees.

The sugar concentration of a nectar has to do with the plant species and its physical condition, but it is also dependent upon other factors. Nectar may dry out in plants which have open flowers and where the nectar is exposed to the wind or the sun; the sugar concentration is also affected by humidity. For example, in the case of birdsfoot trefoil, on a typical summer day, one finds that the nectar usually contains about 20 per cent sugar at 9:00 A.M., 30 per cent sugar at 12:00 noon and 40 per cent sugar at 3:00 P.M. By 6:00 P.M. the sugar concentration of the nectar may decrease to about 30 per cent. Flowers in which the nectaries are not so exposed will not show such a great change in the sugar concentration of the nectar during the day.

Pear growers are alert to their special pollination problems. They circumvent these problems by proper orchard plantings so that the varieties needed for cross-pollination are immediately adjacent to one another. Pear growers are especially watchful of the weather and are prepared to bring in additional colonies of bees if needed. Delaying the movement of colonies into the orchard until the pears are in full flower increases the chances of cross-pollination in the case of those trees close to the colonies.

Alfalfa

Alfalfa is a popular forage plant, especially for dairy cattle. Most of the alfalfa seed is produced in western states on irrigated land. Alfalfa appears to benefit from being cross-pollinated, and in any event, the blossoms must be physically tripped in order to be pollinated. Tripping involves the release of the sexual parts of the flower which are contained within the keel and are kept under pressure until released; it is one of the few instances in plants where we may observe physical movement of a plant part. The sexual parts of a flower are released as a bee straddles the keel and extends its proboscis into the throat of the flower. When tripping occurs, the bee's head may be caught between the large standard petal, typical of legumes, and the tip of the sexual column. The bee is actually hit in the process, and a patch of pollen is visible on the hairs of the bee's head where it is hit. If the bee goes on to trip another flower, the sexual parts of the second flower come into contact with the pollen left by the first, and thus cross-pollination is accomplished.

Experimenters have observed that honey bees soon learn to avoid being hit by the alfalfa's sexual column. Instead of straddling the keel as they normally would while collecting nectar or pollen, they seek the flower's nectar from the side of the keel. While naive honey bees trip many flowers before learning to avoid this explosive mechanism, on the average, honey bees trip only 1 per cent of the alfalfa flowers which they visit. The only way in which alfalfa seed growers may be able to make up for this lack of tripping is to have more bees in their alfalfa fields; often three to five colonies of honey bees are used per acre for alfalfa pollination.

Interestingly, certain solitary bees do not learn to avoid the explosive-type mechanism found in the alfalfa flower. At least two species, the alfalfa leafcutter bee, *Megachile rotundata,* and the alkali bee, *Nomia melanderi,* are very effective alfalfa pollinators and are used commercially in many parts of the West for this express purpose. The leafcutter bee is so named because it cuts pieces of leaves from plants to line its cells. The alkali bee nests in alkaline soil. Methods of encouraging both species have been studied, and in certain areas they have replaced honey bees as commercial alfalfa pollinators.

Several works have been devoted to the biology of wild or solitary bees. One of the more recent, which contains a lengthy bibliography, is that by Stephen, Bohart, and Torchio (1969).

Apples and other fruits

Apples are our most valuable orchard fruit in the Northern United States, and unfortunately for apple growers, most apple varieties must have pollen from another variety in order to set fruit. The McIntosh apple is an excellent example of this; McIntosh pollen will not serve to pollinate a McIntosh apple. As long ago as 1917, Arthur J. Heinicke pointed out that it would be helpful to produce apple varieties which did not require cross-pollination. He stated that there was often inclement weather during apple blossom time. He was also aware that, with most apple varieties, the number of seeds in a fruit affect both the size and shape of the fruit. Fruits with fewer seeds were more likely to drop from the tree before maturation. If one examines a misshapen apple, it will usually be found that some of the seeds are not fully developed.

Probably seven years out of ten apple growers do not need to rent colonies of honey bees for apple pollination. If the weather during fruit bloom is favorable, there are usually a sufficient number of flies, beetles, wild solitary bees, and colonies of honey bees in buildings, trees, and hobbyists' apiaries to set a crop of fruit. Of course, this is not true of every apple orchard, but the facts apply to many areas where apples are grown commercially.

If the weather during fruit bloom is favorable for bee flight, most growers find that too many fruits are set on their trees, and they must use a thinning spray to remove some of them so that the remaining apples will be of marketable size. It is perhaps in only one year out of ten that bees are absolutely needed in an apple orchard throughout most of the Northeast; few people are willing to gamble and to decide which year will be a good year or a poor year for pollination. Certainly everyone agrees that without adequate cross-pollination there will be no fruit.

Apple pollination time is difficult for both the fruit grower and the beekeeper. Much of our fruit in New York State, for example, is grown in the vicinity of large lakes, and winds from these lakes may stop or slow bee flight. A wind of more than about 12 miles per hour stops bee flight.

Honey bees begin to take short flights at about 18°C (65°F), but full bee flight does not occur until the temperature is 21°C (70°F) or higher.

The flight of bees is also affected by their location within the orchard. If colonies are placed on the ground and have damp bottomboards, which tend to cool them, there will be fewer bees in the air than if the hives are warm and dry. In a damp hive a greater number of bees are needed to maintain normal hive temperature and humidity. Colonies exposed to full sunlight will have their field force active earlier in the morning and later at night than those which are shaded. For these reasons we recommend that bees be placed in groups of about three to six colonies within the orchard, taking advantage of local environmental situations including windbreaks and the absence of trees. Under favorable conditions a greater number of bees will fly from the hives; this is in the best interest of both the fruit grower and the beekeeper.

A serious problem for the fruit grower is that in most of the northern states, two plants—dandelion and yellow rocket—are in flower during fruit bloom. Both produce nectar which competes with apple nectar insofar as their respective sugar concentrations and abundance are concerned; all three plants also produce a large quantity of attractive pollen. As a result, many of the bees from hives moved into the orchard spend time visiting these weed plants, not apples. For this reason it is recommended that fruit growers mow their orchards or use a weed killer to remove these plants, at least from the orchards themselves. These same weeds in adjacent fields may also attract bees from the orchards.

A fruit grower once told me that honey bees did not visit dandelions in his orchard; he went on to say that he was not going to remove the dandelions, and thought it was foolish to suggest that it be done. He said he had spent over half an hour one day examining his orchard for bee activity and found most of the bees in the apple trees and on the apple blossoms, not visiting the dandelions. It was difficult to understand why bees would not visit dandelions in his orchard. The answer lies in research by John B. Free (1970), who discovered that dandelions produce the greatest quantity of pollen between 9:00 A.M. and 3:00 P.M.; 63 per cent of dandelion pollen is produced between 11:00 A.M. and 12:00 noon. Thus, dandelions are much more attractive to bees during the forenoon

11.7. The dandelions in this flowering apple orchard in New York State are sufficient in number to attract bees away from the fruit bloom. Thus, this grower would need to rent more than the usual number of colonies for apple pollination.

than at other times. Furthermore, Free found that apples produce pollen from about 8:00 A.M. to 5:00 P.M. but that 67 per cent of apple pollen is produced between 12:00 noon and 4:00 P.M. Free's observations were made in England, but we presume they have application in North America. Thus, during the day the number of bees actively foraging on various plants may vary depending upon the food available to them (see fig. 11.7).

Apple blossom time is a difficult period for beekeepers who move bees to the orchards. While they are compensated for their efforts, they run the risk of spray losses, usually brought about by bees collecting insecticide-contaminated water from wheel ruts and puddles in the orchard. Additionally, the time when colonies are in the orchard is followed by the time when most swarming occurs in the northern United States. Because the colonies are widely scattered throughout the orchards, beekeepers cannot give them the attention which they require to prevent swarming. Movie and television programs portray apple blossoming as a romantic period and picture loving couples tripping through the fragrant, flowering orchards; beekeepers will testify that this is not precisely correct. They will say that, when apples bloom, orchards are often cool, wet, muddy places, and the beekeeper who does not have to ask the orchardist to pull his truck out of a mud hole is fortunate (fig. 11.8).

Beekeepers measure the strength of the colonies they rent in terms of the quantity of brood present in the colony. For apple pollination, colonies should contain 30,000 to 40,000 bees. It is difficult to count the precise number of bees in a colony, but it is easy to determine the number of frames containing brood. Since the brood nest takes the shape of a sphere within a colony, and at apple blossom time this sphere is just slightly smaller than a basketball, it is an easy matter to state how much brood a colony should have. For apple pollination, I recommend that a colony should have brood in six frames. Note that this is quite different from saying that a colony should have six frames of brood. When a colony has brood in six frames, and the brood nest is the shape of a sphere, it is obvious that the two outside frames will not contain much brood. A colony which has brood in six frames will have a population of at least 30,000 bees.

A few apple growers buy package bees to use for apple pollination in the spring. This is not a good practice. Not only do packages contain fewer bees than are desired but during the first several weeks after installation the population of the packages decreases; thus, packages of bees do not have enough field bees to perform the job which must be done.

Apple growers would prefer to plant their apples in solid blocks. Like the growers of many other commodities, they would prefer to have whole areas devoted to a single variety. Not only is it important to keep apple varieties separate for growing and selling purposes, but there are also differences in the keeping and storage qualities of certain apples. Since, however, apples require cross-

11.8. This worker honey bee is taking nectar from the base of the flower's male and female parts without coming into contact with them. The pollen in her pollen basket indicates she is a pollen collector, too. (Photo by New York State College of Agriculture and Life Sciences, Cornell University.)

pollination, this practice is not practical. It is recommended that every third row, or every third tree in every third row, be of a variety that will pollinate adjacent trees. If every third tree in every third row is a pollinator, then no single tree in the orchard will be more than one tree away from a pollinator.

Interestingly, however, some growers continue to plant solid blocks. Despite the fact that books and bulletins on apple growing devote some attention to the importance of cross-pollination, not all growers heed this advice and plant new orchards accordingly. For the long run, we recommend that orchards which have been planted as solid blocks be replanted in part, or that other varieties be grafted onto the existing apple trees. Replanting is best, for if the occasional branch is grafted into existing trees on a random basis, there is again a picking problem. As stated above, it is best to replace every third tree in every third row.

Remedial measures exist for providing pollen for cross-pollination in orchards where growers have planted solid blocks. The best technique is to carry into the orchard, at the time the apples are flowering, large bouquets of apple blossoms, which are positioned around the orchard. Open-head, fifty-gallon drums are used as containers to hold the bouquets. The branches in the bouquet should be one and one-half to three inches in diameter to provide a sufficient number of flowers so that cross-pollination can be accomplished. We recommend one such bouquet for every four to six trees. Obviously, cutting and carrying such a large number of flowering branches to the orchard is a difficult task, and it behooves the grower to move as rapidly as possible to replant or graft in pollinator varieties.

A second technique which may be used for cross-pollination in solid blocks in emergency situations is to distribute hand-collected pollen (pollen collected by men, not bees) on open flowers. Hand-collected pollen is available from firms in the State of Washington where the pollen is collected, mixed with a diluent, and frozen for use the following year. It is possible to place a pollen-distribution apparatus on the entrance of a colony of honey bees in such a way that the bees exiting from the hive are forced to walk through the hand-collected pollen and thus dust their bodies with it. Research undertaken by several persons has shown that the bees will carry some of this pollen from the hive to the flowers and the cross-pollination will be accomplished in this manner. However, we know it is the natural habit of the honey bee to clean its body whenever it becomes covered with pollen or pollen-like material. Thus, we are also aware that a large quantity of the hand-collected pollen is moved into the honey bee's pollen basket and is returned to the hive where it is used for food by the bees and not for the purpose for which it was intended. M. V. Smith and G. F. Townsend (1951) of Guelph University found they could mix flourescent dye with the hand-collected pollen, and using a black light at night, could check on the distribution of the hand-collected pollen throughout the orchard. Smith and Townsend showed that a large quantity of the pollen was properly distributed under these circumstances. They also noted several apple leaves which were covered with flourescent dye, indicating that the bees had stopped to rest and had cleaned themselves before proceeding further. Clearly, the use of hand-collected pollen is costly, and its distribution is time consuming. It should be considered as an emergency measure, to be used for cross-pollination of solid blocks only until corrective measures can be taken.

Singh and Boynton (1949) showed that pollen collected by bees from apple trees, and presumably other plants as well, lost its viability within about two hours after the bees collected it. Presumably it is the addition of honey (or some head gland secretion) to pollen which causes it to lose its viability. In any event, the question has been examined thoroughly and bee-collected pollen is not suitable for redistribution from the hive for the purpose of cross-pollination.

The idea that hand-collected pollen might solve all pollination problems has been carried to extremes by some people. One may, for example, buy shotgun shells loaded with pollen. The thought is to "shoot" the tree, thus saving all the bee and human effort which is normally associated with apple pollination. Clearly, the idea is not practical, for when one calculates the area of the receptive part of the female flower, versus the area being shot, it is obvious that most of the pollen is wasted. People have also suggested dusting apple trees with hand-collected pollen from helicopters flying above them, or by placing the hand-collected pollen in the air stream of an air blast sprayer directed at the tree. These methods are again not recommended from the practical point of view.

Pollination in greenhouses and cages

Some colonies of honey bees are used for the pollination of crops, both on an experimental and commercial basis, in both greenhouses and outdoor cages. In the northern United States and in Canada, a small industry is devoted to the greenhouse production of cucumbers. A few melons of various sorts are raised under greenhouse conditions; these plants must be cross-pollinated to set fruit, and honey bees are the easiest animal to use under these circumstances. Vegetable seed companies in many northern states confine bees in cages to pollinate carrot and onion seed in stock or foundation plantings. In many instances the seed produced under cage conditions is shipped to the western states where it is sown in isolation in irrigated areas to produce the seed which is finally marketed. Flies have been used as agents for cross-pollination under these same circumstances, but most growers and experimentalists prefer honey bees. Flies are less effective as pollinators, and more important, few people know how to raise and manage flies for this purpose.

Experimentally, both in greenhouses and cages, honey bees have been used with most plants which require cross-pollination, including cabbage, broccoli, alfalfa, and birdsfoot trefoil.

Bees confined in greenhouses or cages soon exhaust their pollen reserves. Without pollen to supply the necessary protein, brood rearing stops. As a result, the average age of the bees in the hive increases, and after several weeks the beekeeper has a colony of old bees. Egg laying by the queen may continue, but the larvae are discarded (removed by house bees) as soon as they are hatched. However, by the time this occurs the crop being pollinated has usually passed the flowering stage and the task for which the colony was needed has been completed. Depending upon the time of year and the length of confinement, the colony may or may not survive when it is once again placed in its normal environment.

From a practical, though perhaps cruel, point of view, colonies placed in greenhouses for more than five or six weeks are usually not worth saving. However, if they are removed from the greenhouse cage in the late spring or early summer, the bees may possibly have time to recover.

As a rule, colonies used for greenhouse and cage pollination are single story, containing 10,000 to 15,000 bees and a queen. Adding pollen reserves, that is, combs with pollen, can be helpful and may allow brood rearing to go on for a slightly longer period. There has been little research on the use of pollen substitutes and pollen supplements under such harsh conditions as cage or greenhouse confinement, and whether or not the use of these materials for such small colonies would be worthwhile is questionable. In the normal course of events the bees in such colonies are discarded after a period of five or six weeks though, of course, the equipment may be reused.

It is advisable to provide water for the bees under greenhouse conditions. Bees need water to dilute honey, and they also use it to cool their hive in warm weather. In the greenhouse, the routine watering of plants will usually leave some water on the greenhouse surfaces which bees can collect. In an outdoor cage, especially in a warm summer, it is advisable to place shallow pans or trays of water within the cage.

When a colony is confined in a limited space, only a few bees actually visit the flowers and are responsible for the cross-pollination that occurs. A fascinating and unresolved aspect of the biology of the honey bee is how such bees are designated or determined. Under cage conditions one may actually observe a few bees gathering enough pollen so it is visible in the pollen baskets on their hind legs. Still, the great majority of bees in the same cage continue to hit against the wall, glass, or screen and make no attempt to visit the flowers. Those few bees which do collect pollen under these conditions make trip after trip and apparently are not discouraged by the confined condition.

One cannot leave the question of greenhouse pollination without mentioning an opposite problem. As has been pointed out earlier in this chapter, flower fertilization shortens the period which that flower will remain open or in bloom. A flower which a greenhouse grower is producing for a corsage is expected to remain open and brilliant for several days. Flowers which are cross-pollinated wither sooner than those which are not, and a withering bouquet or corsage can be a disaster. The greenhouse grower of flowers wants precisely the reverse of what is wanted by the seeds-man or vegetable grower; he wants no bees visiting his flowers! Over the years we have been asked many times by greenhouse growers how they can keep bees, especially bumble bees, out of their greenhouses in the early spring. At this season, as the temperature warms, the growers are forced to increase the ventilation in their greenhouses, and they open the doors and louvers to do so. While it is not true of all flowering plants, many of those grown in greenhouses are odoriferous and highly attractive to any insects flying in the vicinity. Greenhouse growers of flowers for the fresh flower market do not use pesticides at this stage, and there are no repellents which will keep pollinating insects away. Their only recourse is to screen their greenhouses or those parts of the greenhouse which they open, an expensive and time-consuming process.

Flower fidelity

The Greek philosopher and scientist, Aristotle, was the first to record that honey bees show flower fidelity. Aristotle observed that bees would fly from a flower of one kind to the same kind and very rarely would they make a mistake and visit a flower of another species. If one observed the activity of honey bees in a field with mixed flowers, it will be noted that this is true; however, occasionally a bee will make an error. Another method of demonstrating that honey bees show flower fidelity is to examine the pollen loads which they bring back to the hive. It will be noted that each individual load is remarkably uniform in color, even though different bees from the same colony may return to the hive with loads of different colors.[2] At certain times of the year it is not difficult to find bees from the same hive collecting pollen from five to ten food sources in the field.

Some species of solitary bees do not show the same flower fidelity, and they may visit several flowers on a trip to the field. This has biological significance both to the bee and to the flower.

Some plants produce pollen which is deficient in certain nutrients when it is used as bee food. Honey bees collect and use pollen from many plant species during the year which means they are unlikely to suffer nutritional deficiencies. A few of the solitary bees feed on only one plant species; we presume that, where this occurs, the pollen and nectar from the plant in question must contain all the amino acids and nutrients needed in the bee's diet. In the case of solitary bees whose biology is not tied to a single flowering species, we presume the mixing of pollens overcomes any potential deficiencies.

Insofar as the biology of the flower is concerned, the flower fidelity of bees is important. For example, dandelion pollen will not fertilize yellow rocket. Each clover species must have pollen from its own kind for cross-pollination to take place. Plants, by distinctively marking their flowers with color, odor, and taste, take advantage of the fact that honey bees may detect these differences. If the food offered by a plant is more attractive than that offered by other plants, bees will continue to visit the more attractive species.

2. In 1963, Free studied the question of flower constancy in honey bees and found that only about 6 per cent of the pollen loads (pellets) he took from bees returning to the hive contained pollen from more than one plant species, indicating that most bees visit only a single flowering species on a trip to the field.

Behavior of pollen and nectar-collecting bees

Where does a honey bee go when she leaves the hive? We know that certain bees are scouts. Scout bees spontaneously leave the hive and search for acceptable food sources, both pollen and nectar (and additionally water, propolis, and hive sites when these are needed). Successful scouts dance in the hive conveying this information to other bees (recruits) in the hive. Our information on scouts suggests that they range over large areas in their search for food.

Research by Sardar Singh, published in 1950, shows that many bees work in a small area only. Singh marked bees which were collecting pollen and nectar and then studied their activities. Of course, Singh followed only those bees which remained in a small area, and we still wonder how typical such bees are.

Singh found that a bee might spend one field trip on a single apple tree; this same bee might later return to the same tree and still not visit a second tree. In a single field trip to alsike clover, Singh noted that a bee might work a plot as small as eight feet by nine feet; during a day the bee might visit an area not much larger than 20 feet by 25 feet. Singh was able to follow five bees for 23 to 25 days each. He noted that all of these bees visited relatively small areas over this whole time; one bee, for example, did not move outside of an area ten feet by seventeen feet for a period of eight days. Singh noted that weather had a profound effect on the area over which bees would forage. When flowers were producing a large supply of nectar and/or pollen, the area visited would be much smaller than when less pollen or nectar was being produced.

The practical implication of the work by Singh is simply that when cross-pollination must be undertaken either because the plant varieties in question have sterile pollen, or the plants are some distance apart, or for some other reason, the source of pollen must be relatively close to the plant to be pollinated. A bee which visits a single McIntosh apple tree is of little value to a fruit grower except that she might redistribute some pollen from another tree brought there by a second bee. In the case of onions, where hybrid seed involves the use of male sterile plants (plants which do not produce pollen), there is a tendency for bees to work along rows rather than across rows. While there will be some crossing between rows, Singh's work points out that the area worked by bees will remain relatively small and the disrupting of rows or interplanting of pollenless plants with the others would be helpful.

Singh's work is often referred to, for indeed it is unique. Observing individual bees for long periods of time, as he did, requires infinite patience and time. Primary among the many questions raised by Singh's work is whether or not bees mark their foraging areas or territories and perhaps deter other bees from entering them.

Size of the insect as a consideration in pollination

In certain instances a large bee is needed to trigger the pollinating mechanism of the flower. Two examples are the legumes alfalfa and birdsfoot trefoil, which have similar flower structures. There is a large standard petal, and the nectary lies at the throat of this petal. Additionally, two wing petals surround the keel, which contains the male and female flower parts. In alfalfa, there is physical movement of the parts within the keel, and a fairly large bee, one at least approaching the size of the honey bee, is necessary to trigger the mechanism. In the case of birdsfoot trefoil the bee must weigh enough to force the male and female parts out of the tip of the keel and into contact with the bee.

Over a period of several years I have collected, by sweeping, pollinating insects from many flowering plants in the Northeast. It has been observed that there are twice as many solitary bees as there are honey bees. However, the great majority of these bees that I found were very small.

In one instance, for example, on white sweet clover (*Meliotus alba*) 1,255 solitary bees which weighed 5.1 grams were collected. At the same time the 58 honey bees which were collected in the sweep net weighed 4.8 grams. Thus, the weight of these two groups of insects was almost the same, but in this instance the wild bees outnumbered the honey bees more than 20 to 1.

This was an exception; in no other instance were so many wild bees, and so few honey bees, collected on a single day. However, there were instances which were not totally dissimilar as a result of collecting on yellow sweet clover (*Melilotus officinalis*), yellow rocket (*Barbarea vulgaris*), raspberry (*Rubus* sp.), and alfalfa (*Medicago sativa*).

These data may come as a surprise to those who are familiar with bumble bees and the large, bumble-bee-like carpenter bee. These large insects are not so numerous as they would appear, and in using the sweeping technique to collect wild bees, one obtains only a few of them. However, when one looks at a large field, the presence of these large insects is most obvious, and they are credited with accomplishing much more cross-pollination than they actually do. But, this is not to say that these large insects are useless for, indeed, they are very important. Bumble bee biology has been studied by many people in hopes that they might be used commercially, or semicommercially, as pollinators. However, several problems have arisen, and bumble bees have not yet been exploited for this purpose.

The future for pollination

In this chapter we have discussed only a few pollination problems and certain of the peculiar habits of bees as regards pollination. Each plant has different pollination requirements and these, as well as special climatic conditions, soil types, and cultural practices, must be taken into account when considering how one is to undertake the pollination of a particular crop.

The number of bees rented for pollination varies from state to state and area to area. In New York State less than 10 per cent of the bees are used or rented annually for commercial pollination purposes. In California a great number of colonies are used for the pollination of alfalfa and almonds. In Arizona too, many bees are rented for commercial pollination. In Michigan there has been an increased number of bees rented for the pollination of cucumbers and blueberries. However, in the country as a whole, not much more than 10 per cent of our honey bee colonies are used commercially for pollination, and the beekeepers compensated for their efforts. Thus, the emphasis in the commercial beekeeping industry in the United States is on the production of honey and beeswax.

In many areas, the role of honey bees in the pollination of the wild fruit, nut, and berry crops essential for wildlife is underestimated. Wild bees are often important in this regard, but they are not abundant in all areas. Generalizations on the subject of pollination are difficult to make, but as the agricultural system in the United States is intensified, there will clearly continue to be a need for pollination specialists, beekeepers, and researchers who devote exclusive attention to this aspect of agriculture.

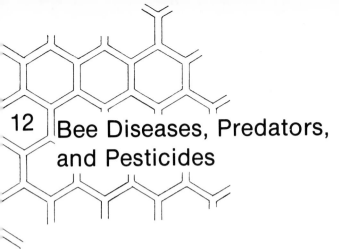

The reproductive potential of all free living plants and animals is such that, if any one of them were allowed to reproduce unchecked, it would soon overpopulate the earth. Diseases and predators may be regarded in two ways. They are destructive, and it is in this context that we normally think of them. Their benefit, of course, is that they prevent overpopulation by other species. At the same time, disease organisms and predators are themselves plants and animals that are only trying to survive on earth as best they can.

The thrust of modern agriculture, which is increased production per unit of land, investment, and per grower, involves not only the intense use of the land but the control of diseases, pests, and predators that might make such agriculture unprofitable.

Pesticides, an important part of our modern agricultural system, include insecticides, herbicides, rodenticides, and other chemicals which kill or slow the growth of harmful or destructive organisms, or at least those organisms that men consider in this light. Since honey bees are insects, they are adversely affected by certain of the modern-day pesticides which are designed to kill insects. In areas where agriculture is intense, the bees must be removed if they are to survive; however, not all pesticides have proven injurious to honey bees. Pesticides safe to use when bees are flying in the vicinity, and methods of applying them, are discussed below.

It is perhaps remarkable that there are so few diseases and predators of honey bees. Generally speaking, crowding is considered deleterious to a plant or animal species, for under these conditions communicable diseases can spread rapidly. Honey bees in a colony are crowded together more closely than most animals. The fact too, that honey bees maintain a constant, high temperature in their brood nest, 33°C (92°F) or higher, and a high humidity, suggests that their nest might provide an excellent environment for a number of parasites and pathogens. The reserves of pollen and honey could be useful to a wide range of animals; one hundred pounds of honey, not an uncommon quantity to be found in a honey bee colony, plus several pounds of pollen, could supply the energy needs of a great many pests and predators. Still, honey bees have evolved a highly efficient system to protect themselves, their young, and their food reserves.

Natural systems protecting honey bees and their food

Although honey bees have problems with some bacteria, fungi, viruses, protozoa, and predators, they have several natural systems of protection. These include their weapon, the sting, a routine of cleanliness unsurpassed in the animal world, and special methods of preserving and protecting pollen, honey, and royal jelly, which are their food.

The sting is clearly the first line of defense against other insects, including other honey bees, which would rob the hive, and bigger predators, such as skunks, bears, and men. Colonies have guard bees which post themselves at the entrance(s) of the hive and which are apparently able to differentiate between those which should enter and those which should not.[1] The sting is useful in

1. A colony normally has one entrance. However, a colony in an old tree or house, or even in an old beehive, may have many entrances merely because there are holes. Having several entrances does a colony no harm, but each entrance must be protected. The number of guard bees varies. When nectar and pollen are available in quantity, there are few guard bees; when there is a dearth, and colonies might rob one another, there are many guards. Likewise, if a skunk starts to feed nightly in an apiary, the number of guards will increase in the disturbed colonies.

wintertime as well as in the summer. This has been discussed in Chapter 7.

Honey bees are fastidious about removing any debris or materials that should not be present in the hive, and their method of doing so can be observed if small pieces of grass, straw, or sticks are introduced into an observation hive. This system of cleanliness seems to have to do with the division of labor within the colony. The fact that worker bees of house age are continually inspecting all parts of the hive interior suggests, to speak anthropomorphically, that they are looking for work to be done. Usually, a bee will grasp a foreign object within a few seconds after it has been introduced into a hive, and will start to move it toward the entrance. In a single frame or two-frame observation hive, it is seldom more than five minutes before an object inserted into the top of the hive appears at the entrance. Even more interesting, instead of dropping debris immediately at the entrance, the bees carry it some distance from the hive. Honey bees treat their dead in the same way; they are removed promptly. There are exceptions to this statement, and beekeepers should become familiar with them so as to better protect their bees. One may find a natural accumulation of dead bees on the bottomboard or in front of a hive in the spring. The accumulation may come about because inclement weather prevented removal of the bees or because poor food caused an excessively high death rate. Weak colonies do not always remove their dead promptly. In the case of a pesticide loss, large numbers of bees often accumulate at the hive entrance. (Not all bees affected by pesticides die in the field; this varies with the pesticide.) Under normal circumstances, however, the bees carry the dead some distance from the hive, and thus remove from the vicinity of the colony a possible source of infection. Worker bees may fly 50 or 100 feet from a hive before dropping a foreign object such as a stick or a dead bee.

Spaces within the colony that are too small to be used for brood rearing or food storage are sealed off and so are not available to harbor disease organisms or predators. Bees collect propolis from the gums and resins of trees and use it, as one might use varnish, to seal rough areas and cracks and crevices in the hive. Gums and resins from pine and poplar trees contain terpenes which have both a bacteriostatic and bactericidal effect. They are, for the honey bee, natural disinfectants. These substances are readily available in most parts of the world and form an important part of the internal protection system in the bee hive.

Honey is the chief food of the adult honey bees and their source of carbohydrates, but in addition to honey, bees also store large quantities of pollen, which provide them with protein and fat. The third food item found within the honey bee colony is royal jelly, a glandular secretion from worker bees that is used to feed both young worker larvae and queen larvae. Investigations have revealed that all three of these food items contain natural protective systems which function both physically and chemically.

When one examines a honey bee colony, it will be noted that pollens of a like color, and presumably from the same source, are stored in the same cells. Rarely is pollen of two colors found in one cell. The same is true of honey. This is especially evident when bees gather honey from two markedly different sources at the same time. When comb honey was a common product several decades ago, one of the problems faced by its producers was that the end of the clover season in the northern states often overlapped with the beginning of the buckwheat nectar flow. If there happened to be unfilled cells in a comb of clover honey, the bees might fill these with the coal-black honey made from buckwheat, and the light, white, cells of clover honey made a sharp contrast to the cells with buckwheat honey. This was often little understood by the consuming public. While it is conjecture, we presume that the separation of food in this manner served as a safeguard; if certain pollens or honeys are contaminated, the fact that they are not mixed within the hive would lessen the spread of the contamination.

Stored pollen is protected in at least two additional ways within the hive. First, bees never fill the pollen storage cells to more than about 80 per cent of their capacity. If the pollen is then stored for a long period, honey is added on top of it and serves as a safeguard. Pain and Maugenet (1961) found that several microorganisms worked together to form a natural ensilage in stored pollen. *Pseudomonas* (a bacterium) acts to consume the oxygen present. Yeast causes a fermentation which partially digests the pollen. Most important is *Lactobacillus,* another bacterium that produces lactic acid, which is a good preservative. The action of these bacteria and yeast have little or no deleterious effect on the food value of stored pollen; in fact, the action of the yeast is probably useful.

Of the several natural factors which offer honey protection, perhaps most important is that it is an acid medium with a very low pH, and as such it is an inhospitable medium for the growth of most microorganisms. This low pH, of course, also gives honey a tart taste and is part of the reason that it is so appealing to man as a food item. Also, honey is a supersaturated sugar solution and has a very high osmotic pressure. A classic paper pointing to the value of honey's high osmotic pressure was written by Walter G. Sackett (1919). He introduced several microorganisms into honey and found that they all died, in a relatively short time, simply because the high osmotic pressure extracted water from their systems. Thus, the reason for the reduction of the moisture content of the honey is clear; in addition to saving space, it is part of the natural defense system.

Sackett observed that diluted honey is also an unsatisfactory medium for the microorganisms which he introduced into it. However, it was not until 1963 that Jonathan W. White and his colleagues discovered that honey contains an enzyme, glucose oxidase, presumably added to it by the worker bees. Glucose oxidase attacks glucose, one of the two common sugars in honey, and in the process forms gluconic acid and hydrogen peroxide. Hydrogen peroxide is a powerful bactericidal agent. While glucose oxidase is present in honey, it is not active in normal honey for in this case the low pH and the osmotic pressure appear to be sufficient to protect the honey. Only when additional moisture is added to honey does the enzyme become active. The glucose oxidase system becomes important when honey bees dilute the honey which they feed to the larvae.

Blum, Novak, and Taber (1959) found that royal jelly contains a fatty acid which has antibiotic properties one-fourth as active as that of penicillin and one-fifth as active as chlortetracycline. This activity is sufficiently high to give the royal jelly protection against several forms of bacteria.

There is one group of microorganisms which live in honey. These are the so-called osmophilic yeasts belonging to the genus *Zygosaccharomyces*. There are several species of these yeasts, and they appear to be very common in nature. One never finds nectar that does not contain at least a few active yeast cells. While the osmophilic yeasts can grow in liquids with high osmotic pressure, they cannot multiply when the moisture content of honey is reduced below about 19 per cent. Depending upon the local environment, honey normally contains 14 to 18 per cent moisture and so, under most circumstances, is protected against the growth of these yeasts.

Honey is hygroscopic (it absorbs moisture from the air with ease). In part, it is for this reason that bees control the humidity within the hive; if they did not do so, the honey might pick up moisture at its surface, and at this point the osmophilic yeasts might grow. The hygroscopicity of honey may pose problems for both bees and beekeepers. The honey at the surface of a cell may contain more moisture than that deeper in the cell, and this moisture may encourage yeast growth at the surface. In a beekeeper's open storage vessel, a barrel, a can, or even a one-pound jar, honey on the surface may pick up moisture and ferment — whereas the honey just beneath the surface may not be attacked by the yeast. Most beekeepers and packers pasteurize their honey to kill any yeast spores it may contain, even then they keep the storage vessels tightly sealed and in an unheated building where fermentation is less likely to occur.

The osmophilic yeasts, genus *Zygosaccharomyces,* will grow in diluted honey; the glucose oxidase system, even though it is active, is apparently only strong enough to slow their growth, not to stop it. If the stored honey is not protected by bees or men, it may ferment, producing carbon dioxide and alcohol, and under these circumstances a portion of the stored food may be lost. The osmophilic yeasts are quite different from those yeasts used to produce normal ethyl alcohol, and they have no useful purpose insofar as man is concerned. The yeasts used commercially, including the bread yeasts and those used to make beer, wine, and distilled beverages such as whiskey and gin, belong to the genus *Saccharomyces*. It is sometimes stated that the natural yeasts found in honey are used to make mead, but this is not correct: *Saccharomyces* will not grow in sugar solutions with more than about 30 per cent total solids; *Zygosaccharomyces* grow in solutions containing about 30 to 81 per cent solids.

American foulbrood

The most destructive of the bee diseases is American foulbrood, an infectious disease of honey bee larvae which kills in the late larval or the early pupal stage. It affects only honey bees and is found in almost all countries where they are kept.

The terms "American" and "European" have no special meaning insofar as the origin and distribution of the two foulbrood diseases are concerned. Although in a few isolated regions and countries no American foulbrood is found, European foulbrood is found everywhere honey bees are kept. The diseases acquired their names because much of the early research on their respective biologies was done in America and Europe.

The causative organism for American foulbrood is *Bacillus larvae*. It is especially interesting to the biologist because, in the spore or resting stage, the microorganism may remain alive for several decades — no one is sure precisely how long. For this reason, control is extremely difficult. Apiary inspectors report cases of American foulbrood occurring in equipment which has been in storage for periods of ten, twenty, or more years. The information suggests that the equipment may have been stored after the original colony had died of American foulbrood, and that the disease reappeared when the equipment was put back into use.

Because of American foulbrood, many states spend thousands of dollars annually for apiary inspection. This disease is the reason that bees on combs are not allowed to cross the Canadian border and certain state borders. Most states require that colonies of bees which are brought across their borders, sold, or moved, must be examined by an apiary inspector. Most states also require that apiaries which produce and sell queen bees and package bees be inspected and the packages and queens carry certificates of inspection.

American foulbrood is relatively simple to identify for the symptoms are quite uniform, and the stage at which the bacillus kills is rarely affected by other bee diseases. Since the insect is killed in the late larval or early pupal stages, it lies flat on its back in the cell, whereas larvae killed by European foulbrood usually die at a younger age and are still coiled in their cells. Often, in the case of American foulbrood, the remnants of a leg or the mouthparts are visible, protruding upward from the dead body. As time progresses, the glistening white larva turns brown and finally, as it dries in the bottom of the cell, becomes a black scale.

Resistance to American foulbrood

Several researchers and beekeepers have attempted to breed a honey bee resistant to American foulbrood. Resistant bees have been found, but unfortunately they often show weaknesses such as susceptibility to other diseases, particularly European foulbrood, and this has made their use questionable. One of the reasons for actively pursuing research on reproduction and mating in honey bees is so that we might make better use of the resistant strains that already exist.

For a number of years, Walter C. Rothenbuhler (1968) of Ohio State University has used a strain of bees resistant to American foulbrood in his research work. He has studied the genetics of resistance to American foulbrood in honey bees and has found that at least two genes are involved. One gene allows the bees to remove the sticky, gummy, dead larvae or pupae from their cells; the second makes it possible for the bees to uncap the cells that contain them; not all bees are able to do this. It has been found that the larvae from some resistant strains of bees are less susceptible to the pathogen.

Control by burning

Most state apiary inspectors, and most state apiculturists, believe that the best method of controlling American foulbrood is to burn and destroy infected colonies. First the bees are killed, usually with a gas in the late evening or in the early morning, and then the dead bees and the combs are burned in a deep pit. All equipment made of wood which is three-quarters of an inch or more thick is scorched to disinfect it; the rest is burned. Many people find it hard to accept the destruction of whole colonies of honey bees by fire, including those that may contain only a single larva dead from American foulbrood. This is especially a problem when a colony contains a hundred or more pounds of honey. However, the consensus is that this is the only effective method of control.

New York State has had a rigorous burning program in effect since 1929. During the first five years, between 5 and 7 per cent of the colonies inspected were found to be infected and were destroyed. However, by 1943, only 1.07 per cent of the colonies were diseased. Unfortunately, at this time the problems associated with the Second World War left less money and fewer men available for apiary inspection. During this time, too, beekeeping became a popular avocation engaged in by many persons not familiar with honey bee biology. American foulbrood spread to such an extent that in 1946 nearly 4 per cent of the colonies inspected were burned. As the number of colonies inspected increased during the next several years, the degree of infection decreased, and in 1958, for the first time in the history of New

York State, fewer than 1 per cent of the colonies inspected had to be destroyed. The strict program has continued since that time, and each year the percentage of colonies found infected with American foulbrood and destroyed by fire has been either slightly above or slightly below 1 per cent, which is considered to be a tolerable disease rate. Because so many people go into and out of the beekeeping business, including those who are knowledgeable about bee diseases and those who are not, we probably cannot hope to improve the situation greatly. The records of the State Apiary Inspector show that inspectors may work for several days without finding disease only to find a number of colonies with a high rate of infection in a single abandoned or unattended apiary.

There is usually less disease in rural than in urban areas. One finds many disease organisms in the vicinity of city dumps, and it is presumed that bees may pick up American foulbrood from discarded honey carrying the *Bacillus larvae*. Any exposed honey is attractive to bees. Although honey infected with American foulbrood is perfectly safe for human consumption, bees exposed to it can be infected. In urban areas there are also more beekeepers, including beginners, who know little about disease. Swarms which escape in urban areas usually have little difficulty in finding a suitable homesite, usually an abandoned or old building where they may nest in walls or under eaves. Such colonies are not inspected for American foulbrood because of their inaccessibility, and they may harbor the disease; when the colonies are finally killed by foulbrood and robbed out by bees from nearby colonies, the disease is spread. For these reasons some apiary inspectors believe that bee inspection in or near large cities is futile. In the southern states the wax moth is a great aid to the apiary inspector and the beekeeper; this moth will enter and consume the comb in any weak or dying colony, thus lessening the chances that the infected residual honey will be stolen.

Shaking diseased colonies

If the bees, including the queen, from a colony infected with

American foulbrood are shaken from the combs into a box, confined there for four to six hours, then put into a hive containing new frames and foundation, with no old drawn comb, they will usually survive and not carry the infection to the new hive. If, on the other hand, bees are shaken from an infected hive onto old comb, brood in the new hive is most likely to show the disease several weeks after the bees are settled in their new home. We believe that, in the process of being shaken, confined in a box and subsequently placed on foundation, the bees consume any honey they are carrying, and with the honey, any American foulbrood organisms. Since at least a few days are required for the bees to draw out new comb foundation, and it will presumably be several days before larvae appear in the new hive, there is thought to be little likelihood of bees carrying the disease with them. This method works well for those who believe that the bees are worth saving.

The rate of occurrence of American foulbrood in colonies properly shaken is usually less than 1 or 2 per cent. Still, most commercial beekeepers do not feel that it is profitable to shake colonies. Shaking, of course, requires a certain amount of time and effort, and whether or not it is worthwhile depends upon the time of year and whether or not the colonies have time to construct new combs and gather the honey required for the following winter or dormant season; it also depends upon the availability and the cost of labor. Apiary inspectors do not encourage shaking because they know that unless the process is carefully undertaken it will not be successful.

Drugs for American foulbrood control

In 1944 it was discovered that sulfathiazole would control American foulbrood. Since that date the subject has been researched by hundreds of persons around the world, and there have been almost endless discussions about whether or not drugs should be used for disease control. Good arguments have been made by persons on both sides. In print, the more conservative dogma of those who prefer to control American foulbrood by burning, dominates; in practice, it is known that many commercial beekeepers, and hobbyists as well, use various drugs to control American foulbrood. Apiary inspectors report that hobbyists are seldom effective in treating the disease because of their lack of knowledge of the biology of the honey bee.

Those in favor of treating American foulbrood with drugs point to the tremendous cost of destroying 1 or 2 per cent of the colonies of honey bees in the United States annually. Those who advocate burning point out that this is a relatively low degree of infection and that the beekeeper must also take into account the cost of treatment. This last argument is immediately countered with the thought that inspection costs are high, too. In return, one may point out that even the use of drugs does not negate the need for inspection.

There are two major arguments against the use of drugs for the control of American foulbrood. First, the colonies must be routinely treated, usually two or three times a year. In states where there is no inspection service, commercial beekeepers report that, because of the high cost of labor, it is cheaper to use drugs than to make routine inspections for disease. Labor costs are not so important for beekeepers with only a few colonies; I take the view that such beekeepers should spend their time keeping their equipment in good repair and carrying out a sound management scheme. Under these circumstances, burning infected colonies is the cheapest and most effective way of controlling American foulbrood.

Second, drugs might sometimes be found in honey which is offered for sale on the market. Beekeepers are proud that their production of honey involves the use of very few, and in many cases none, of the modern chemicals or pesticides so commonly used in other agricultural pursuits. This has special appeal among those people who are interested in producing and consuming only natural foods. At the same time, those persons who advocate the use of drugs for the control of American foulbrood have data to show that, if a drug is properly applied, there is no danger of contaminating the honey. Drugs for the treatment of American foulbrood are usually used only in the early spring and late fall. If the drugs are properly applied then, there is no need to use them immediately before, or at the time, that the honey flow is in progress. The concern, of course, is that not every beekeeper will understand this, especially those who are new to the industry. Meanwhile, research for new and more effective drugs for the control of American foulbrood continues, as do the arguments concerning their use.

Ethylene Oxide Fumigation

A. S. Michael of the U. S. Department of Agriculture reported in 1964 that ethylene oxide fumigation of combs killed wax moth larvae, and after 18 hours of exposure, the *Bacillus* in American foulbrood scales. His tests were conducted under precise laboratory conditions and on a small scale. Subsequently, other researchers attempted to sterilize combs and equipment infected with American foulbrood by fumigation under polyethylene tarps or in polyethylene bags. However, these treatments were not effective as some active *Bacillus* survived the fumigation.

Robinson, Smith, and Packard (1972) reported on experiments conducted with 32 nucleus (small) colonies. They treated infected American foulbrood combs with a mixture containing 12 per cent ethylene oxide and 88 per cent freon. The pressure in the autoclave which was used for the treatment was held at 30 pounds per square inch after preheating. After the combs had been fumigated, they were used to make up the 32 new colonies; only treated combs were used in the test. Fifteen months after the nucleus colonies were established, all the combs were combined into six, two-story colonies which were kept under observation for more than three years. The disease did not recur in any of these colonies. Thus, under precise conditions it has been shown that ethylene oxide fumigation can be used to sterilize infected beekeeping equipment.

Several eastern states, including Maryland, Virginia, and New Jersey, have fumigation chambers of varying sizes which they use to treat diseased combs. While some consider these units experimental, others believe that they are successful and practical. Most of the chambers are converted autoclaves and are fixed in position. Both beekeepers and inspectors bring equipment to them for treatment.

It is possible that elaborate equipment, mounted on a truck, could be developed to fumigate and thereby sterilize equipment and combs infected with American foulbrood microorganisms, but whether the equipment would be useful enough to justify its purchase price and maintenance costs is questionable.

The stress diseases

Three diseases of bees are often considered as a unit. These are called stress diseases since they are most common in the spring when colonies are weak, or when colonies become weakened. Often, at the end of winter, there are too few bees to form a cluster to adequately cover the brood and to protect it against fluctuating temperatures and dampness. The stress diseases often appear soon after colonies have lost a large number of adults because of pesticides. These diseases are European foulbrood and sacbrood, both of which kill in the larval stage, and nosema, which attacks adult bees and may shorten their lives.

All three of the diseases are less common in the South than in the North, though they may be found almost everywhere on earth where honey bees are kept.

Drugs and antibiotics are available for the treatment of two of these diseases, but for the third, sacbrood, a virus, there is no known treatment. The use of drugs for European foulbrood and nosema is perhaps justified and even necessary under certain conditions, for example, when commercial beekeepers are forcing colony development in Canada and other northern areas, and the short production season is further shortened by adverse weather. However, treatment with drugs has the same drawbacks that it does in the case of American foulbrood.

The most important point is that the beekeeper can do much to relieve or eliminate certain stresses which may be placed on colonies, especially in the spring. The rules are simple. Colonies should be located where they are exposed to a maximum of sunlight and where there is good air and water drainage. A desirable apiary site has a slope to the east or south. Providing the bees with a supply of fresh water prevents water collectors from returning to the hive with water contaminated from bee fecal matter and disease organisms. Placing colonies on hive stands or on some other device which keeps the bottomboards off the ground and dry is helpful since evaporation from the wet or damp bottomboards may cool the hive interior. During the parts of the year when the bees are more or less inactive, especially in the early spring, late fall, and winter, the colony entrances should be restricted to prevent rain from being driven into the hive entrance and to reduce any adverse effects which might be brought about by strong winds. Colonies can also better protect themselves from robber bees if their entrances are reduced.

These measures, which are just common sense and good management practice, not only help to protect the colonies against the stress diseases, but otherwise serve to encourage colony prosperity.

European foulbrood

European foulbrood, like American foulbrood, has a name which is not descriptive of the disease. European foulbrood affects larval bees but kills much earlier in the larval life than does American foulbrood. Larvae killed by European foulbrood are usually still coiled in their cells, and thus the dead larvae do not lie flat as do larvae killed by American foulbrood.

According to L. Bailey (1963), *Streptococcus pluton* is the primary causative organism in the case of European foulbrood. However, several secondary invaders (bacteria) are also found in association with European foulbrood, including *Bacterium eurydice, Bacillus alvei, Bacillus laterosporus,* and *Bacillus para-alvei.* Three other bacilli have also been found in association with European foulbrood, but their roles are not understood. At various times the secondary microorganisms associated with European foulbrood have been thought to be the primary invaders, but proof of this is lacking.

The causative microorganism of European foulbrood, unlike that of American foulbrood, does not form a long-lived resistant spore. However, larvae killed by European foulbrood or fecal matter from larvae which have survived an infection will remain infective for up to approximately three years, according to Bailey.

A larva killed by European foulbrood does not form a gummy, sticky mass as is the case with American foulbrood. Furthermore, since the larvae are killed at an earlier stage and usually before the cells are capped, house bees are able to detect the dead and remove them from the hive before the infection becomes widespread. This is true, of course, only if the colony is not under stress, and if the bees are free to undertake the task of removing dead larvae.

The first bees brought to the United States in the 1600's and used throughout the country were from northern Europe. These included the bees from western Europe, called "black bees" or "German bees," which are quite susceptible to European foulbrood. This was one of the primary reasons for the importation of the Italian bee in the late 1800's. The Italian bees are remarkably resistant to European foulbrood. They are referred to by beekeepers as being "good housekeepers," and quickly and easily remove the dead larvae from their cells (see races of bees, Chapter 1).

Recommendations for the control of European foulbrood include requeening, relocating, or improving the apiary site so as to provide more sunlight and better water drainage, and last, and only if necessary, the feeding of certain drugs. Requeening is most important since a young, vigorous queen will lay more eggs than an old queen and thereby help to build the colony population.

Nosema disease

Nosema disease is caused by a microsporidian, called *Nosema apis*. Several insects have nosema microorganisms which live in their gastrointestinal tracts, but *Nosema apis,* like other bee diseases, affects only honey bees. (However, it does appear that many of the microorganisms which will affect *Apis mellifera* will affect the other species of *Apis* as well.) *Nosema apis* was described by Zander in 1909 in Germany.[2]

An excellent biology on *Nosema apis* was prepared by Kudo (1924). He makes no recommendations concerning the treatment of nosema disease, but the papers which he cites seem to confirm that the best defense lies in the use of preventative measures.

In 1952 Katznelson and Jamieson discovered that Fumidil B, an antibiotic produced by Abbott Laboratories, was effective in the control of nosema disease. This discovery touched off a controversy between beekeepers north and south which is still raging. According to complaints from the northern states and Canada which are directed at the package bee producers from the southern states, bees arriving from the South are infected with *Nosema apis,* and this affects the subsequent development of the colony in the North. Perhaps more important, queens produced in the southern states may also be infected with nosema, and northern beekeepers claim that this, in large part, is the cause of queen supersedure in

2. E. F. Phillips of Cornell University had a favorite story about *Nosema apis.* Soon after the disease was discovered, Zander and others in Europe were certain that it would destroy the beekeeping industry. Phillips, then head of the USDA Bee Culture Laboratory in Beltsville, Maryland, sent G. F. White, who had done much of the early work on brood diseases of honey bees, to Germany to work with Zander for several months. Immediately upon his return to the United States, White and Phillips had a long conversation concerning nosema; White had become convinced, while he was working with Zander, that nosema is highly destructive, and he urged Phillips to take steps to halt the importation of bees from Europe so that nosema could not gain entrance into this country. After several hours of conversation, Phillips asked White how one would diagnose nosema. Thereupon, the two men went into the nearby experimental apiary, and White pulled the gastrointestinal tract from a bee to show how simple it is to make a nosema diagnosis. Much to his surprise, the first bee which White pulled apart contained the microorganism. The apiary was carefully inspected and nosema was found to be present in all colonies. Subsequently, White traveled around the United States and found nosema almost everywhere. Phillips, laughingly, at this point acknowledged that he had been duped by the worrisome letters from Zander. As a result of their experience, Phillips and White suggested that the best defense against nosema disease was good management and the same methods which would protect colonies from European foulbrood and sacbrood. While Phillips did not use the term "stress diseases," he certainly thought along these lines.

the early spring. For the person who uses package bees in the northern states for honey production, this can be a serious matter. The season is short and if colonies do not develop rapidly, or if queens fail, the colony is lost as a production unit. Persons who use package bees for honey production usually order about 20 per cent more packages than they need; they recognize that about this number will fail because of nosema and other problems. When the queen in a package unit fails, the only recourse is to combine the queenless colony with a queenright one. Still, this is a tremendous loss for any beekeeper to sustain, and naturally the northern producers want steps taken to eliminate nosema infections.

Package bee producers in the southern states, on the other hand, state that nosema is not a problem in their areas and that the feeding of drugs is expensive and at the same time has not been shown to be effective. The question appears to be one of coordinating the research, north and south, so as to determine the best course of action.

Sacbrood

Sacbrood is caused by a virus. In most areas it is not a serious disease despite the fact that it is fairly common. It is usually more severe in colonies already having difficulty with European foulbrood and nosema.

Sacbrood gets its name from the fact that the larvae it has killed may be lifted from the cells like sacks. They lie flat in their cells, and the cells are usually capped. The outer skin of the dead larvae becomes crusty and hard, and their interior disintegrates into a watery mass. I have never seen a bee killed in the prepupal stage by sacbrood, that is, with appendages developed, and it does not appear that this occurs.

Only a few people have studied sacbrood. Bailey devotes two pages in his text to the subject. He states that the virus survives for only about three weeks in dead larvae or honey, and he wonders how it persists from year to year. According to him, there is some evidence that susceptibility to the disease is inherited. Sacbrood is probably present everywhere that honey bees are kept.

Mammals which are pests

Bears, skunks, opossums, raccoons, and certain squirrels and mice sometimes may ravage bee hives and are a nuisance for the beekeeper; skunks and mice are especially abundant and are a problem for nearly all beekeepers. Some people consider all wildlife a national heritage; the beekeeper who suffers financial loss because of these animals often views the problem in a different light.

Bears

Bears, in certain areas, north and south, east and west, in both the United States and Canada, can be more destructive in an apiary than thieves, fire, weather, or disease. Bears destroy only a small percentage of our honey bee colonies annually, but the beekeeper who suffers such damage does not soon forget it. In fact, the only recourse most beekeepers have is to sell a few pictures of the bear damage to a journal or magazine which might publish a story about the problem because of its interesting aspects.

Bears are fascinating animals. Their food habits are not unlike those of a pig; they will eat almost anything. They roam over large areas in search of food. Although bears eat some honey, they seem to prefer the brood, both larvae and pupae. Of course, to admit this is heresy, for the popular image of a bear eating honey has sold many pounds of honey. Beekeepers who have had bears ravage their apiaries will testify that they find many supers turned upside down, the bottombars torn out, and the contents of the brood nest consumed.

Bears feeding in an apiary seldom take more than one or two colonies a night. Their habits suggest that they learn that bees flying from a moved hive return to the old site if it is nearby. The author has been in apiaries where bears have carried supers of comb and frames of brood and honey several hundred feet from the site before feeding upon them. By doing so they avoid many stings.

Not all bears attack bee hives, in fact, the number which do so is small, but once a bear starts to feed in an apiary, it does not stop until the food supply is exhausted. A bear may take several weeks to consume all the food available to it in a large commercial apiary. Many beekeepers do not visit their apiaries more often than six to twelve times a year, and it may be several weeks before a beekeeper visits an apiary being torn apart by a bear.

There is no good defense against a bear except to remove the hives or the bear. Colonies have been placed on high platforms, and electric fences have been used against bears with some success. Bears which have never fed on a beehive may be driven away by an electric fence, but an experienced bear will dig under an electric fence to gain access to the apiary. In some states, conservation departments have trapped offending bears with humane-type, live traps and carried them to a new territory. However, since most bears may roam over an area twenty-five or more miles in diameter it is necessary to move them a great distance.

Four states, Pennsylvania, Vermont, New Hampshire, and Minnesota, compensate beekeepers who lose bees because of bears. In most instances beekeepers cannot claim compensation for bees lost a second time in the same apiary, even though the losses are several years apart. Beekeepers have no objection to this for bees are not normally kept in the areas which harbor bears. There are some exceptions, but generally, the type of terrain which will support a bear is not good beekeeping territory. The beekeeper's major problem comes from those bears which wander several miles from their normal habitat and into good farming territory.

It is claimed that there is some illegal killing of bears by shooting, trapping, and poisoning by beekeepers in certain states, especially states which license bear hunters, protect bears, and will not admit that bears may damage property. In the eastern states, where bears have been a problem for beekeepers, their numbers have been declining gradually, and will probably continue to do so. It is expected that bears will be less of a problem in the future.

Skunks

Skunks will eat adult bees. To capture the bees they approach the entrance of a hive, scratch on it, and when a guard bee appears at the entrance, the skunk swats and kills it and then eats the bee. The skunk then repeats the process and will feed for an hour or more a night, night after night, in this manner. Most feeding on bees by skunks takes place in the early evening or morning hours just after sunset or before the sun rises. Of course, it is the rare hive from which only one bee will emerge at a time when the entrance is rapped upon by a skunk; thus, skunks are often severely stung when feeding on hives. Persons who have watched skunks feeding on hives report that the skunk will move up and down rows of hives in an apiary, seeking hives from which only a few bees will emerge at a time. Skunks which select weaker, or less populous hives of bees, will be stung less than those feeding on hives with a greater number of bees. Thus, the ravages of skunks are especially troublesome since they make the weak colonies weaker.

Skunk feeding is easy to detect. The front of the hive being ravaged by a skunk will be muddied. The grass in front of a hive will be torn up and matted down by the skunks fighting stinging bees. Persons who have seen skunks feeding report that they will roll, twist and turn in the grass or mud trying to remove one or more stinging bees from their bodies. Skunks which have fed on bees have been dissected, and stings have been found in their mouths, throats and stomachs; obviously, being stung does not deter a skunk from feeding on bees.

Not all skunks will eat bees. Some are apparently driven away by stinging bees and others never learn to do so. Mother skunks have been observed with young, presumably teaching them to feed on bees at a colony entrance. Skunks will feed on bees at any time of year. Interestingly, skunks which are stung in the act of feeding at a colony entrance do not release their defensive odor.

There is no defense against skunks except to move the bees or do away with the skunk. Since skunks are protected fur-bearing animals is most states, killing them is illegal. This poses a problem for the beekeeper since a skunk that is allowed to continue to feed will do so *ad infinitum.* Colonies of bees which are being preyed upon by skunks are kept in a state of alarm for long periods of time;

beekeepers report that such colonies are most difficult to manage because bees from them are apparently more prone to sting than bees from unscathed colonies.

Opossums

Opossums, or possums, as they are more commonly known, have migrated into the northern states, especially in the eastern United States in the past several decades. The possum is not especially well suited to life in the rigorous north, and it is not uncommon to find possums which have lost their tails and the tips of their ears from frostbite. The animal is not territorial, but it migrates, apparently aimlessly, in any direction.

Possums are not a serious threat to beekeepers. While they will attack a hive in much the same manner as a skunk, they are less inclined to do so. In many years of observing activities in the University apiaries, I know of only one possum which worked its way into the top of two colonies wrapped for winter in black paper. For several days the possum apparently fed on bees emerging from the hole in the inner cover, which was on top of one of the hives. The possum was detected and removed before it had done much damage.

Squirrels

Squirrels may nest in a house, barn, or in the case of a beekeeper's establishment, a remote storage building. In the north, beekeepers often store their combs in unheated buildings for winter. Storing combs in a cold building is the best way to protect them against moths since the moths cannot survive freezing temperatures. However, a remote building is a desirable haven for a red squirrel which may destroy hundreds of combs in a winter if it is undetected. Not only will the squirrels build nests in hives without bees, but they will also chew stored combs, presumably obtaining food from the cells of pollen which are present in almost all old combs.

The best protection against squirrels is a tight building which prevents their entry. However, rats will often open holes in buildings which may later be used by squirrels. Stored combs may be protected against rats and mice by poisons which may be left in storage buildings for that precise purpose; interestingly, at least in my experience, squirrels are not inclined to eat ordinary rat and mouse poisons. Squirrels will eat certain nuts, and these may be used as baits to capture them.

Mice

Mice probably cause more damage to beekeeping equipment than all the other mammals together. Not only will mice nest in, chew, and destroy unprotected, stored combs, but they will also live in active beehives during the winter season.

In the late fall, mice move from their field nests to better protected cavities — stone walls, fallen and hollow trees, buildings, and beehives. Apparently, a mouse is able to walk into the entrance of a hive when the bees are cold and clustered and to construct a nest within inches of the clustered bees. How they do so without being attacked and driven away by the bees is not known, but thousands of beekeepers will testify to finding mice, with nests five or six inches in diameter, in their hives in the spring. While building its nest, a mouse may chew holes several inches in diameter in three to five adjacent combs, and by the time the nest is finally found and removed by the beekeeper, the comb is ruined. Supers of mouse-riddled combs may be placed on strong colonies of bees during the honey flow; at this time of the year the bees will clean the comb thoroughly, but will usually build drone comb, rather than worker comb, in the portion of the comb that has been chewed away by the mouse.

Mice sometimes rear a litter of young within a hive in the spring. A mouse nest is surrounded by an inch or more of insulation made from bits of grass, bark, leaves, old rags, and so forth. The bees may remove this material, given sufficient time, but in the spring the bees in a colony are much less numerous than in the summer and fall, and it takes several weeks for the colony population to increase to the point that it can remove such a large object as a mouse nest. By the time the colony is able to remove the nest, it has been abandoned by the mouse or mice.

Observations of mice living in hives suggest that the mice enter and leave their nests when the bees are inactive, presumably at night. It is possible that mice obtain some food by eating dead bees from the bottomboard or the front of the hive. They may also consume the pollen, and perhaps the honey, in the area where they nest; however, mice will not attempt to capture or eat live honey bees. A mouse which builds a nest in a bee hive usually constructs it near the entrance and bottom of the hive, well away from the stored food. Furthermore, in observations of hives in which mice have lived in the winter, I have not seen chewed combs outside of the mouse nest proper. Apparently, too, mice close the entrance of their nest while they are inside the hive so that bees cannot enter and attack them.

There is sharp disagreement about how best to protect a hive against mouse damage. Many people advocate screening the colony entrance with hardware cloth so small that mice cannot move through it. This has several disadvantages. Small mice may still enter the hive. If the colony entrance is reduced too much, it may be easily clogged by dead bees during a severe winter. It is also possible that a skunk, or just the action of freezing rain and snow, may move the entrance reducer slightly so that a mouse may gain entrance. A beekeeper who has only a few colonies is in a better position to construct a mouse-proof entrance guard than is a beekeeper with several hundred or several thousand colonies of bees. A hobbyist, too, often has more opportunity to inspect colonies during the winter and to make adjustments to protect the hive.

Most beekeepers protect their stored equipment and hives against mice by placing poisoned wheat under, on top of, and often in the hive. A small quantity of poison is sufficient since most formulas are made so that only one or two grains of wheat will kill a mouse. The danger in using mouse poison is that the dead animals may later be eaten by another animal, though this does seem a remote possibility. Poisons which may be used to kill harmful mammals are closely regulated in many states, and persons who use these materials must often obtain a license or permit.

Birds as honey bee predators

Only rarely will one observe a bird feeding on live honey bees in the United States or Canada. However, in other parts of the world, especially Africa and Asia, there are several species of birds which prey on bees as they fly to and from their hives. My experience is limited to the Philippine spine-tailed swift, *Chaetura dubia,* a bird which would come in flocks of several hundred to the apiaries in the Philippines. The fast flying birds would swoop down over barren fields adjacent to the apiaries and catch the bees on the wing, flying to and from their hives. When we examined the stomachs of captured birds, we found parts of over a hundred *Apis mellifera* in some. The birds also feed on *Apis indica, Apis dorsata,* and other stinging Hymenoptera. In one bird we estimated there were parts from over 260 *Apis indica* (Morse and Laigo, 1969).

We found several birds which had been stung in the buccal cavity, or mouth. The protective membrane of the muscular stomachs of the birds often contained a hundred or more stings (figure 12.1). These had no apparent adverse effect on the birds.

In the Philippines, the swifts I observed were unable to avoid small nets which were flung up at them as they swooped in to capture the bees. The nets were usually one meter by two meters and were raised on long bamboo poles. The birds weighed slightly less than 200 grams and were consumed by the people in the area where meat was not too plentiful. It is difficult to estimate precisely how much damage the birds might do over a long period of time but they did appear almost every day and feeding would last from half an hour to an hour.

Wax moths

There are a number of moths which infest honey comb and, if present in sufficient numbers, destroy it. Among these, one species, *Galleria melonella,* is especially destructive; it has been given

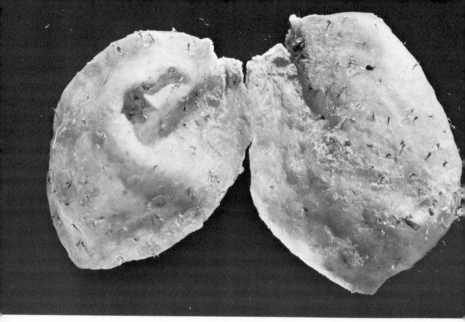

12.1. An everted stomach of a Philippine bee-eating bird. Several of the bees were swallowed alive and stung the bird on the inside of its muscular stomach. Clearly this caused the bird no difficulty for it continued to eat bees. The stings are in various stages of digestion.

several names, including "greater wax moth," "wax moth," and "bee moth." The wax moth is Asian in origin, but men have carried it, together with bees, to all continents. It is especially destructive in the southern areas in the United States. Although it cannot survive the rigorous winters much north of North Carolina in the eastern United States, it is a good flier and moves north rapidly in the summer. In New York State, in most years, we can expect wax moth infestations to be common in August and September. Additionally, wax moths are unquestionably overwintered in the North in heated or semiheated warehouses and buildings where combs are stored. The beekeeper's best protection against wax moths is to place the combs in storage buildings where they will be subjected to freezing temperatures, which will kill the moth in all stages — egg, larva, pupa, and adult. Wax moth larvae are large, about an inch long, and make very good fish bait, they are reared by a certain number of fish-bait producers and sold for this purpose. No doubt wax moths escaping from rearing rooms aid in spreading the infestation in the northern states.

It appears that the adult female wax moth usually lays her eggs on the outside of hives. The first instar larvae are good crawlers and are able to move through small spaces, including the cracks between supers, into the inside of the hives. The European honey bee will seize and remove any wax moths which it finds within its hive. However, the colony must be populous enough for the bees to do a thorough job of housecleaning, and in weakened colonies wax moths have been known to be very destructive.

On an expedition to the Philippines and other parts of Asia, I found wax moths infesting colonies of *Apis dorsata*. In fact, *Galleria melonella* were found in about half of the thirty nests of *Apis dorsata* observed in the Philippines. Weak or partially abandoned nests of *Apis dorsata* were very heavily infested with wax moths. Strong, populous colonies with 30 thousand to 70 thousand bees might have only two or three larvae or half a dozen pupae. The fact that the wax moth is Asian in origin and can coexist with *Apis dorsata* suggests that the moths probably have some protective mechanism which disguises them and prevents the *Apis dorsata* house bees from removing all of them from a colony.

The chemical most popular with beekeepers to protect combs in storage is paradichlorobenzene (P.D.B.). This material has a low mammalian toxicity and does not affect honey bees adversely. In areas where beekeepers are especially fearful of wax moths, such as the southern states, the usual procedure is to place pieces of newspaper on the floor with approximately a tablespoon of paradichlorobenzene crystals on the paper and then to stack supers of combs for storage on the paper. At a height of about four supers, a second piece of newspaper is placed in the pile, again with a similar quantity of paradichlorobenzene. If the supers are stacked more than eight high, a third dose should be placed in the pile. Beekeepers who use paradichlorobenzene find it is not necessary to air the supers prior to placing them on colonies; however, airing the supers for a short time, perhaps an hour or more, will remove much of the unpleasant odor from the combs and make them more acceptable to the bees. Other chemicals are also available for fumigation of stored combs, but regulations concerning their sale and use vary from state to state; it is advisable to check with the state specialist in apiculture to determine what is approved locally. At the present time there are no chemicals approved to protect comb honey (see Chapter 10).

Acarine disease and bee importations

Acarine disease is caused by a mite, *Acarapis woodi,* which infests the prothoracic spiracles of adult honey bees. Female mites may be found in the tracheae of adult bees within a day after they emerge from their cells. The mites lay their eggs within the tracheae, and the young complete their whole development there. It is interesting that a bee may sometimes have only one of its two prothoracic tracheae infested with mites. Mites migrate from one bee to another by leaving a spiracle, climbing onto a thoracic hair, and grasping the hair on another bee as it brushes past the first bee.

Acarine disease is fascinating in that it may be a relatively new bee disease. It was found in Scotland in 1919 by persons searching for an ill-defined bee disease. There is a possibility that it comes from the Isle of Wight, but there is good reason to question even that much as regards its origin. However, from that general region it spread over much of England and then into Europe proper. Within the last decade it has been reported in Russia and India.

Acarine disease is not found in North America, Australia, or New Zealand, and all of these areas have a strict quarantine against the importation of honey bees so the mites cannot be introduced. L. Bailey suggests that the mites perhaps do not survive in North America, but this suggestion is debatable.

In addition to *Acarapis woodi,* there are three other Acarine mites, including *Acarapis dorsalis, Acarapis vagans,* and *Acarapis externus,* all of which live externally on honey bees and are probably world-wide in distribution. Each of the three species is morphologically different and is usually found at a specific place on the bee's body.

Several treatments for acarine disease have been suggested. Most of these involve a differential fumigation of the colony, that is, a fumigation with a material that will affect the mites and not affect the adult honey bees. The only good fumigant appears to be chlorobenzilate, which is sold under the commercial name of Folbex. This material is reasonably effective in reducing, but not eliminating, infestations of *Acarapis woodi*. Bailey has suggested that treatment is not necessary and that populous colonies can effectively protect themselves against the mite; in this regard, he suggests that acarine disease might be treated as we treat the stress diseases of honey bees.

The Asian bee diseases

Apis mellifera has been introduced into tropical Asia many times; it has never been established there, though the other three *Apis* species are very successful throughout most of Asia. The difficulty in Asia appears to be mites, which are of limited consequence to Asian species but are highly destructive to European bees. The mites probably attack in the larval stage and they kill the developing bees in the pupal stage. Although in recent years, several persons, including myself, have studied the mites, little is known about their biology, and the theory that they are the principal problem of *Apis mellifera* in Asia may be erroneous.

The situation seems to be as follows. *Varroa jacobsonii* was first described in 1904. The mite may be found in the adult stage on the dorsal (top) surface of dead *Apis mellifera* pupae; the mite has been found in Asian bee colonies but is not so destructive in these colonies as in those of the European bee. The position of the mite and the presence of some adult *Apis mellifera* with deformed wings suggest, but do not prove, that these mites may deform those bees which they do not kill, if indeed they do kill some individuals.

A second mite, *Tropilaelaps clareae,* discovered in 1961, has also been found in association with dead *Apis mellifera* pupae and in the nests of other Asian species as well; although its biology has not yet been written, this mite, too, is suspected of killing the introduced European bee.

Apis mellifera has replaced the native bees in Japan. The entry of Red China into the world honey market in the 1960's would not have been possible without the introduction of the European species into that country. The production, or at least the export, of honey from Red China is erratic, suggesting problems within its beekeeping industry. At about the same time (after World War II) that the European bee was being successfully introduced into Japan, China, and Korea, it was being reintroduced into the Philippines, Viet Nam, Thailand, India, and perhaps elsewhere; in these countries it again failed to survive. The Asian mites may possibly be present, or at least destructive, in the tropics only.

One experience of mine in the Philippines is worth relating. In cooperation with F. M. Laigo of the University of the Philippines, College of Agriculture, I introduced five colonies onto the campus in Los Banos. One of these superseded its queen almost immediately and produced two virgin queens, which were separated and placed in two small nucleus colonies. One of the five colonies had a few drones, probably no more than eight or ten. The queens did not mate; probably they could not do so because they could not find males. It was a frustrating experience for us because we were making a strong effort at the time to increase the colony populations by feeding both sugar syrup and pollen taken from *Apis dorsata* colonies. However, the mite problem was so serious that the colony populations could not expand, and the weak colonies produced few drones. Our present scanty information on honey bee mating suggests that for every successful drone, it is probably necessary that there be a thousand or more in the area. One queen and one drone do not constitute a sufficient number for mating to take place, so far as we are aware.

This cautionary tale is directed to those who would take bees to remote areas and expect normal matings when supersedure or swarming takes place. Perhaps this should have been obvious. For every queen which is produced by a colony, that colony and others, even those not growing queens, produce large numbers of males.

It was not until 1961, when *Tropilaelaps clareae* was discovered

12.2. Bees in this colony have blocked much of the entrance with propolis; in this way the colony can better protect itself against intruders. Certain races of bees use much more propolis than others.

and described, that bee researchers came to realize that mites limited the success of the European bee in Asia. Additionally, birds, wasps, and toads destroy many bees; however, this last is true in the tropics everywhere.

Other predators, pests, and diseases

In addition to those mentioned, there are several hundred other predators, pests, and diseases of the honey bee. Most of these are of a minor nature and are little known by beekeepers, who rather infrequently call them to the attention of researchers and others interested in predation and parasitism among animals. Only a few of these will be discussed (fig. 12.2).

Several years ago I was dissecting adult, field bees, checking the contents of their honey stomachs to determine the sugar concentration of the nectar they were carrying. The method involved removing the head of the bee and then the contents of the abdomen. It is a relatively simple matter to remove the honey stomach by means of a pair of fine forceps. One day, while making a routine examination of honey stomachs, I took, from the abdomen of a bee, a nematode nearly eight centimeters (three inches) long. It was coiled within the abdomen and, of course, nearly filled the cavity, leaving little room for nectar in the honey sac. Other bees were examined, and that year the nematode incidence in honey bees was less than one per thousand. The parasites probably had little effect on colonies as a whole. The nematodes were still in the larval form and as such could not be identified to species. It is presumed that an adult bee, when she is feeding on flowers, accidentally picks up the eggs or young larvae of the nematode, and development in the bee's abdomen follows.

An interesting bee predator that occurs occasionally in Florida is the dragonfly, which is reported to be especially serious on the east coast. In that part of the state a large and sudden emergence of dragonflies in the spring sometimes causes serious difficulties for queen breeders. The dragonflies show some selectivity and prefer queens and drones, presumably because they are larger. One queen breeder told me that in some years when the problem was especially serious, he had been forced to stop his queen rearing operations for as long as two weeks. Another beekeeper who has had considerable experience in Florida described being in an apiary where several hundred dragonflies were feeding; he said that the bee parts falling to the ground came in such quantity as to make one think it was raining. The dragonflies did not consume the whole bee but rather appeared to prefer the thorax, allowing the abdomens and heads to fall to the ground.

In certain parts of the world giant toads, belonging to the genus *Bufo,* are troublesome to beekeepers. Articles from Australia, South America, and parts of Europe have appeared on the subject (Roff, 1966; Lescure, 1966). Apparently the toads are severely stung in the process of collecting bees but still return to the hives and take the bees as they move to and from the entrance. One defense against toads is to place the colonies on hive stands which are too high for the toads to reach.

A great many insects and spiders are found associated with bee hives. For the most part, it seems, these arthropods find the honey bee hive a good place to live. Certain of these, including some spiders, will capture a few bees. In some parts of the world predatory wasps capture a number of live, flying bees and are reported as being a serious problem.

In his text on the infectious diseases of honey bees, Bailey lists a number of little-known brood diseases that have been mentioned in the literature, including chalk brood, addled brood, stone brood, and bald brood. In some cases the organisms responsible for these diseases are known. There has never been a complete compilation of all the animals and pathogens that have an adverse effect on honey bees.

Pesticides

Although insecticides are formulated to kill insects, not all insecticides will kill honey bees. One of the more interesting chemicals in this regard is DDT. The major concern among entomologists immediately following the discovery of the toxic powers of DDT in the mid-1940's was what it might do to the beekeeping industry in the United States. Extensive testing was undertaken, and beekeepers soon came to understand that DDT has little or no effect on honey bees. In fact, there is no record of a colony of honey bees being killed by a single application of DDT.

The honey bee-pesticide problem predates the discovery of the chlorinated hydrocarbons for insect control. In the late 1800's, Paris green and London purple were both used in apple orchards, and to a lesser extent on other plants for the control of insect pests. These materials contained arsenic and often contaminated the water in wheel ruts, and in low areas in orchards; as a result there were some bee losses. In the late 1940's, when lead arsenic was still a popular insecticide in apple orchards, there were serious losses as a result of honey bees collecting lead arsenic-contaminated pollen. Lead arsenic has a relatively low toxicity to adult honey bees, and field bees are able to carry large quantities of contaminated pollen back to the hive where it is stored. The lead arsenic in the stored pollen remains toxic, and beekeepers found that it was necessary to destroy combs containing arsenic-contaminated pollen lest the loss of young bees within the hive continue.

As a result of losses of honey bees from lead arsenic in New York State, the legislature in 1948 outlawed the spraying of fruit trees and other crops, including alfalfa and clover, with poisons while they are in flower. At the same time, the New York State College of Agriculture changed its recommendations concerning lead arsenic, advocating that it be used in apple orchards as a postbloom spray only. The law was probably unnecessary since no cases have ever been prosecuted under it, and fruit growers are well aware of the importance of honey bees in setting fruit during the flowering season in May.

Many people in the beekeeping industry have condemned the use of pesticides by modern agriculture, but many beekeepers have found that they, too, must use certain chemicals in their management routine. While small beekeepers may be able to exist without these materials, the beekeeper with many hives finds it difficult to do so. It is one thing to be a hobby beekeeper and to lose a hive of bees to moths, skunks, or bears. It is another thing to own a thousand colonies of bees and to suffer the loss of many hives which could have been easily protected. The most commonly used chemical in the beekeeping industry is pentachlorophenal, an excellent wood preservative which is especially helpful in treating hive stands and bottomboards. Stands and bottomboards made of soft pine will usually rot within three to five years if exposed to the ground, but the same items treated with a cold soak of pentachlorophenal will have a life of 25 years or more. Paradichlorobenzene is widely used to protect combs from wax moths and is favored over several other chemicals because of its low toxicity to man and honey bees. Beekeepers use strychnine to control rodents, and warfarin is also an excellent rodenticide. In areas infested with ants and termites, chlordane is placed underneath hives to kill these insects; it is highly toxic to honey bees but, if placed on the ground under the hive, has no effect on them. Some beekeepers use sulfa, terramycin, and others drugs to control brood diseases. Several states, including New York State, have enacted legislation directed at the use of pesticides within their boundaries.

Present problems with pesticides

Since the discovery of DDT in the mid-1940's, the pesticides which we have seen developed may be grouped into three categories: the chlorinated hydrocarbons, the phosphates, and the carbamates. While certain insecticides in each group cause beekeepers losses, the carbamate insecticides, especially Sevin, produced by the Union Carbide Corporation, have caused the greatest losses in the last several years. The situation in New York State is reviewed below since it is the one with which I am most familiar.

During the past decade in New York State, the majority of honey bee losses have resulted from the spraying of sweet corn for corn borer control, alfalfa for alfalfa weevil control, and forests, especially in eastern New York, for protection against the gypsy moth. Many persons have researched and suggested alternate methods of controlling these pests; in recent years parasites introduced for the control of the alfalfa weevil have been quite successful, and there has been much less spraying of alfalfa. The spraying of fruit trees, which over the years has been a problem in New York State for beekeepers, poses no serious threat today. In part, this is true because the apple and fruit producing areas of New York State lie outside of the primary beekeeping areas; however, many apiaries are near large, commercial orchards that are sprayed on a routine basis.

Pesticide legislation

New York State has been the only state to recognize its obligation to beekeepers who lose bees as a result of state spray programs. Special legislation was enacted in 1965, and the money appropriated was used both to compensate beekeepers who lost bees (and their honey crop) and also to move bees out of spray areas. The act was intended to cover losses incurred in the gypsy moth spray program but has been extended to compensate bee-keepers for losses encountered when insecticide spraying for other forest insects causes difficulty. No other state has followed New York's lead. In 1971, the United States Congress passed laws which would compensate beekeepers who lost bees as the result of the use of any registered pesticide anywhere in the United States. Thus, the New York State law was superseded.

The amounts and types of pesticides used varies greatly from one state to another. Also, the attitude of legislators and state officials toward bees and beekeeping problems is dissimilar in every state. In part, the attitude of persons in a position to make and carry out legislation is influenced by the type and intensity of the agriculture in a state. My observation is that in those states where large num-bers of honey bee colonies are rented for pollination there is more concern about protecting bee populations than in those where the crops grown do not need to be cross-pollinated.

It behooves beekeepers to be familiar with legislation, as well as to be active in county and state agricultural and beekeeping organizations. Beekeepers do not own the land or the plants on which their bees forage. However, tradition and our knowledge of agriculture and biology demonstrate that the honey bee is impor-tant to our overall economy. The beekeeper must understand that the grower has a right to protect his crops to continue our high level of productivity, and the grower must understand that the honey bee is important insofar as pollination is concerned, if not of his own crop, certainly of those produced by others. While bee-keepers make most of their money producing honey and beeswax, it is through pollination that they make their most important con-tribution to our economy.

Protecting honey bees from pesticides

F. R. Shaw and A. I. Bourne (1944) of the Massachusetts State College of Agriculture, in a paper that is often referred to, described attempts to combine repellents with pesticides so that bees would not visit sprayed plants and thus might be protected from the pesticides. Their paper reported on the testing, of such materials as creosote, carbolic acid, and another phenol compound which was new at the time. While the results of their study were negative, the idea that we might someday find a repellent which could be combined with an insecticide has been suggested and studied by many people.

In the late 1940's the dinitros, used as thinners on apples, were found to be highly toxic to honey bees, at least in laboratory tests. However, when these same materials were applied in the field, bees were not killed. It was discovered later that the dinitros cause the anthers on apple flowers to wither and make them unattractive to bees. Thus, the bees will not visit the apple blossoms and do not come in contact with the toxic material. However, the use of phytotoxic materials to dissuade bees from visiting blooms has obvious drawbacks.

The formulation of an insecticide has much to do with its toxicity. In preparing an insecticide, a variety of stickers, spreading agents, wetters, and emulsifiers are added, and these affect honey bees and other insects differently. Insecticides are formulated in various ways because of this fact. According to recent studies, certain formulations of Sevin, for example, make it much less toxic to honey bees without affecting its ability to control the gypsy moth. Further testing of this and similar materials is needed.

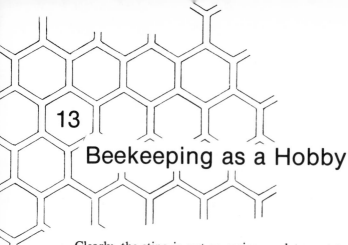

13

Beekeeping as a Hobby

Clearly, the sting is not so serious a deterrent to beekeeping as some people believe. Thousands of commercial beekeepers and researchers around the world will testify that one can soon gain immunity to the swelling from the sting of the honey bee, and that the pain is minor. Parts of a honey bee's sting shaft are shown in figures 13.1 and 13.2.

People take up beekeeping for a variety of reasons. Most of them think in terms of the honey they might produce. This is not unreasonable, and a knowledgeable beekeeper should expect a financial return of 25 to 50 per cent on his investment each year. Of course, there are shortcuts in making and using beekeeping equipment which will lessen the investment and not reduce the return.

The hobby beekeepers

As noted previously, the majority of beekeepers are hobbyists. The chief requirement for the hobbyist is adequate space to keep his colonies in a location with sufficient honey plants so that his bees may produce a surplus of honey. Many city beekeepers own an acre or more in the country which they use as a weekend retreat and consider an investment in land.

One of the virtues of beekeeping as an avocation is that in most parts of the country it may be expected to bring a reasonable return on an investment; equally important, since the hobbyist may

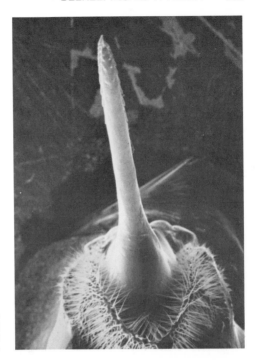

13.1. An electron micro-
scope view of the sting shaft
of a worker honey bee. Barbs
are visible on the shaft's tip.

buy one hive or many, he need invest only as much money as he
cares to in bees and beekeeping equipment. Many beekeepers
make their own hives and hive parts. It is necessary to build equipment of standard dimensions, to insure its resale value, and to
allow the beekeeper to exchange equipment from one hive to another. At the same time, it is important to build the proper spacing
between combs in the hive.

Where may bees be kept?

One or two hives of bees may be kept almost anywhere in the
United States. Of course, bees will not flourish in the deserts or
mountains, but even there, certain locations can support a hive or
two. Bees have been kept in cities such as New York, sometimes on

13.2. The tip of a worker honey bee sting showing the barbs.

rooftops. If the flight lanes of the worker bees in cities are above the heads of people working or walking in the vicinity, the bees will pose no problem (see figure 13.3).

As a guideline, those hobbyists who consider expanding their operation should be aware that commercial beekeepers feel that they should have a minimum of 40 to 50 hives per apiary for a profitable operation. Locations where bees can be kept in these numbers are limited, and commercial beekeepers spend a great deal of time searching for good apiary locations.

Water for bees

As has been indicated earlier, honey bees use water both to cool the hive and to dilute the honey which they feed to larvae. At

13.3. An apiary in the fall. This apiary is surrounded by a heavy hedge which forces the bees up in the air and above the heads of people who might be walking in the vicinity. The colonies are on hive stands which are placed on cement blocks. While such precautions are not necessary, they do help to keep the hives level and to keep them dry during wet weather.

certain times of the year, when it is excessively warm or when bees are rearing large quantities of brood, they may collect great quantities of water, sometimes three liters (approximately a gallon) per colony per day. A beekeeper whose hives are located in or near a village or a city should provide a source of clean water for his bees.

Providing water for bees is a simple matter. The water does not necessarily need to be fresh. Many beekeepers use 55 gallon drums with floats, which they fill periodically. It is important to have a float in a container in which water is held, for otherwise many bees may drown. A water faucet dripping over a long board will provide a satisfactory source of water for bees.

Under certain circumstances, especially in desert areas, bees may expend great energy in collecting water. Again, beekeepers should provide them with water to save them time and energy in collecting it. Honey bee colonies have been known to survive under very high temperatures in desert areas if they have a sufficient water supply. Even in the East, summers can be long, hot, and dry, and many commercial beekeepers locate their apiaries near permanent streams or rivers where water will be readily available. In the selection of a permanent apiary site, water is an important consideration.

The need for honey plants

Before one makes an investment in bees and beekeeping, it is well to check with other beekeepers and county agricultural agents, and perhaps with the state specialist in beekeeping, to determine what is both possible and reasonable in an area. All too often professional apiculturists receive letters from persons in New York City, for example, stating that they would like to go into beekeeping and that they have purchased some land within 50 or 100 miles of the city for the express purpose of having a summer home and a place where they might have a small farm, including bees. Many of these people want to know what plants they should grow or encourage which will be of greatest benefit to their colonies. It is not profitable to make plantings for the sole purpose of nectar or pollen production, and unfortunately, the area within 100 miles of New York City is poor beekeeping territory. While one might produce 50 to 75 pounds of honey per colony in that area, the number of colonies which can be kept in a given area is limited and so is the amount of honey that can be produced. A beekeeper who locates his hives in a primary honey-producing area in New York State, or some other state, may expect to produce two or three times the quantity of honey, with the same effort, as does the one locating near the New York City area.

If one studies honey production in the United States and those areas which produce the greatest quantity of honey, it is clear that the successful beekeepers have moved to the honey-producing areas. These areas have a profusion of nectar and pollen-producing plants early in the year, before the primary honey flow, which serves to increase colony populations, and large populations can produce a surplus of honey.

However, this is not meant to discourage beekeepers from planting interesting and attractive nectar and pollen-producing plants around their homes and farms. Observation of these plants throughout the year serves to alert the beekeeper to the activities of bees and may well serve to guide his management program. Sometimes the flowering plants found in a sizeable village or city collectively provide sufficient forage for a large number of colonies of bees. In Florida, for example, many commercial beekeepers move their apiaries into some of the big cities before the citrus honey flow. Many persons who live in these city areas enjoy gardening and have planted a variety of flowering, tropical plants which bloom prior to the citrus and serve as excellent build-up plants for beekeepers. It is interesting how many gardeners strive to produce flowering plants early in the spring; this can be a great benefit to the beekeepers. In certain villages and towns in the northern part of the country, city fathers have lined the streets with flowering plants, sometimes in sufficient numbers to provide a surplus of nectar. Basswood trees, which provide excellent shade, line the roads and streets in many New England towns. Some bee clubs have prepared brochures and/or mimeographed lists of flowering trees which their members can distribute to garden groups, park superintendents, and city and town planners. Such plantings serve to enhance the beauty of any area and also provide food for bees.

How to start in beekeeping

The best time for a beginner to start in beekeeping is in the spring — in January or February in the southernmost states, and in April in the North. The primary point is that a colony of bees must have sufficient time to store the food it will need to carry it through the inactive (winter) season. In the northern states, the bees in an average colony will consume 60 or 80 pounds of honey during the winter and in the early spring before it is unpacked;

even after the packing is removed in the spring, the colony will not be able, for several weeks, to collect the food it needs for day-to-day existence. Colonies may be fed sugar syrup to make up for a deficiency of honey, but this is both costly and time-consuming.

Buying colonies

Buying an established colony of bees is probably the best way to start in beekeeping, and spring is the best time to buy such a unit. In the spring the beekeeper knows the colony has survived the winter. He can observe the queen's brood pattern, check the colony for disease (American foulbrood), and satisfy himself as to the food reserves in the colony. In mid-April, in New York State, for example, a two-super colony with a normal complement of bees should have 20 to 25 pounds of reserve honey.

The chief advantage of buying an established colony is that the unit will produce a surplus in the first year, if properly managed and provided there is a honey flow. The chief disadvantage is that overwintered colonies will have a larger and more alert guard force than packaged bees have, and the beginner is more likely to be stung in making manipulations. However, since getting stung is inevitable for all beekeepers, there is no real reason to delay the matter. An important part of the bargain of buying a hive of bees might well be the privilege of acquiring some first-hand advice, and especially the right to work with the seller, in his apiary, in order to gain the necessary know-how.

Another advantage of buying an established colony is that the combs which are needed for both brood production and honey storage will be drawn and ready to use. Making new frames, adding the foundation, and placing the combs in hives so that bees will draw foundation are not difficult operations; however, colonies which are forced to draw foundation devote considerable effort to the task, and they have less time to collect and store their honey. It is advisable to buy one or two extra supers for each two-story colony, if possible, and if they are not too expensive. A good colony of bees will occupy four to six hive bodies during the active honey producing season in a good beekeeping territory.

Not all colonies which are purchased second-hand have frames, supers, and other hive parts that are in good physical condition. However, a hive with poor equipment may still be a good buy if the bees themselves are in good condition, that is, if they have a good queen, a food supply, and are free of disease. Old equipment may be scraped, renailed, painted, and made to serve as well as new in most instances.

It is worthwhile to take a few extra steps in preparing equipment so as to protect a beekeeping investment as much as possible. Most beekeepers do not nail their equipment with enough nails, or large enough nails. The holding power of a nail has to do with its length, not its diameter or coating. The nails which bee supply manufacturers sell, with their hives, are too short, and usually there are too few of them. When buying old equipment, or when visiting an apiary owned by another beekeeper, it is advisable to note the condition of the hives. Hives and hive parts have weak points, places which need more and longer nails, wood preservative, an extra coat of paint, and so forth; beekeepers who are aware of these facts, and of special problems in their area, such as termites or wood-eating ants, are in a position to act to protect their equipment.

Buying packages

Bees are sold in packages of varying weights, but the best package for the beginner to buy is one containing three pounds of bees and a queen. Package bees usually arrive well-fed but should be fed an additional pint or so of sugar syrup before installation. Feeding bees makes them gentle, and it should be possible for the beekeeper, in most instances, to place the bees in a hive without being stung. However, while package bees may be very gentle, the same bees, with an organized brood nest a few days later, may not be so gentle. Here again, it cannot be stressed too much that having an experienced beekeeper on hand the first few times a colony is inspected is helpful. Some of the steps in installing a package of bees are shown in figures 13.4–13.9.

One disadvantage of starting beekeeping with package bees is

13.4 Bees in this wooden, wire-bound box, called a package, are being fed sugar syrup which is "painted" onto their cage.

that the beginner may also have to start with all new frames and foundation. This can be done, and it is done by thousands of new beekeepers each year. Bees need food to make wax. A three-pound package of bees may very well consume 30 or more pounds of sugar, made into a sugar syrup, during the first two months after it is installed. Between the time the package is placed in the new hive, and until young bees are emerging in numbers, and until the colony has reserves of at least ten pounds of honey and some pollen, the unit should never be without feeder pails, or some other feeding units, full of syrup. While the new colony would probably not starve to death under most circumstances, the production of brood, the secretion of wax, and the building of new comb are dependent upon an abundance of food.

One may circumvent the drawing of foundation by giving a

13.5. A package of bees from a southern state is shipped north with a can of syrup so the bees will have some food enroute. The first step in installing the package of bees is to remove the block of wood which covers the can within the package. Before placing these bees in their new home, sugar syrup should be painted on the wire cloth on the side of the package so as to make certain the bees have ample food. (Photo by New York State College of Agriculture and Life Sciences, Cornell University.)

package of bees drawn comb, if it is available. There is one drawback in giving a package old comb. Bees from the south may come from colonies infected with American foulbrood. They may be carrying, in their honey stomachs, infected honey. If they should store this honey in drawn comb upon installation, this could serve as a reservoir of infection; however, if the bees are placed on foundation, and have no cells in which to store food, it is thought that they will consume any food they are carrying to supply energy for building new comb. Package bees from the South are less likely to be carrying disease today than they were many years ago.

Hiving swarms

Established colonies of bees, especially those which are crowded and congested, may cast off swarms of bees; this usually occurs

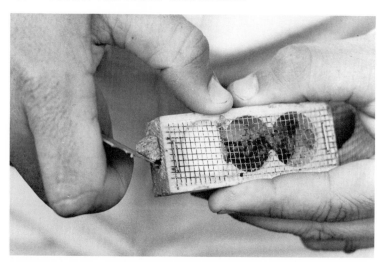

13.6. The queen in a package is caged separately with about six workers, thus allowing the beekeeper to whom she is sent to determine if she arrives safely. Before bees in the newly hived package can release her, by eating the sugar candy shown in the right-hand cage hole, the cork in the queen cage must be removed. (Photo by New York State College of Agriculture and Life Sciences, Cornell University.)

every two or three years in the average colony. Swarming occurs in March and April in the South, and in late May, June, and early July in the north.

Hiving a swarm is much like hiving a package. Bees which swarm engorge before they leave the hive and carry sufficient food to sustain the members of the swarm for several days. However, should the swarm run out of food, it becomes what is called a "dry swarm." Bees in dry swarms can be extremely vicious, and most of the severe stingings recorded in the literature have happened to people who were trying to hive such swarms. An experienced bee-keeper can usually tell the condition of the swarm without any difficulty. We hive many swarms in the vicinity of Ithaca each year and have no trouble. If the weather is warm and pleasant, it may be assumed that bees are flying and collecting food normally, and the swarm should not be dry or without food. A swarm which is

13.7. Shaking bees into their new home in a northern state. This package contains three pounds, or approximately 12,000 bees. The queen, which is caged separately, has been placed between two frames.

13.8. This newly installed package is fed sugar syrup from two cans inverted over the new brood nest. The covers in the cans have about 20 small holes large enough for the workers to insert their proboscises to obtain the sugar syrup.

found after several days of inclement weather, especially two or three days of cloudy, cool weather, may very well have exhausted its food and should be handled with extreme care.

There are basically two ways to hive a swarm. One is to shake the swarm into a burlap bag or a cage and to carry the bees to the apiary. A plastic bag should not be used for the bees might suffocate. A better way is to place a hive body, preferably with some drawn combs, immediately under the swarm and to shake the bees into the hive. They will usually accept the new hive, which may be picked up that night and carried to the apiary.

Occasionally a swarm will not stay in a hive into which it is shaken. Sometimes, within minutes of being shaken into the hive, a swarm will reemerge and again settle on a bush or in a tree. We do not fully understand why bees in a swarm may behave in this manner, but we suspect that swarms which reemerge under these

13.9. An alternate method of feeding bees. A division board feeder, is inserted along the side of the super in place of a frame.

circumstances have already selected a home site and are perhaps in the early stages of moving to it. It is also possible that such swarms may contain multiple queens. A swarm which does not remain in the super into which it is shaken may be shaken a second time (and, rarely, a third time!). Usually a swarm shaken into a hive at dusk, or after dark, will be more inclined to remain in the new home. Sometimes well-fed swarms will have a few bees which will sting after dark, and shaking bees at this time of day is a little more difficult than it is during the daylight hours. In shaking a swarm from a bush, it is best to give the branch one hard shake, sufficient to dislodge the swarm from the branch it is on.

Swarms appear to be more inclined to accept a new home if it has a beehive odor, that is, if used supers and combs are employed. In East Africa, where swarm collecting is practiced extensively, and bait hives are popular, the natives smear hot wax and honey on the inside of new bark hives. This apparently gives the hives an attractive odor, and hives so treated catch more swarms than untreated ones do.

An almost certain way to force a swarm to accept a new hive is to place a frame of brood in the hive. It is probably brood phero-mones which stabilize the bees, but in any event a swarm shaken into a hive with a frame of live brood will almost certainly remain in place. Of course, brood cannot be taken from a hive and carried any great distance before bees are placed on it. Brood which is unattended for more than about ten to fifteen minutes will probably start to starve. Temperature is also important in this regard; the brood must not be chilled.

Removing bees from a tree or house

Swarms will often take up residence in a hollow tree or inside the wall of a house or barn. The bees can be removed from such a place, but it should be done for fun, not profit. Considerable time is involved in capturing bees from an inaccessible place. Figures 13.10–13.12 show natural bee trees cut apart.

To hive a swarm which has settled in a tree, it is first necessary to fell the tree and to cut out that section containing the swarm. The process of felling a large tree may cause considerable damage to the comb, and may result in the death of some bees; however, there is no alternative.

That section of the tree containing the colony is next placed in an upright position. The top of the nest is opened as much as possible. In other words, wood is removed so that the bees can move in an upright direction. The beekeeper next places a hive body of combs on top of the tree. The super of combs is covered with an ordinary hive cover. In nature, the queen and the brood nest move in an upward direction. It is hoped that after several weeks the queen will be active in the super(s) of combs. At this time one may place a queen excluder below the super and allow the brood in the old nest below the excluder to emerge. Since worker bees emerge in three weeks and drone brood in 24 days, there should be no brood remaining after this period of time, and the ac-tive brood nest will occupy the added super(s). The bee tree may then be discarded, or one may attempt to salvage any wax and

13.10. A cross section of a bee tree showing the bee space. In this case, the combs are evenly constructed.

honey which remain in it; again, this may not be worth the effort from a financial point of view, but it can be a fascinating exercise.

Bees may be removed from a box or crate in the same manner. It is only necessary to open the top of the box, or the unit containing the bees, so that there can be uninhibited movement up into the super which has been placed above. Unless the queen migrates into the super of combs, the method will not work.

An alternate but little-used method of removing a swarm of bees from a house is to place a colony of bees containing a queen and only a few thousand bees just outside of the house. The new, weak hive must be within a few feet of the entrance of the colony in the

13.11. Examining a bee tree in winter. This photograph was taken in February and the bees have some brood. Unfortunately, colonies removed in this manner cannot survive. (Photo by New York State College of Agriculture and Life Sciences, Cornell University.)

building. All the entrances to the colony but one are then blocked. A bee escape, or wire gauze funnel, is placed over the nest entrance in such a way that bees may exit but not reenter the nest. Thus, the bees will be trapped outside of their home and will slowly enter the new hive placed there for them. The greatest danger is during the first day when a large number of bees may be trapped outside and may not accept the queen in the alternate hive; however, even if she is killed, the bees will rear a new queen from eggs or young larvae in the hive. As the field force is trapped from the hive in the building, brood rearing will decrease. After six to eight weeks the population within the parent colony will be too depleted to survive. The bulk of the bees should now inhabit the new hive, and it may be carried away. The nest in the building may be opened and the combs removed.

One word of caution about removing swarms from buildings is

13.12. Removing a piece of honey from a bee tree in midwinter. The bees are cold and find it difficult to fly, but if they hit one's bare hand, they might sting. It was in this manner that our ancestors in North America harvested bee trees. (Photo by New York State College of Agriculture and Life Sciences, Cornell University.)

in order. Since bees prefer to nest where bees have nested previously, and presumably are attracted by the odor emanating from an old nest, after a swarm is removed from a house, the area which it occupied should be packed with insulation, or some other material, so that the site cannot be used again by a swarm. It is not satisfactory merely to block or cover the old nest site for even after many years a swarm may gain entrance through a crack or crevice, still attracted by the residual odor.

Drumming

Drumming is a process seldom practiced and little understood. If one beats rhythmically on the side of a hive, or a tree or some other container that holds a colony of bees, the bees will move upward, and out of the hive. It is interesting that if a hive is kicked once or twice or otherwise disturbed, bees will rush from the entrance and sting anyone in the vicinity. However, drumming does not appear to have such an effect on bees, and drummed bees remain gentle.

We do not know why bees move upwards and abandon their nest when drummed. We know bees do not hear sound, but they do detect substrate-borne sound. We suspect that drumming somehow mimics substrate-borne sound, but what message is being conveyed is unclear. In any event it is an interesting and reliable method of removing bees from a hive with fixed comb.

Collecting swarms

From time to time, every police department needs the services of a knowledgeable beekeeper. Swarming is a natural process for honey bees that occurs every spring, and when a swarm alights in a public area or proceeds to build a nest between the studs in a home, it is usually to the police department that people turn for help. Most departments have a list of beekeepers, usually hobbyists, who will assist them in an emergency such as removing a swarm from a telephone pole, a parking meter, an automobile, or a house.

Early in the year swarms of honey bees are valuable to the beekeeper, that is to say, they can be installed in a normal hive and moved to an apiary where the colony will grow in population and eventually store a surplus of honey. In certain states collecting swarms of honey bees for pay or service falls into the area of pest control, and these states insist that pest control operators be licensed. In such areas it is necessary to obtain a license for the express purpose of handling and removing colonies of honey bees that are a nuisance. Since most professional pest control operators are expert in dealing with ants, termites, and other destructive insects but not with the stinging kind, they are often glad to leave to the beekeepers the removal of unwanted colonies. A few hobby beekeepers specialize in the control of honey bees, bumble bees, carpenter bees, and the social, nest-building wasps, as pests; this, too, can be a profitable avocation.

13.13. A two-frame observation hive by a window. (Illustration by V. L. Kellogg in Anna Botsford Comstock's *How to Keep Bees,* 1905.)

Observation hives

An observation hive contains a single comb between two panes of glass; the hive may be made using one frame or several, one above the other, in a single plane (see figure 13.13). The panes of glass are usually about one and one-half to two inches apart; thus, there is room for the comb between the panes as well as ample bee space between the comb and the glass. The amount of space the beekeeper leaves between the glass and the comb depends upon the function the hive is to serve. A narrower space allows one to follow the activities of individual bees with ease; if too much space is left between the comb and the glass, the bees will add wax. Most observation hives are designed to be used indoors only; because of their small size, the bees would have difficulty keeping brood warm if the hives were exposed to the elements. The observation hive entrance should connect to the outdoors so that the bees may enter and exit from the building. In this way people in the building may see the bees without fear of being stung. The top covers for observation hives are fitted with holes, usually about one inch in diameter, so that feeder jars or pails may be placed on them to feed the bees when necessary.

In our experimental work we find a three-frame observation hive is a convenient unit. We place the three frames, one above the other, with a bee space between the top bar of one frame and the bottom bar of another so that the bees may move freely from one side of the hive to the other.

An observation hive may be fitted with an entrance closure so that one may close the hive at night and take it to a classroom or lecture the following day or evening. It is only necessary to provide two or three ventilation holes on the ends of the hive so that the bees have fresh air. These holes should be about one inch in diameter and covered with wire screening. In time, the bees may coat the screen with propolis, and when this does occur, a new piece of wire screening should be placed over the holes.

The major problem with an observation hive is that it becomes congested in a relatively short time, and as a result the bees will swarm. In observation hives containing more than two frames, some of the bees may remain behind, but in those containing only one or two frames all of the bees usually leave when the colony swarms. There is no effective way to stop a queen from laying eggs if the temperature is normal and the bees have food. Since a normal colony of bees occupies a hive with 30 or more standard frames during the active season, it is obvious that providing the bees with only one or a few frames will soon lead to congestion. Some bees, and perhaps some brood, must be removed from an observation hive once every four to six weeks. If the hive is fitted with a device for closing the entrance at night, one may carry the hive to an apiary, make the necessary changes, and then return it to its original location. Any bees which become lost will enter another hive in the apiary.

Hives which are to be moved should be closed at night, after the bees have stopped flying, so that the bees will be retained within the hive. Interestingly, a few honey bees stay outdoors all night; they become chilled in the late evening and are unable to return to their hive. Bees have been observed returning to a hive in the early morning hours, before others are taking flight from a hive; these are bees which were caught outdoors and were warmed by the early morning sun so that they might fly again.

Many experiments can be performed with an observation hive. Egg laying and larval feeding may be followed if one cuts a piece of comb so as to expose the side of a cell and places it in an observation hive perpendicular to the glass. Although a queen is reluctant to lay eggs in cells bounded on one side by a pane of glass, she will lay in such cells when the hive is crowded.

Dancing bees may be followed with ease through the side of an observation hive and individuals can be distinguished if they are marked with paint or numbered discs, which may be glued onto their thoraxes. It is easiest to mark the bees while they are at a feeding station. An alternate method is to introduce marked, young bees, which have emerged only a few hours earlier from a comb in another hive, to the observation hive, in the hope that they will become scouts within a few weeks. Introducing young bees also gives one an opportunity to follow the life history of a bee.

The observation hive serves many functions for the beekeeper. It may be a source of amusement, a tool for instruction or a means of conducting research. Few animals lend themselves to experimentation so readily as does the honey bee. Despite our accumulation of knowledge much remains to be discovered about the bee, and the observation hive will always be an important means of discovering it.

A local beekeeper—the best source of information

Since there are so many hobby beekeepers in the United States, the beginner should be able to find one willing to help him with his problems. Although an established beekeeper may not want to visit a new apiary, he would probably not object to a visitor in his own apiary. In many areas beekeepers have cooperated in such tasks as moving bees and extracting honey, which require costly equipment.[1] Although a honey extractor of almost any size can be purchased, it is still a great deal of work to extract a large volume of honey with small machinery not suited to the task. Thus, insofar as moving bees and extracting are concerned, there are additional reasons for searching out local beekeepers who might be willing to exchange work.

State apiculturists, entomologists, and apiary inspectors

All states hire entomologists who study and work to control insect pests within their state's boundaries. More than half of the states also employ a beekeeping specialist and most of these same states have a state apiary inspector. One may write to these men even if their names are not known, addressing them by title and mailing the letter to the state capitol or the state college; they are usually located at one or the other, and some states have men working in these areas in both locations.

Most states have bulletins, brochures, and mimeographs which pertain to beekeeping and special problems within the state. Some of the states which have limited bee populations may depend on other nearby states for this information. Persons in state positions are usually willing to send literature to other states, and by writing to several states, a beekeeper may build a good library which will serve as a source of information. Most of this literature is available without charge.

Additionally, the federal government operates six bee research laboratories; these are in the states of Maryland, Wisconsin, Wyoming, Arizona, Louisiana, and Utah. Men working at these laboratories are usually research specialists devoting their efforts

1. The two largest bee supply companies in the country have dealers throughout the United States. A post card to the A. I. Root Co., Medina, Ohio, or the Dadant and Sons Co., Hamilton, Illinois, will bring a list of their dealers. In addition to selling supplies, including texts, these companies will know about area meetings, literature from the state colleges, and where local beekeepers reside.

to particular problems. Some of these men also teach and write literature which is distributed from the laboratory or through the state college.

Most states have state beekeeper's organizations. The state apiculturists and apiary inspectors are usually active in these associations and will provide information about the meetings so that anyone may attend. State meetings are a good place to learn some of the fundamentals of beekeeping.

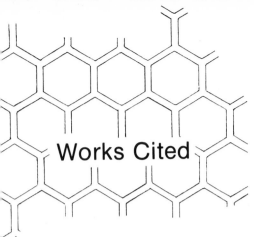

Works Cited

Alfonsus, Erwin C. 1933. Some sources of propolis. *Gleanings in Bee Culture* 61:92–93.

Anderson, Edwin J. 1958. Honey candies. *Pennsylvania State University Progress Report* 186.

Bailey, Leslie. 1963. *Infectious Diseases of the Honey Bee*. Land Books, London.

Bertholf, L. M. 1925. The moults of the honeybee. *Journal of Economic Entomology* 18:380–4.

Bisetsky, A. R. (see Frisch, 1967*b*)

Blum, M. S., A. F. Novak, and S. Taber III. 1959. 10-hydroxy- Δ^2-decenoic acid, an antibiotic found in royal jelly. *Science* 130:452–453.

Boch, R. (see Lepage; Hopkins; or Frisch, 1967)

——, and D. A. Shearer. 1962. Identification of geraniol as the active component in the Nassanoff pheromone of the honey bee. *Nature* 194:704–706.

——, and D. A. Shearer. 1964. Identification of nerolic and geranic acids in the Nassanoff pheromone of the honey bee. *Nature* 202:320–321.

——, D. A. Shearer, and B. C. Stone. 1962. Identification of iso-amyl acetate as an active component in the sting pheromone of the honey bee. *Nature* 195:1018–1020.

Brown, G. Douglas, and Frank V. Kosikowski. 1970. How to make honey yogurt. *American Dairy Review* 32(4):60–62.

Burgett, D. Michael, and Roger A. Morse. 1974. The time of natural swarming in honeybees. *Annals of the Entomological Society of America* 67:719–20.

Butler, C. G. 1956. Some further observations on the nature of "queen substance" and its role in the organization of a honey-bee (*Apis mellifera*) community. *Proceedings of the Royal Entomological Society* A 31:12–16.

——. 1972–1973. The queen and the "spirit of the hive." *Proceedings of the Royal Entomological Society of London* 37:59–65.

——, R. K. Callow, and N. C. Johnston. 1961. The isolation and synthesis of queen substance, 9-oxodec-*trans*-2-enoic acid, a honeybee pheromone. *Proceedings of the Royal Entomological Society* B 155:417–432.

Cheshire, F. 1886–1888. *Bees and Beekeeping.* Vol. 1. L. Upcott Gill, London.

Comstock, Anna Botsford. 1905. *How to Keep Bees.* Doubleday, Page & Co.

Combs, Gerald F., Jr., and Roger A. Morse. 1972. Package bees: their installation and immediate care. *New York State College of Agriculture and Life Sciences at Cornell University, Information Bulletin* 7.

Demuth, George S. 1919. Commercial comb-honey production. *United States Department of Agriculture Farmer's Bulletin* 1039.

——. 1921. Swarm control. *United States Department of Agriculture Farmer's Bulletin* 1198.

Doolittle, G. M. 1888. *Scientific Queen-Rearing.* George W. York, Sandpoint, Idaho.

Dyce, Elton J. 1931. Fermentation and crystallization of honey. *Cornell University Agricultural Experiment Station Bulletin* 528.

——, and R. A. Morse. 1970. Wintering honey bees in New York State. *New York State College of Agriculture and Life Sciences at Cornell University, Extension Bulletin* 1054. Revised edition.

Fowler, C. E., and M. J. Pritchard. 1918. Two remarkable odor experiences. *Gleanings in Bee Culture* 46:422–423.

Free, J. B. 1963. The flower constancy of honeybees. *Journal of Animal Ecology* 32:119–131.

——. 1968. Effect of the time of day at which colonies are first allowed flight in a new location on their choice of flower species. *Nature* 218: 982.

——. 1970. *Insect Pollination of Crops.* Academic Press, London.

Free, J. B., and M. V. Smith. 1961. The foraging behavior of honeybees from colonies moved into a pear orchard in full flower. *Bee World* 42:11–12.

Frisch, Karl von. 1967a. *A Biologist Remembers.* Translated by Lisbeth Gombrich. Pergamon Press, Oxford.

——. 1967b. *The Dance Language and Orientation of Bees.* Translated by Leigh E. Chadwick. Harvard University Press, Cambridge.

——. 1971. *Bees, Their Vision, Chemical Senses and Language.* Cornell University Press, Ithaca, New York. Revised edition.

Gary, Norman E. 1962. Chemical mating attractants in the queen honey bee. *Science* 136:773–774.

Gary, Norman E., and R. A. Morse. 1962. The events following queen cell construction in honey bee colonies. *Journal of Apicultural Research* 1:3–5.

Goncalves, Lionel Segui. 1969. A study of orientation information given by one trained bee by dancing. *Journal of Apicultural Research* 8:113–132.

Harbo, John. 1971. Annotated bibliography on attempts at mating honeybees in confinement. *Bee Research Association Bibliography* No. 12. Mimeographed.

Heard, H. F. 1946. *A Taste for Honey.* Vanguard Press, New York. 1941. Reprinted: In *Murder with a Difference,* edited by Christopher Morley. Random House, New York. pp. 177–306.

Heinicke, Arthur J. 1917. Factors influencing the abscission of flowers and partially developed fruits of the apple (*Pyrus malus* L.). *Cornell University Agricultural Experiment Station Bulletin* 393. pp. 41–114.

Hess, Gertrud 1942. The effect of queenlessness and the fertility vitamin E on the ovaries of worker honey bees (translated title). *Beihefte zur Schweizerischen Bienenzeitung* 1:33–109

Hopkins, C. Y., A. W. Jevens, and R. Boch. 1969. Occurrence of octadeca-*trans*-2, *cis*-12-trienoic acid in pollen attractive to the honey bee. *Canadian Journal of Biochemistry* 47:433–436.

Jay, C. S. 1970. The effect of various combinations of immature queens and worker bees on the ovary development of worker honey bees with and without queens. *Canadian Journal of Zoology* 48:169–173.

Jeffree, E. P. 1956. Winter brood and pollen in honeybee colonies. *Insectes Sociaux* 3:417–422.

Johnson, John A., Philip Nordin, and Donald Miller. 1957. The utilization of honey in baked products. *The Bakers Digest* 31(2):33–34, 36, 38, 40.

Karlson, Peter, and Adolf Butenandt. 1959. Pheromones (ectohormones) in insects. *Annual Review of Entomology* 4:39–58.

Katznelson, H., and C. A. Jamieson. 1952. Control of nosema disease of honeybees with fumagillin. *Science* 115:70–71.

Kelley, Walter T. undated (ca. 1940's). *How to Grow Queens.* Walter T. Kelley Co., Paducah, Kentucky.

Kerr, Warwick E. 1969. Some aspects of the evolution of social bees (Apidae). *Evolutionary Biology* 3:119–175.

Killion, Carl E. 1951. *Honey in the Comb.* Killion and Sons Apiaries, Paris, Illinois.

Kudo, Roksabro. 1924. A biologic and taxonomic study of the Microsporidia. *Illinois Biological Monographs* 9(2–3):1–268.

Laidlaw, Harry H., Jr., and J. E. Eckert. 1962. *Queen Rearing.* Dadant and Sons, Hamilton, Illinois. Revised edition.

Laigo, F. M., and R. A. Morse. 1968. Control of the bee mites, *Varroa jacobsoni* Oudemans and *Tropilaelaps clareae* Delfinado and Baker with chlorobenzilate. *The Philippine Entomologist* 1:144–148.

Lepage, M., and R. Boch. 1968. Pollen lipids attractive to honeybees. *Lipids* 3:530–534.

Lescure, J. 1966. The predatory behavior of the common toads towards bees. *Annales de L'abeille* 9:83–114.

Lindauer, M. 1957. Communication among the honeybees and stingless bees of India. *Bee World* 38:3–14, 34–39.

——. 1971. *Communication among Social Bees*. Harvard University Press, Cambridge. Third printing with appendices.

Lindenfelzer, L. A. 1967. Antimicrobial activity of propolis. *American Bee Journal* 107:90–92, 130–31.

——. 1968. In vivo activity of propolis against *Bacillus larvae*. *Journal of Invertebrate Pathology* 12:129–131.

Maeterlinck, Maurice. 1901. *The Life of the Bee*. Dodd, Mead and Co., New York.

Mautz, D. 1971. Communication effect of wagtail dances of *Apis mellifica carnica* (translated title). *Zeitschrift für vergleichende Physiologie* 72:197–220.

Mautz, D., R. Boch, and R. A. Morse. 1972. Queen finding by swarming honey bees. *Annals of the Entomological Society of America* 65:440–443.

Michael, A. S. 1964. Ethylene oxide. A fumigant for control of pests and parasites of the honey bee. *Gleanings in Bee Culture* 92:102–104.

Michener, Charles D. 1974. *The Social Behavior of the Bees*. The Belknap Press of Harvard University Press, Cambridge.

Miller, C. C. 1903. *Forty Years among the Bees*. George W. York and Co., Chicago.

——. 1911. *Fifty Years among the Bees*. A. I. Root Co., Medina, Ohio.

Morse, Roger A. 1960. The abundance of wild bees (Apoidea) in the Northeastern United States. *Journal of Economic Entomology* 53:679–680.

——. 1963. Swarm orientation in honeybees. *Science* 141:357–358.

——, George E. Strang, and Jan Nowakowski. 1967. Fall death rates of drone honey bees. *Journal of Economic Entomology* 60:1198–2202.

——, and F. M. Laigo. 1969. The Philippine spine tailed swift, *Chaetura dubia* McGregor as a honey bee predator. *The Philippine Entomologist* 1:138–143.

——, and R. Boch. 1971. Pheromone concert in swarming honey bees (Hymenoptera: Apidae). *Annals of the Entomological Society of America* 64:1414–1417.

Morse, Roger A., D. Michael Burgett, John T. Ambrose, William E. Conner, and Richard D. Fell. 1973. Early introductions of African bees into Europe and the new world. *Bee World* 54:57–60.

Nixon, H. L., and C. R. Ribbands. 1952. Food transmission within the honeybee community. *Proceedings of the Royal Entomological Society* B 140:43–50.

Nowakowski, Jan, and Roger A. Morse. 1971. Attempts at mating queen honeybees in confinement. *Gleanings in Bee Culture* 99:216–218.

Oertel, E. 1971. Queen mating experiments fifty years ago. *Gleanings in Bee Culture* 99:369.

Pain, J. 1961. The pheromone of queen bees and its physiological effects (translated title). *Annales de L'abeille* 4:73–158.

——, and J. Maugenet. 1966. Biochemical and physiological study of pollen stored by honeybees (translated title). *Annales de L'abeille* 9:209–236.

Pellett, Frank Chapman. 1938. *History of American Beekeeping*. Collegiate Press, Ames, Iowa.

Pessotti, I. 1972. Discrimination with light stimuli and a lever-pressing response in *Melipona rufiventris*. *Journal of Apicultural Research* 11:89–93.

Phillips, E. F. 1928. *Beekeeping*. The Macmillan Company, New York. Revised edition.

Reinhardt, Joseph F. 1952. Some responses of honey bees to alfalfa flowers. *The American Naturalist* 86:257–275.

Robinson, F. A., and A. H. Krezdorn. 1962. Pollination of the Orlando tangelo. *American Bee Journal* 102:132–133.

——, K. L. Smith, and P. M. Packard. 1972. Gas sterilization of beekeeping equipment contaminated by the American foulbrood organism, *Bacillus larvae*. *The Florida Entomologist* 55:43–51.

Roff, C. 1966. Beating the toads. *The Australasian Beekeeper* 67:266.

Rosch, G. A. (see Frisch, 1967*b*)

Rothenbuhler, Walter C. 1958. Genetics and breeding of the honey bee. *Annual Review of Entomology* 3:161–180.

Rothenbuhler, W. C., J. M. Kulincevic, and W. E. Kerr. 1968. Bee Genetics. *Annual Review of Genetics* 2:413–38.

Ruttner, F. 1966. The life and flight activity of drones. *Bee World* 47: 93–100.

Sackett, Walter G. 1919. Honey as a carrier of intestinal diseases. *Colorado Agricultural Experiment Station Bulletin* 252.

Schwarz, Herbert F. 1948. Stingless bees (Meliponidae) of the Western Hemisphere. *Bulletin of the American Museum of Natural History* 90: 1–546.

Shaw, F. R., and A. I. Bourne. 1944. Observations on bee repellents. *Journal of Economic Entomology* 37:519–521.

Shearer, D. A., and R. Boch. 1965. 2-heptanone in the mandibular gland secretion of the honey-bee. *Nature* 206:530.

——, and R. Boch. 1966. Citral in the Nassanoff pheromone of the honey bee. *Journal of Insect Physiology* 12:1513–1521.

Simpson, J. 1960. The age of queen honeybees and the tendency of their colonies to swarm. *Journal of Agricultural Science* 54:195.

Singh, Sardar. 1950. Behavior studies of honeybees in gathering nectar and pollen. *Cornell University Agricultural Experiment Station Memoir* 288.

——, and Damon Boynton. 1949. Viability of apple pollen in pollen pellets of honeybees. *Proceedings of the American Society for Horticultural Science* 53:148–152.

Smith, Jay. 1923. Queen rearing simplified. A. I. Root Co., Medina, Ohio.

Smith, M. V. 1961. A note on natural mating under artificial conditions. *Bee World* 42:182.

——, and G. F. Townsend. 1951. A technique for mass-marking honeybees. *The Canadian Entomologist* 83(12):346–348.

Snodgrass, R. E. 1956. *Anatomy of the Honey Bee.* Comstock Publishing Associates, Cornell University Press, Ithaca, New York.

Stephen, W. P., G. E. Bohart, and P. F. Torchio. 1969. *The Biology and External Morphology of Bees.* Agricultural Experiment Station, University of Oregon.

Strang, George E. 1970. A study of honey bee drone attraction in the mating response. *Journal of Economic Entomology* 63:641–645.

Taber, Stephen III, and Roy J. Barker. 1974. Honey bees collect caulking material as propolis. *American Bee Journal* 114:90.

Velthuis, H. H. W. 1972. Observations on the transmission of queen substances in the honey bee colony by the attendants of the queen. *Behaviour* 41:105–129.

Watson, L. R. 1927. *Controlled mating of queen bees.* American Bee Journal, Hamilton, Illinois.

White, J. W., Jr., M. H. Subers, and A. I. Schepartz. 1963. The identification of inhibine, the antibacterial factor in honey, as hydrogen peroxide and its origin in a honey glucose-oxidase system. *Biochimica et Biophysica Acta* 73:57–70.

Wilson, Edward O. 1971. *The Insect Societies.* Harvard University Press, Cambridge.

Woyke, J. 1973. Experiences with *Apis mellifera adansonii* in Brazil and Poland. *Apiacta* 8:115–6.

Zmarlicki, Cyprian, and Roger A. Morse. 1963. Drone congregation areas. *Journal of Apicultural Research* 2:64–66.

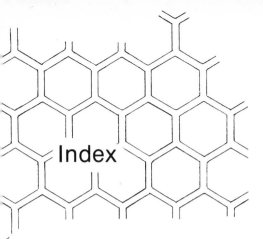

Index